A VOICE FOR
NONPROFITS

A VOICE FOR NONPROFITS

Jeffrey M. Berry

with

David F. Arons

BROOKINGS INSTITUTION PRESS
Washington, D.C.

Copyright © 2003
THE BROOKINGS INSTITUTION
1775 Massachusetts Avenue, N.W., Washington, D.C. 20036
www.brookings.edu

Library of Congress Cataloging-in-Publication data

Berry, Jeffrey M., 1948–
  A voice for nonprofits / Jeffrey M. Berry, with David F. Arons.
    p. cm.
  Includes bibliographical references and index.
  ISBN 0-8157-0912-9 (cloth : alk. paper)
    1. Nonprofit organizations—United States. 2. Nonprofit
organizations—United States—Political activity. 3. Nonprofit
organizations—Political activity—Law and legislation—United States.
I. Arons, David F. II. Title.
  HD2769.2.U6B47 2003
  322'.3—dc21   2003012547

                         9 8 7 6 5 4 3 2 1

The paper used in this publication meets minimum requirements of the
American National Standard for Information Sciences—Permanence of Paper
for Printed Library Materials: ANSI Z39.48-1992.

Typeset in Sabon

Composition by Oakland Street Publishing
Arlington, Virginia

Printed by R. R. Donnelley
Harrisonburg, Virginia

Contents

Acknowledgments

A *Voice for Nonprofits* would not have been possible without the partnership of the Strengthening Nonprofit Advocacy Project (SNAP), a collaborative research effort of Tufts University, OMB Watch, and Charity Lobbying in the Public Interest. Although the statements made in the book are to be attributed solely to the authors and not to their respective institutions, each organization generously supported our work and enabled the research to move forward. Gary D. Bass, Matthew F. Carter, and Kay Guinane, all at OMB Watch, played a crucial role in all phases of the survey, elite interviews, and focus group research. Gary Bass was also instrumental in the fund-raising that sponsored this rather extensive and complex research undertaking.

There were many other members of the SNAP research team, and we are profoundly grateful to Melissa Brennan, Erin Desmarais, Heather Hamilton, Patrick Lemmon, Catherine Ma, Carolyn Nelson, Kelly Patterson, Louis Tavaras, Ryan Turner, Mo Twine, Barbara Western, and Jean Intoppa.

We would also like to thank the following individuals who participated as advisers to the SNAP project: Jim Abernathy, Audrey Alvarado, Nancy Amidei, Marcia Avner, Srilatha Batliwala, Robert A. Boisture, Neil Carlson, Porthira Chhim, Rick Cohen, Pat Conover, Pablo Eisenberg, DeeAnn Friedholm, Joe Geiger, Matthew Hamill, Kim Hsieh, Frances Kunreuther, Jeff Kirsch, Sharon Ladin, Jim Masters, John McNutt, Debra Minkoff, Rick

Moyers, Thomas H. Pollak, Susan Rees, Elizabeth Reid, Judith Saidel, Doug Sauer, Margery Saunders, Cinthia H. Schuman, Peter Shiras, Vince Stehle, Debbie Stein, Carmen Delgado Votaw, and Susan Weiner. For their partnership and organizational contributions to the focus groups conducted for the SNAP project, we thank the following organizations: California Association of Nonprofits, Council of Michigan Foundations, Massachusetts League of Community Health Centers, Michigan Nonprofit Association, Minnesota Council of Nonprofits, McConnell Foundation, Nonprofit Resource Center, Tennessee Conference for Social Welfare, and United Ways of Texas.

For their critically important assistance with the IRS tax form 990 data set and for answering what may have seemed to be an endless number of questions, we are indebted to Elizabeth Boris, Jeff Krehely, Elizabeth Rowland, and Amy Stackpole from the National Center for Charitable Statistics at the Urban Institute. Thanks, too, to Heather Gorski and Durwood Marshall for statistical consultations. For their initial advice and constant encouragement we thank Alan Abramson and Cinthia Schuman at the Aspen Institute. At Tufts University we are grateful for the administrative support we received from Badi Foster, then the director of the Lincoln Filene Center, and James Glaser, chairman of the Department of Political Science.

Our Tufts colleague, Kent Portney, was enormously helpful in advising us from the time we conceived of the project to the time the last version of the manuscript was sent to Brookings. We cannot say enough about how helpful Bob Smucker and Tom Troyer were in contributing time to the research effort and for their wisdom about the legal framework surrounding lobbying by nonprofits.

This manuscript was reviewed for Brookings by Elizabeth Boris, Burdett Loomis, and Steven Rathgeb Smith. They made numerous suggestions for improving *A Voice for Nonprofits*, and we incorporated many of their ideas into our final draft. We deeply appreciate their efforts and thank them for taking time away from their busy schedules to help us.

This project would not have been possible without the generous support of the following foundations: the Aspen Institute's Nonprofit Sector Research Fund, Atlantic Philanthropies, Nathan Cummings Foundation, Ford Foundation, Robert Wood Johnson Foundation, David and Lucile Packard Foundation, and the Surdna Foundation.

Finally, we thank the many fine people at the Brookings Institution Press who have been involved with this book. Robert Faherty, director of the

Press, and Chris Kelaher, our editor, have been extremely supportive since we first discussed the project with them a few years back. We also appreciate the contributions of Rebecca Clark, Christopher O'Brien, Theresa Walker, Tanjam Jacobson, and Susan Woollen to the publication of this book. Carlotta Ribar proofread it, and Julia Petrakis prepared the index.

A VOICE FOR NONPROFITS

CHAPTER ONE

The Age
of Nonprofits

$\mathbf{A}$merica loves nonprofits. They represent what is best about our country: generosity, compassion, vision, and the eternal optimism that we can resolve our most serious problems. Unlike the for-profit sector that employs most Americans, nonprofits have a higher calling, a more noble purpose. Each week millions of people volunteer their time to nonprofits, reading to the blind, raising money for the Cancer Society, mentoring adolescents from troubled backgrounds, or doing countless other good deeds. Nonprofits show loving kindness to the most vulnerable and the most wretched in society. Nonprofits keep homeless alcoholics from freezing to death on cold winter nights and make sure that people dying of AIDS can spend their last days in the familiar surroundings of their home. We love nonprofits because they embody the caring, charitable side of us.

Everyday we come across nonprofits that we admire, like New York's City Harvest, which donates food to pantries and shelters; or Chicago's Bottomless Closet, which provides professional clothing and interview training for women trying to escape welfare; or the Codman Square Health Center in the Dorchester section of Boston, which not only provides health care to the poor but also offers free computers to parents and their children who take a ten-week training course together; or the Genesis Women's Shelter in Dallas, where women and their children arrive in the middle of the night with just the clothes on their back; or Beyond Shelter in Los Angeles, which finds housing for the homeless and provides the social services that, it is hoped, will keep its clients from becoming homeless again; or the Transitional Work Corporation in Philadelphia, which takes the hard-core unemployed and gives them part-time work and support from a mentor while training them for something better; or Newark's New Community Corporation, which operates 3,000 units of low-income housing as well as day care centers, a nursing home, and a supermarket; or Movers, a faith-based nonprofit trying to combat AIDS in the poor Liberty City section of Miami; or Somerville-Cambridge Elder Services, which provides Meals-on-Wheels, homemaker assistance, personal care, and other services that enable frail elderly to remain in their apartments and out of nursing homes. These organizations are a mere handful of the hundreds of thousands of non-profits that do similar work.

Besides these kinds of health care and social service providers are the nonprofits that enrich our lives with beauty and art. The Seattle Symphony, the San Francisco Ballet, and the Lyric Opera of Kansas City add to the vitality and appeal of those cities. The Friends of the Mill Valley Public Library, a tiny organization in a small California town, earns our gratitude too. Even in this day and age of the Internet, libraries are nothing less than the repositories of our civilization, and members are passionate about their town library. Many nonprofits, like the Friends of the Mill Valley Public Library, are rather small, run out of people's homes, and depend entirely on volunteers. Neighborhood-based nonprofits like parent-teacher associations (PTAs) build community within our communities. At the other end of the spectrum are nonprofit behemoths like the United Way, the Salvation Army, Catholic Charities, and the Red Cross. If these organizations did not exist, would the government step in and provide the same services? Maybe. Or perhaps the government would offer those services but not perform them as well. It is hard to answer the question because it is hard to imagine America without these public charities.

Americans' devotion to nonprofits is reflected in their generosity. In 1998, 109 million Americans volunteered for nonprofits, approximately 56 per-cent of the adult population. On average they volunteered 3.5 hours per week, representing an annual aggregate of $226 billion in donated time.[1] In actual dollars contributed, Americans' commitment to nonprofits is equally impressive. Total giving from all sources in 2001 was $212 billion. Approx-imately 75 percent of the donated money came from individuals.[2] Giving to nonprofits rose sharply through the 1990s, though the subsequent down-turn in the stock market tempered the rate of increases.[3]

As essential as nonprofits are today, current trends suggest that they are going to grow even more significant in the years to come. Increasingly, scholars and pundits have drawn our attention to the importance of civil society, community, and civic engagement in American life.[4] When discussion turns to improvements, to ways of enhancing a sense of community, nonprofits are inevitably at the heart of visions of what the good society should look like. Building a better society means working together to solve problems. When we work with others in the community, we usually do so in organizations—nonprofit organizations. Whatever the problem, nonprofits seem to be part of the solution.

Government: Tough Love

America's love affair with nonprofits includes the affections of its government. Although not all nonprofits carry out functions of critical importance to government, a surprising number of them deliver services that ordinary Americans depend on. Indeed, the modern welfare state has largely been subcontracted to nonprofits. Appropriately, scholars emphasize the partnership between the agencies of government and nonprofits.[5] In many ways it is an ideal relationship. Government provides a significant portion of the financial resources but by subcontracting the actual administration of programs to nonprofits, it is able to take advantage of the dedication, imagination, and private fund-raising capacity of these public-spirited organizations.

Consider, for example, the Idaho Youth Ranch. Begun in 1952 with a lease of four square miles of government land from President Harry Truman, the nonprofit has grown over time and now runs several residential facilities in the state. The initial site, located in southern Idaho, is a working ranch, and the troubled youth who are sent there not only go to school but also work with the staff raising thoroughbred horses. The young men and women at the Youth Ranch take part in all aspects of the horse program, including foaling, imprinting, and halter breaking. They take classes on breeding and horse care, show horses to prospective customers, and attend sales. Those youth sent by either corrections or welfare bureaucracies are paid for under a contract with the state.[6]

Alternatively, the state of Idaho could run its own home for troubled youth. It is a virtual certainty that the state would not build and run a horse farm as a residential facility for children with serious behavioral problems. Most likely, the state government would construct something modest, in deference to taxpayers' concerns about the cost of government. The nonprofit Idaho Youth Ranch, with its tax-deductible status, raises a significant amount of private money to supplement the contractual payments it gets from government. Donors to the Youth Ranch give with the certain knowledge that they will get part of their charitable contributions back from the federal government when they file their tax returns. In contrast, a state facility for troubled youth would receive no private support, and taxpayers would have to fund 100 percent of its budget.

The financial incentive for contributions to nonprofits comes at a price to those organizations. In exchange for tax deductibility, nonprofits must accept a serious restriction on their right to lobby legislative bodies at the federal, state, and local levels. Under the tax law governing nonprofits, lobbying is considered an unsavory and suspect activity. Although legislative advocacy is not forbidden, almost all tax-deductible nonprofits fall under a regulatory standard that restricts them from doing any "substantial" amount of lobbying. The government may love nonprofits, but when it comes to political activity it is a case of tough love.[7] Nonprofits must comply with government's restriction or risk losing the crown jewel of fund-raising: tax deductibility.

In the chapters that follow we argue that the consequence of this regulation is that it deters nonprofits' participation in public policymaking. This, in turn, harms the most vulnerable populations, who are denied effective representation in the political system. Although nonprofits serve a cross-section of all Americans, they are crucial elements in serving the hungry, sick, disabled, and frail. What nonprofits are not supposed to do is to represent their clients before legislators. Feed them, just don't lobby for better antihunger programs. Heal them, just don't try to lobby for changing the health care system. This is the essence of American law on nonprofits.

To measure the impact of tax law on political participation, a mail survey was conducted of a random sample of nonprofits from all over the United States. The survey was supplemented by interviews with the executive directors from nonprofits from around the country and by focus groups with executive directors and board members of nonprofit organizations. All the interviews and focus groups were done on a not-for-attribution basis and were conducted between the fall of 2000 and the spring of 2001. More detail on the survey and interview methods is offered in chapter 2, and the appendix offers a more complete review of the study's methodology.

This study's emphasis on nonprofits offering social services reflects their predominance in the population of all nonprofits. As figure 1-1 shows, approximately half of all nonprofits are involved in either health care

Figure 1-1. *America's Nonprofits*

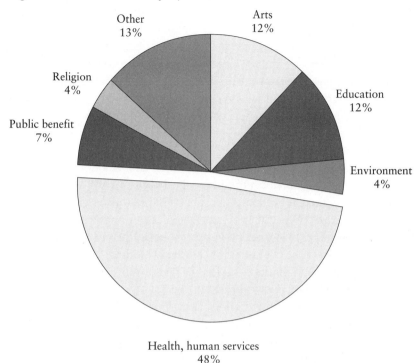

Other
13%

Arts
12%

Religion
4%

Education
12%

Public benefit
7%

Environment
4%

Health, human services
48%

Source: Authors' survey; see appendix.
Note: N = 583. "Religion" is religion-related nonprofits and excludes individual con-gregations.

(11 percent) or human services (37 percent). More accurately, these organizations are half of all charitable nonprofits, eligible to receive tax-deductible donations.[8] "Nonprofit" is an inherently ambiguous term.[9] Indeed, it is rather a misnomer because it is perfectly legal for a nonprofit to make a profit. There are restrictions on what a nonprofit can do with a profit, principally that it cannot distribute the profit to shareholders or employees, but profits are not prohibited.[10]

"Nonprofit" is also a relatively elastic term as it covers an enormous range of organizations in America.[11] Under section 501(c) of the IRS code, there are twenty-six different types of nonprofits.[12] They include nonprofit cemetery companies [section 501(c)(13)]; labor unions [sec. 501(c)(5)]; and employee-funded pension trusts [sec. 501(c)(18)]. These diverse organizations have only one thing in common: they are tax exempt. That is, they pay no taxes on income related to their exempt purposes. But when we think of nonprofits we usually do not have in mind nonprofits like the AFL-CIO (a c5) or the American Petroleum Institute (a c6). Only one type of the 501(c) nonprofits can offer donors a tax deduction for their contributions. Section 501(c)(3) encompasses those nonprofits considered to be public charities, such as religious organizations and educational institutions. It is these organizations, the c3s, that we are usually referring to when we talk about nonprofits. The same is true of this study: unless otherwise indicated, a reference to nonprofits is a reference to only those that qualify under 501c3 and thus offer donors tax deductibility for contributions.[13]

Distinguishing nonprofits is more than a bit of methodological housecleaning. The tax-deductible nonprofits, the 501c3s, have a different story to tell because their legal status as public charities gives them a unique financial structure. When in 1917 the federal government created the tax incentive for people to donate money to charities, there was little controversy because everyone is in favor of charity. Over time, however, the vast majority of organizations applying for 501c3 status from the Internal Revenue Service have not been charities in the colloquial sense of the term. They are public-spirited organizations to be sure and do work broadly supported by Americans. But the fact that half of tax-deductible nonprofits are now health or human service providers creates a public policy dilemma. The nonprofits envisioned in the original legislation creating the tax deduction—churches, charities, and educational institutions—were not seen as having much stake in public policy. That is not true of today's community health centers, multiservice centers, Community Development Corporations, job training facilities, housing collaboratives, and the like. They have an enormous stake in what government does and therein lies the problem.

Growth Sector

Economists offer a straightforward explanation of the rise of nonprofits in areas in which government itself directly offers services, such as health care, social services, and education. In their view, when government offers services it will aim to satisfy the demand of the median voter. (In plain English: government will offer what the typical consumer wants but nothing more extensive than that.) Economists also say that nonprofits will emerge in areas served by for-profit organizations when consumers have difficulty evaluating the quality of service and are worried that the for-profits will pursue greater earnings at the expense of quality service. For example, when a family must place a loved one in a nursing home and cannot monitor that nursing home closely because it is far away, the family might feel more comfortable utilizing a nonprofit facility. A 501c3 does not have the same profit incentive as a private sector nursing home and, presumably, there is little pressure on its managers to cut corners or keep services to a minimum.[14] Finally, of course, economists point out that nonprofits are a response to market failure, where neither government nor business steps in to provide necessary services.

Political scientists offer a different perspective for examining the growth of nonprofits. They focus on the political process that leads to agenda change. In some cases, new social problems emerge and government feels a responsibility to address them. When AIDS became an issue Congress enacted the Ryan White Act and federal agencies responded with new initiatives too.[15] For the most part, though, the nonprofit sector has grown because of increased attention to problems that have long existed, such as malnutrition, inadequate job skills, or family violence. Consequently, political scientists also look at the events and trends that raise our awareness of problems. In this vein they will emphasize the role that advocacy groups play in drawing our attention to various social problems and in lobbying legislatures, agencies, and executives to address them.[16]

These differing perspectives are not mutually exclusive. Political advocacy can cause government to begin funding a service, but then support it only to the degree it satisfies the median voter. Given that the nonprofit sector has expanded by hundreds of thousands of organizations in recent years, surely many cogent explanations could explain all or part of this population explosion. Documenting the growth, however, is relatively straightforward since the Internal Revenue Service provides population figures for 501c3s and all other types of nonprofits. Whatever the underlying reasons, the proximate cause of the rising number of nonprofits is the expansion of government's commitment to social services. The sharp rise of 501c3s is evident in figure 1-2. Between 1977 and 1997, a period of just twenty years, the number of public charities shot upward from 276,000 to 693,000. In 1998 (the last year for which figures are available), the number of 501c3s increased by another 41,000, or 5.9 percent, above the previous year. This is even more robust than the already high (5.1 percent) annual growth for the previous decade.[17]

The phenomenal growth of public charities is further evidenced by comparisons with other types of nonprofits and with all organizations in general. All major types of organizations have been growing in number—

Figure 1-2. *The Nonprofit Surge*

Thousands of 501c3s

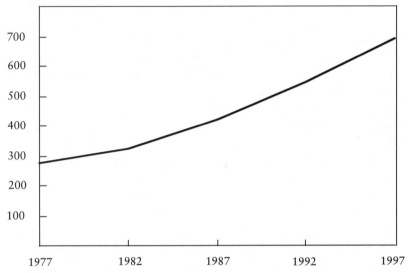

Source: Murray S. Weitzman, Nadine T. Jalandoni, Linda M. Lampkin, and Thomas H. Pollak, *The New Nonprofit Almanac and Desk Reference* (Jossey-Bass, 2002), pp. 4–5.

hardly surprising since the American population is growing, and the nation's collective wealth continues to expand. Conceivably, nonprofits could simply be growing at the general rate of growth for all organizations. Figure 1-3 shows that this is not the case. Between 1987 and 1997, all other types of nonprofits have grown only incrementally while 501c3s grew by 64 percent. Even more striking is that 501c3s have grown at about two and one-half times the rate of new businesses. Clearly, the 501c3s are not simply riding the crest of a wave of growth of all kinds of organizations.

The financial resources fueling the growth of 501c3s are imposing. Excluding health care nonprofits, total revenue for all other public charities in 1997 was $338.5 billion.[18] The nonprofit sector share of GDP is close to 7 percent, and it employs 10 percent of the work force in the United States.[19] Government is a significant source of funding and constitutes just over 20 percent of all revenues for non-health-related public charities. As a proportion of revenue, government funds have dropped slightly from 21.6 percent of 501c3s' revenues in 1977 to 20.7 in 1997.[20] When we look at human service providers, government support is far more important. As figure 1-4 demonstrates, these nonprofits depend more heavily on govern-

Figure 1-3. *America's Growth Sector*

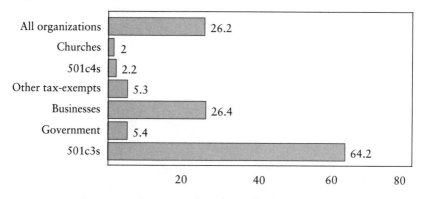

Percentage change, number of organizations 1987–97

Source: Weitzman and others, *The New Nonprofit Almanac and Desk Reference*, pp. 4–12. "Other tax-exempts" are all nonprofits except 501c3s, 501c4s, and church congregations. Although churches are tax deductible, they do not file the same tax return as 501c3s and are counted separately by the Internal Revenue Service. The 501c4s are social welfare organizations but lack tax deductibility.

Figure 1-4. *Sources of Income for Human Service Providers*

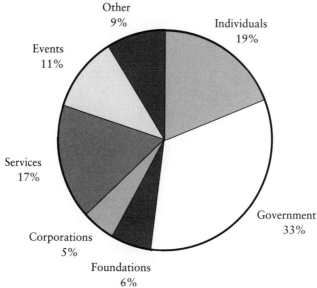

Source: Authors' survey.
Note: *N* = 539.

ment, receiving 50 percent more than other non-health-care-related public charities. The 33 percent figure for government support for human service providers underestimates the true level of assistance since some of the income that nonprofits count under services are fees paid through government programs.

The nonprofit sector has clearly developed substantial sources of support beyond government. The 501c3 population expanded sharply during a period when there were federal budget cuts in many social service programs. The Reagan-Bush years (1981–92) were characterized by a philosophy calling for more reliance on private charity. Nonprofits were aggressive in seeking out additional private sources of revenue, and they even found ways of getting one part of government to make up for the funds cut by other parts. As Lester Salamon notes, nonprofits profited from "repackaging traditional social services as behavioral health services [to] secure government support through the rapidly expanding health programs."[21] After adjusting for inflation, revenues for nonprofits grew by 144 percent between 1977 and 1997 while the nation's economy grew at just 81.[22]

The growth of nonprofits did not just happen because funds were available and needs became more evident. This growth reflects an intellectual ferment about the substance of domestic policy and the process by which it is made. Two enormously important ideas that took hold in the second half of twentieth century America had a profound impact on the nonprofit sector. The first is the belief that welfare should be directed at fighting dependency. The government's basic approach to welfare, born in the New Deal, was to provide income maintenance to the needy. Social Security, unemployment compensation, and Aid to Dependent Children (ADC) were the cornerstones of this approach. As ADC (later AFDC, Aid to Families with Dependent Children) became a general welfare program for the poor, criticism began to mount that it did little to resolve the underlying problems that kept people impoverished. There was also growing recognition that macroeconomic policy, after years of Keynesian fine-tuning, was not enough to cure poverty either. Beginning in 1962, the federal government moved toward the rehabilitation of the poor through social services. It was a philosophy of helping people by giving them skills and (noncash) support to supplement their welfare payments.

Second, American federalism was fundamentally changed by a devolution of responsibility for domestic programs from the national to the state and local levels. Presidents Richard M. Nixon and Ronald Reagan each called for a "new federalism," and money and authority were transferred out of Washington. The primary structural change was the replacement of numerous categorical programs with block grants. The accent was on creativity. Each local government could fund programs it saw as uniquely well suited to solve the problems of the community. What wasn't attached to these grants was administrative capacity. Consequently state and local governments needed to develop a means of carrying out their new mandates. They quickly came up with a solution.

The Revolution in Welfare

There is nothing new about nonprofits providing assistance to the poor in this country. Before there was government-sponsored welfare, there were nonprofits offering assistance—charity—to the dispossessed. But change in the American welfare system changed the nonprofit sector. The transformation of welfare from a system oriented around income maintenance to a system relying on social services is at the heart of the transformation of the nonprofit sector from being largely a source of private charity to being an arm of the government.

A Turn toward Services

President John F. Kennedy was encouraged to move welfare toward a social services approach by his transition Task Force on Health and Social Security and by its chair, Wilbur Cohen, who continued to shape policy as the assistant secretary for legislation at the Department of Health, Education, and Welfare (HEW). Cohen's views reflected the current thinking of many academics and social work professionals.[23] The administration proposed legislation that was designed in the words of Abraham Ribicoff, secretary of HEW, "to wage war on dependency." In testimony before Congress he declared, "The byword of our new program is prevention— and where it is too late—rehabilitation."[24] Ribicoff then asked rhetorically, "Now how, you may ask, is this accomplished? The answer is through professional, skilled services. We believe that services represent the key to our efforts to help people become self-sufficient so that they no longer need assistance."[25]

Social services were certainly not an entirely new approach to welfare as the federal government was already providing a small amount of funding for various programs, especially in child welfare.[26] Yet the 1962 amendments initiated a sea change in the American welfare system. Surprisingly, "services" was not defined in the legislation, and HEW did not offer a specific definition in the initial regulations either. Martha Derthick writes, "Ultimately [services] could mean anything that would help troubled, handicapped, and dependent people."[27] The new program was attractive to the states because the federal government committed itself to paying 75 percent of the cost of services states provided to its welfare population. For states already providing services, it was found money since they could just turn around and bill HEW for programs they were already offering.[28] The three-for-one matching formula thus provided a strong incentive for states to support a continuation of the services program, which would become known as Title XX.

The social services approach was spurred on by the mounting criticism of AFDC. Conservatives complained that dependency was being passed on from welfare mothers to their children and that something must be done to break the cycle of poverty.[29] As pressure grew to do something to get people off AFDC, "self-help" became the guiding philosophy. Those who were just receiving a check became the unworthy poor, while those who were actively trying to escape welfare deserved job training, day care, and other government-sponsored services.[30] As the War on Poverty was being designed inside the White House, Lyndon B. Johnson summed up his philosophy succinctly when he gave an aide instructions for a meeting with antipoverty czar Sargent Shriver: "You tell Shriver no doles."[31]

When the 1962 amendments came up for renewal in 1967, social services were strongly endorsed despite the lack of any concrete evidence that the approach was working. As the nation's economy picked up steam, escaping from the terrible recession of the late 1950s, unemployment dropped to a record low. Perversely, AFDC enrollment continued to climb.[32] It is certainly conceivable that AFDC rolls might have been even larger without the new money sent to the states, but it seems unlikely that services had any real effect on dependency since actual spending was still modest. Five years after the program was begun, the federal government forwarded just $281 million in matching funds to the states.[33] The real problem, of course, is that dependency and all its assorted ills are not easily ameliorated. Even so, the 1960s was a time when social scientists thought they knew the solutions to social ills and the federal government demonstrated its strongest activist bent since the darkest days of the Great Depression.

The program was not only renewed but, remarkably, no budget ceiling was prescribed. Also, in what seemed like an innocent oversight, the language from the 1962 statute stating that the HEW secretary could determine what qualified as reimbursable services, was somehow dropped. What followed was an open-ended appropriation for services that HEW could not define. The result was an explosion in spending on social services, jumping from $354 million in 1969 to $1.7 billion in 1972. The agency's inability to control the costs of its matching grants led those in the agency to joke that the agency's operating philosophy was "You hatch it, we match it."[34]

Another feature of the 1967 amendments was the removal of restrictions on subcontracting services to nonprofits. States were no longer required to use a circuitous funding route to use nonprofit service providers. With a mandate in the 1967 law for child care and family planning services for those enrolled in job training programs, lawmakers acknowledged that greater utilization of nonprofits was critical to any expansion of social services. The government was actually having trouble filling social worker positions as salaries for comparable positions in the private sector were higher.[35] Whereas earlier administrators were cautious about contracting to private vendors instead of state agencies, a new regime in HEW "made a wholesale commitment" to using nonprofits to deliver services.[36] A particularly interesting incentive to encourage nonprofits to approach state agencies was that they could donate the money that the state had to put up as its match in the one-for-three formula. If, for example, a nonprofit gave the state $25,000, the state would receive $75,000 from Washington, which it would then send to the nonprofit for the services it was offering. Nonprofits would make in-kind donations in the form of the services they were already offering and would designate private contributions or a United Way allocation as the funding source for the donated services. In effect this meant that a nonprofit "could receive a contract essentially at no cost."[37]

Services Dominant

The loophole leading to the uncontrollable spending was corrected in 1972, and a fixed appropriation was set for the social services match. The spending debacle did little to diminish the enthusiasm of policymakers for finding ways to end dependency. As the reach of Title XX expanded, nonprofits took on increasing responsibilities for administration of social programs. In 1971 subcontracting accounted for 25 percent of all state spending on social services. Five years later it had risen to 49 percent. The true figure was surely higher since some state agencies technically contracted with another state agency, but that second agency then turned around and subcontracted its grant to an array of nonprofits.[38]

Social services continued to expand beyond those programs first funded by Title XX. Over the years besides core areas like job training, day care, and child welfare, the government came to fund programs for the homeless, runaways, battered women, shut-ins, and many other constituencies. Health and nutrition services are funded from other budget lines, and appropriations for these areas have risen exponentially. Government funds had a compounding effect: nonprofits attracting significant federal money gained in stature and used this credibility to expand their private fund-raising. Through individual donations, foundation grants, corporate gifts, United Way contributions, fees for services, and money garnered from fund-raising events, nonprofits multiplied government's investment. Whatever the mix of funding sources, each year more multiservice centers, more mental health centers, more mental retardation centers, and more of just about every kind of nonprofit, open their doors for business and begin offering services to the needy.

The range of services currently offered by nonprofits is so broad and the level of services so vast that there is no way to offer a summary assessment of their effectiveness. Even evaluating an individual service is difficult. Highly qualified analysts can look at the same program, like Head Start, and come to different conclusions about whether it works. And when programs do not work terribly well, the instinct usually is to find new ways of providing that service rather than giving up on the basic approach. Should the government stop funding teen pregnancy programs because progress has been limited? Assessments of the social services approach to fighting poverty and family dissolution often criticize the shallowness of programs and call for more comprehensive services. In this vein Lisbeth Schorr writes, "Programs that are successful in reaching and helping the most disadvantaged children and families typically offer a *broad spectrum of services*."[39]

Although services may not be as effective as hoped, the social services approach has now succeeded income maintenance as the basic means for providing assistance to people in poverty. In 1996, with the passage of the Personal Responsibility and Work Opportunity Reconciliation Act, AFDC was replaced with Temporary Assistance for Needy Families (TANF).[40] Those on welfare are now restricted in the time they may receive cash benefits and face a stiff work requirement. In President Bill Clinton's words, TANF did "end welfare as we know it"—at least for cash assistance. Social services, particularly job training and child care, remain "as we know them" and may become more important in the wake of TANF and its time limits for cash assistance.

No matter what the future holds for TANF, the bull market for nonprofits providing human services should continue. Unlike the income maintenance approach to welfare, social services are highly labor intensive. They typically require a professional staff trained in counseling, social work,

Figure 1-5. *The Transformation of Welfare: State and Local Government Employment in Public Welfare vs. Private Organizations, 1972–95*[a]

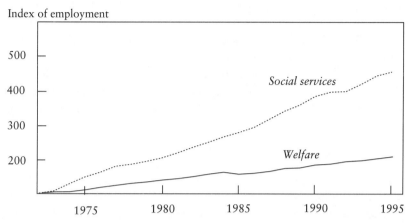

Index of employment

Source: Richard P. Nathan, with the assistance of Elizabeth I. Davis, Mark J. McGrath, and William C. O'Heaney, "The 'Nonprofitization Movement' as a Form of Devolution," in Dwight F. Burlingame, William A. Diaz, Warren F. Ilchman, and associates, *Capacity for Change? The Nonprofit World in the Age of Devolution* (Indianapolis: Indiana University Center on Philanthropy, 1996), p. 33 (reprinted with permission).

a. Private organizations include profit and nonprofit.

substance abuse, special education, or other such field. Quality in services is largely tied to the time that professionals spend with their clients, and thus economies of scale are particularly difficult to achieve. Not surprisingly, the growth in employment for social service nonprofits has far outpaced that of government welfare offices, a large proportion of which are involved with income maintenance programs (figure 1-5).[41]

Changing the approach to welfare not only structurally changed American government by spawning a huge class of government subcontractors, but it also changed the relationship between government and its poorest and most vulnerable citizens. In the United States, when people need help beyond cash assistance they go to nonprofits and do not interact directly with government. Although many receiving services are not unaware that some of the funding for the nonprofit comes from government, the face of compassion, care, and concern they see is the face of private caregivers and community organizations, not bureaucrats and government agencies.[42]

Devolution

Instead of recreating a welfare state built around subcontractors, the federal government could have improved salaries and established multiservice and specialized local offices around the country. This would have provided uniformity in services and alleviated the problem of monitoring the vast number of nonprofits that it now contracts with. During the period of transition to social services, however, the federal government moved toward devolution. There was a growing belief, especially among Republicans, that government would work better if authority as well as revenues were turned over to the states, counties, and cities. Beyond this desire to reinvigorate American federalism, pressure grew on Washington to downsize and to become more efficient—to become in the jargon of the business world, "lean and mean."[43]

The New Federalism and the New Federalism

It is easy to identify reasons why Washington should be shrunk and many of its tasks turned over to local government. The national government is popularly seen as an inflexible leviathan, prone to establishing policies that do as much harm as good. One of the most common criticisms is that Washington prescribes policy on a "one size fits all" basis. Local governments, however, are perceived as more sensitive to the true preferences of citizens and able to tailor policies to fit the unique needs of their constituencies. The imagination and inventiveness of the local citizenry is viewed as an elixir for all that ails the governmental process. As Philip Howard argues, "Whenever the rules are eased, our energy and good sense pour in like sunlight through open blinds."[44]

There is, of course, a simple and compelling reason *not* to ease federal rules in favor of local authority and discretion. Statutes and regulations are drafted in a one-size-fits-all manner to ensure that people are treated equally before the law. If there is a federal program to provide mental health services to those who have no means of paying for them, shouldn't everyone, regardless of where they live, be subject to the same eligibility requirements and receive the same level of services? If federal dollars are paying for those services, shouldn't recipients in Tennessee obtain the same level of counseling and medical care as those residing in California? This is the liberals' concern. But in the face of continuing criticism of the national government, the liberals' rhetoric has not been as convincing and their voices have not been as loud. Liberal legislators in Congress sympathetic to this point of view have also been compromised by Democratic mayors and governors who want greater freedom to spend federal dollars in the way they see fit. They want that freedom as long as those budgets are not cut in the process of devolving programs onto the states and cities.

Within this context of conservative preference for smaller government on the federal level and liberal concerns for protecting funding for social programs, President Richard M. Nixon put forward his "New Federalism." Soon after taking office, Nixon proposed a fundamental alteration in American federalism, offering revenue sharing to state and local governments. Nixon said his proposals "represent the first major reversal of the trend toward ever more centralization of government in Washington."[45] The revenue sharing concept was enormously popular with governors and mayors since such funds could provide badly needed fiscal relief. This step back from categorical grants with their specific mandates gave state and local governments flexibility and additional money. Despite the enthusiasm from state and local officials, Democratic leaders in Congress were wary, and revenue sharing was not enacted until a few weeks before the 1972 election.[46]

Nixon's new federalism did not stop there. He subsequently put forward specialized revenue sharing proposals in broad policy areas. Resistance from Congress resulted instead in new block grant programs, like CDBG (the Community Development Block Grant program). This combined seven different housing and community development programs into just one but still required applications from local municipalities, and the law contained extensive guidelines on the use of the CDBG money.[47] Nevertheless, it was an important step as it gave communities significant flexibility and clearly redefined the role of the federal government in the housing field. Increasingly the Department of Housing and Urban development's responsibility was to evaluate the different approaches each city took with its federal dollars, which typically involved subcontracts with nonprofits. But as Richard Nathan points out, "Nonprofit groups . . . were not explicitly considered in framing Nixon's new federalism."[48] The focus was on the changes in fiscal relations between Washington and the states and cities, and the greater flexibility offered to local government officials. The implications for nonprofits were not yet fully recognized by policymakers at the national level.

When Ronald Reagan took office in 1981 he, too, emphasized block grants as an instrument of change. His similarly labeled "new federalism" was primarily oriented around reducing the size of the national government. Advocating a replacement of AFDC and Food Stamps with a block grant to the states, Reagan said, "In a single stroke, we will be accomplishing a realignment that will end cumbersome administration and spiraling costs at the federal level while we insure these programs will be more responsive to both the people they are meant to help and the people who pay for them."[49] Reagan's true goal was to reduce the size and scope of government rather than to sort out the functions of government among the federal, state, and local levels. Still, in Reagan's mind, cutting the federal budget was the "first step toward returning power to states and communities."[50]

Buoyed by supportive Republicans in Congress, Reagan's initial efforts to implement his new federalism were highly successful. In the momentous 1981 budget act, nine new block grants were created through the merger of seventy-seven categorical programs. In addition sixty categorical programs were abolished.[51] (The proposal to combine AFDC and Food Stamps was not enacted.) The discretion offered to local governments through these block grants ranged considerably, and some programs eventually went through "recategorization." As liberals feared, overall federal spending for the block grants was much less than the combined spending for all the programs they replaced. Between 1980 and 1990, domestic spending for all nonentitlement programs dropped 10 percent in constant dollar terms.[52]

The contrast to Richard Nixon's new federalism was striking. In Nathan's words, "Nixon was a big spender."[53] His goal was to provide money to state and local governments with a minimum of restrictions. He wanted to share the federal largesse in the belief that local control and federal dollars would produce the most effective social policy. For Reagan block grants were a means to reduce federal funding of the same kinds of services and programs that Nixon wanted to support. Reagan's supporters argued that if state and local governments wanted to spend more than the reduced funds Washington was willing to provide, they could raise their own revenues to do it. Reagan also saw a greater role for private charity. He called on individuals and corporations to do more, linking his appeal to a revival of community. In Reagan's mind, America needed to embrace small town values, replacing government paternalism with private voluntarism.[54]

Even though the goals were vastly different, Nixon's and Reagan's versions of the new federalism reshaped intergovernmental relations in America. The expanding discretion deriving from block grants gave state and local government agencies more and more opportunity to experiment and to create competition among potential vendors.[55] Different 501c3 organizations would vie by offering their own program designs for addressing the needs of the community. This was an important change in American government: broad outlines of policy would be developed in Washington, but more detailed program design would, in a sense, be put out for bid. Nonprofits would compete on the basis of their proposals and, over time, on the basis of their performance as well. As in the private sector, competition would presumably produce the optimum outcome: the "best practices" for treating social ills. This competition among nonprofits would be unleashed across the country, in every major city, in every state of the union. The culmination of the two new federalisms was the application of market logic to social services.

False Downsizing

Ultimately Reagan's most enduring accomplishment on domestic policy may have been to make "government" a dirty word. Since he took office in 1981 there has been relentless pressure to keep government small. Democrats and Republicans have been loath to let the size of government expand. Since even in bad times budgets grow inexorably, the coin of the realm in political discussions has been headcounts of government workers. For presidents as well as members of Congress, being able to point to even a small reduction in the number of federal government workers is good enough for the campaign trail.

Head counts may make for good campaign rhetoric but they are a terribly misleading measure of the size of government. Even though its tasks have grown, the federal government has been able to keep its official work force small by subcontracting with the nonprofit and private sectors. The result is what political scientist Paul Light calls the "shadow government." In 1996, the head count of the federal civilian work force was 1.9 million individuals. But that year the federal government indirectly employed 12.7 million full-time equivalent jobs through grants, contracts, and mandates to state and local government.[56] Although there has been a modest decline in the overall federal work force (civil servants plus shadow employees) during the past few decades, there has been a significant rise in employment in the policy areas where nonprofits are most prevalent. For both Health and Human Services and Housing and Urban Development, grant and contract employment has risen sharply.[57]

Subcontracting has been the perfect answer for an electorate that wants services without bureaucrats. More than a government version of Three Card Monte, subcontracting is built on the belief in private sector efficiency. Backed by research demonstrating that the private sector can often deliver services for less money, privatization became another foundation of the Reagan revolution.[58] A variant in the privatization movement is public-private partnership, where corporations and nonprofits form a new nonprofit to coordinate their collaboration with government. The public-private model is undeniably attractive, though the enthusiasm for the concept has always outrun the willingness of businesses to work on social issues.

The dominant trend has been delegation to nonprofits rather than to private sector vendors, although in the past few years more private sector firms like Lockheed Martin and Maximus have become competitors to nonprofits.[59] The role of private sector vendors in human services does not represent a belief that the ideology of efficiency has been compromised by the increasing subcontracting of government services to nonprofits. Rather, the growing competition is more an indication of the money now available to government social service subcontractors.

Although there is no one broad measure of efficiency to use in comparing direct government service providers or private sector vendors to comparable nonprofit organizations, nonprofits' heavy reliance on volunteers and their employees' low salaries are, by themselves, significant sources of efficiency. When fiscal problems squeeze government, demands on nonprofits grow and their ability to offer services in an environment of shrinking resources has enhanced their image of efficiency.[60] The poster child for nonprofit efficiency could be Louisville Housing Services, which the city created to give itself flexibility. At one time Louisville Housing Services had no full-time employees and was run by a half-time consultant.[61] That office contracts with nonprofits to manage all its housing projects.

For all the reasons highlighted, subcontracting became the principal form of social service delivery in the United States.[62] State and local agencies, reluctant to add bureaucrats for the same reason the federal government avoids head count creep, have utilized nonprofits to do what they cannot realistically do themselves. But the government does not merely delegate policies to nonprofits to implement. As chapter 5 details, nonprofits are collaborators with local agencies at every stage of the administrative process.

Operating through grants and contracts, nonprofits adapt and grow and learn how to anticipate government's needs. Large, successful nonprofits can offer a rather substantial range of services to clients. As table 1-1 shows, a single nonprofit can administer numerous government programs, each with its own separate demands for specialized staff skills and organizational capacities. In 2001–02, the "Front Street Health Center" in Massachusetts operated thirty-five programs funded by various government agencies.[63] For simplicity's sake the table lumps together different grants falling under the same general program, but the reality is much more complicated. For example, Front Street runs three separate Ryan White programs, each dependent on a separate grant and each necessitating a different administrative relationship with agency overseers.

Table 1-1. *One Nonprofit, Thirty-Five Government Programs*[a]

Program	Funding/implementing agencies
ACT Now[b]	Massachusetts Department of Public Health (DPH)
AIDS Transportation Grant	Boston Public Health Commission
Breast and Cervical Cancer Initiative	Centers for Disease Control/(DPH)
Campaign for Excellence[b]	Mass. Dept. of Medical Assistance
Center Care	DPH
Children's Medical Security Program	DPH
Chronic Disease Prevention	CDC/DPH
Community Health Centers (#330)	Bureau of Primary Health Care, Health Resources Srvc Adm (HRSA)
Community Access Program[b]	Bureau Of Primary Health Care, HRSA
Community Health Center Enhancement	DPH
Dental Services	Bureau of Primary Health Care, HRSA
Enrollment and Outreach	Mass. Dept. of Medical Assistance
Free Care Pharmacy Demonstration Project	Mass. Division of Health Care Finance and Policy
Hardship Grant	Mass. Division of Health Care Finance and Policy
Health Access Program	DPH and Mass. Division of Mental Health
Healthy Schools, Healthy Communities	Bureau of Primary Health Care, HRSA
Healthy Start	Health Care Financing Agency/DPH
Home Intervention Program	Mass. Dept. of Mental Retardation
Immunization Program	DPH, Division of Food and Drugs
Mass. Loan Repayment Program	DPH
Medicaid	Mass. Dept. of Medical Assistance
Medicare	Centers for Medicare and Medicaid
New Access Point	Bureau of Primary Health Care, HRSA
New Start Dental Program	DPH, Division of Oral Health
NS AIDS Collaborative	DPH
PACE (all-inclusive elderly care)	Medicaid and Medicare
Perinatal and Pediatric Program	DPH
Proyecto Encuentros[b]	HRSA, Substance Abuse Mental Health Services Administration
Refugee and Immigration Health Program	DPH
Representative Payee Program	Mass. Dept. of Mental Retardation
Ryan White Act	DPH/HRSA
School Based Health Centers	DPH
Tobacco Control Smoking Cessation	DPH
Uncompensated Care Pool	Mass. Division of Health Care Finance and Policy
Women, Infants, and Children	U.S. Dept. of Agriculture/DPH

a. Federal, Massachusetts, and city-funded programs at the Front Street Health Center.
b. Grant is to another nonprofit, and Front Street is a subcontractor.

Devolution has come in different ways to different nonprofits. In an interview a Native American leader described the gradual process by which the tribe's nonprofit came to take over programs previously operated by the Bureau of Indian Affairs and other government agencies:

> For the Bureau, we provide the whole range of their services under federal regulations: realty, social services, 15 programs in all we control. The biggest one is social services, part of which is under the TANF program. We do credit finance, loans. . . . We also do job creation and opportunity for our clients. For the state we deliver medical programs, mental health programs [and so on]. We do forestry work. We have an agent on staff who does the cooperative extension work for the system.

The demand by government for nonprofit services continues to grow. The replacement of AFDC with TANF was another huge step in the devolution of government services to the nonprofit sector. In interviews for this study, TANF contracts were repeatedly cited by respondents as representative of the partnerships they had developed with government agencies. But TANF is but one step along a long road. For both political parties, for policymakers at the federal, state, and local levels, and for officials in the legislative and executive branches, the logic of devolution is incontrovertible. Devolution is a means of pretending that government is lean while at the same time maintaining necessary services. Nonprofits are flexible, efficient, and willing to operate in a competitive environment characterized by tight resources. For the 501c3s, devolution is also a path to growth since agencies' constant search for new approaches and more effective ways of providing services creates ongoing opportunities for entrepreneurial nonprofits. When an individual nonprofit grows, the additional revenue allows the organization to address more problems, serve more clients, and come a little closer to fulfilling its mission. For all concerned, devolution is the ultimate win-win situation.

Conclusion

The sharp rise in the number of nonprofits seems to be a classic case of supply and demand. Since the 1960s demand for nonprofits has soared, and the nonprofit sector has demonstrated little trouble in generating enough 501c3s to meet the growing needs of American society. The source of these needs was the transformation of the nation's welfare system. Social services are labor intensive, and nonprofits provide the lion's share of the counselors, employment specialists, social workers, and others who deliver those services. The devolution of social programs, fueled by the movement toward block grants and the political pressure to keep government bureaucracies small, has pulled nonprofits closer into the web of government.

Underlying these changes were two powerful ideas. As the debate over welfare and devolution developed within academe and government, sharp partisan and ideological divisions were never far from the surface. Yet significant resolution was achieved because liberals and conservatives found some common ground. In the case of welfare, conservatives wanted to find ways of cutting back on the welfare state by reducing people's dependency. Liberals did not focus on dependency, but they liked the idea of providing support beyond income maintenance. Social services offered both sides a means of addressing the welfare problem as they saw it. Devolution also represented a neat meld of conservative and liberal preferences. Conservatives wanted a small national government, believing that the scope of government at the state and local levels would accurately correspond to the preferences of their citizens once these governments were given discretion over social programs. Nixon was a bit of an aberration among conservatives who were also looking for ways to cut the budget. Liberals did not share the cost-cutting goals of the conservatives, but the civil rights movement prompted them to look for ways of giving people in urban centers more control over their lives. In politics ideas have power, and these two ideas led to an unprecedented role for nonprofits in America.[64]

Ironically, the debates surrounding these ideas focused little on nonprofits. Even as government's dependency on nonprofits became clear to policymakers over the years, the capacity of nonprofits to administer the welfare state has not been seriously questioned.[65] Nor has our trust in nonprofits been shaken by the occasional scandal like those involving the United Way and the American Red Cross. And that trust is enormous. Nonprofits are given responsibility for our most vulnerable populations, for people who may not have the sophistication to understand their options in services or treatments. Although nonprofits administer government programs, they are not government agencies and are not accountable in the same way as government officials are.[66] This deep reservoir of trust extends to almost all realms of nonprofits' activity, except for involvement in public policy. In the case of advocacy, the federal government has a policy of restrictive regulation. One thing that has not devolved down to nonprofits is the right to represent those that they serve.

CHAPTER TWO

Nonprofits as Interest Groups

The executive director of an organization included in our survey sample called us to respond to our first follow-up letter, which was reminding her to please fill out our questionnaire and return it. She explained, "Our organization is inappropriate for the study because we are not involved in public affairs." We assured her that was not a problem. We wanted all kinds of nonprofits to complete the questionnaire, and respondents from organizations relatively uninvolved in public affairs were just as valuable to us as those that were highly active. Politely, but firmly, she again said her nonprofit was inappropriate for the study. Finally, our survey director asked her if she or others in the organization ever talked to public officials. She replied, "Oh yes, we harass our state legislator all the time."

Studying the political behavior of nonprofits is a challenge. Nonprofits qualifying as public charities under 501c3 are almost always founded for some purpose other than advocacy in the policymaking process. Their mission is feeding the hungry, sheltering the homeless, raising money for the town library, training the unemployed to use a computer, providing recreation for children, or a million other things. They have a mission and that mission is not politics. At some level, all organizations are mission driven, but nonprofits tend to be mission driven with an attitude. Nonprofit employees are the good guys, the ones wearing the white hats. They work for less money than those in the private sector, and they are the ones who help people and make their communities a better place. They are not the ones who dirty themselves in politics.

Government relations is usually an afterthought in the initial design and focus of a nonprofit even though necessity requires contact between the government and nonprofits. Many nonprofit leaders still believe that their contact with those in government has no political connotation. Interaction is an immaculate conception—nothing naughty happens, but something productive is expected to gestate. Thus nonprofit heads convince themselves that harassing state legislators is somehow removed from public affairs.

Although part of the illusion that involvement with government is apolitical can be attributed to the substantive mission of the nonprofit, the lack of resources, the lack of interest in politics, or even the distaste for government, another source of the attitude of nonprofits toward government is section 501c3 of the Internal Revenue Code. Since it threatens nonprofits that violate the limitation with financial annihilation, leaders want to make sure that any contact they have with government cannot be construed as lobbying. The safest path is to be uninvolved. When that isn't possible, the next safest alternative is to minimize anything that could be interpreted as lobbying. As a result nonprofit leaders are good at convincing themselves that what they just did was not lobbying. And if they don't lobby, they're not an interest group. Or so they think.

Nonprofits as Lobbies

Although the study of nonprofits is not a central focus of any of the traditional social sciences, it stretches easily across them all. Its interdisciplinary nature makes for a rich stew of analytical approaches; that may be what pulls the subject from the center of those fields. Overall, there is an abundant and impressive literature on nonprofits, and scholarly interest is on the rise.[1] Despite this rather bountiful literature on nonprofits, there is relatively little work on how nonprofits represent—or fail to represent—their constituents in the political process.[2] The purpose here is not to review what has been written on their political involvement but to push scholarship toward a broader understanding of nonprofits' role in public policymaking. By emphasizing the role of nonprofits as lobbies, we hope to focus attention on how the lack of political involvement by nonprofits works against the interests of those people who have no one else to represent them.

What Kind of Organization?

Although scholars from other disciplines have written about nonprofits and government, it surely comes as no surprise that most of the work on this topic comes from scholars trained as political scientists. Yet the study of nonprofits has traditionally occupied a tiny sliver of the political science profession. Interest group specialists have done their absolute best to ignore nonprofits. Those who study urban politics have been little better, even though nonprofits are increasingly important in the administration of local government services. One bright spot is in the study of welfare and human services, where policy specialists have effectively documented the involvement of nonprofits in service delivery.[3]

In recent years political scientists have written extensively on civil society and on the importance of the civic associations occupying the space between government and the private sector. This literature, including Robert Putnam's seminal *Bowling Alone,* has examined the extent of citizen involvement in public affairs and raised profound questions about the foundations of American democracy.[4] The organizations that are neither part of government nor part of the private sector are, of course, nonprofits. This research has enriched the field and educated academics and the broader public about the critical importance of civic associations to the ongoing well-being of democratic government. One must be cautious, however, in equating "nonprofits" with the organizations that are the subject of these studies. The focus in this growing literature on civic engagement is on voluntary organizations—the groups citizens choose to join as members. As a point of comparison, the survey taken for this study shows that half of all nonprofits have no individual members.[5]

Some of those respondents indicating that their organizations had individual members were, more accurately, listing their number of donors rather than members. Distinguishing the difference between members and donors is a problem for any study of voluntary organizations. Not unexpectedly, leaders do not use a common definition of membership when they calculate the number of people who, in any sense, belong to their organization. Consequently, many "members" of voluntary organizations may not be asked to vote for the leaders or board members, or ever be asked for their opinions about the direction of the organization. By virtue of their donations, however, the organization considers them members.

This is more than a technical or methodological problem for making calculations about membership trends or distributions. Although voluntary organizations are a subset of all nonprofits, the world of nonprofits is fundamentally different than the world of voluntary associations. Many of the nonprofits with no memberships more closely resemble government agencies than they do voluntary associations. Community health centers, elderly drop-in centers, job training facilities, and many other types of nonprofits typically do not have members.

Although this new work on civic engagement, social capital, and voluntary associations does not address the full universe of nonprofits, many of the normative issues at the heart of that work resonate broadly across the nonprofit world. Like membership nonprofits, nonmembership nonprofits are a link between government and the governed. They can also generate social capital, the trust and relationships that bind societies together.[6] Many nonprofits, with or without members, make heavy use of volunteers, and volunteering is one of the foundations of civil society. But even with all these commonalities with voluntary associations, for many nonprofits the key relationship is not between the organization and its members or donors, but with the poor, dispossessed, or vulnerable who are their clients.

The Black Hole of Political Science

The traditional literature on interest groups has had no problem in making room for lobbying organizations *sans* members. Although some interest group scholarship looks only at voluntary organizations, such works are clearly in the minority.[7] Whole divisions of the interest group army come without individual members: corporations, trade associations, some citizen lobbies, state and local governments, and a wide assortment of nonprofits, including foundations, charities, and service providers.[8] Labor unions have members, but membership is usually involuntary. The general rule of thumb among scholars is that if it lobbies, it's an interest group. And among all the organizations that do lobby, voluntary associations are by no means typical.

As one might guess this "If it quacks like a duck" logic makes for rather vague definitions of the interest group universe in the literature. But this is the messy reality of American politics: just about every type of organization does, in fact, lobby government. The very structure of government invites lobbying, and the political system is remarkably open to advocacy by interest groups. Moreover, there is every incentive to lobby since government freely negotiates with interest groups, and any one organization's competitors will likely be pushing policymakers toward its point of view. For most groups it is dangerous not to lobby. Unfortunately, the interest group sector with the strongest disincentive to lobby is 501c3 nonprofits. It is the only interest group sector to whom the government says "you really shouldn't."

Interest group specialists have long known that 501c3 tax status is an issue for nonprofits even though many of these organizations figure out ways to get around its restrictions or lobby in spite of them.[9] But awareness has not translated into any particular scholarly interest in the political behavior of nonprofits. The most concentrated focus on nonprofits of any type has been the research on citizen advocacy groups in Washington. These citizen groups are a combination of 501c3s, 501c4s (no tax deductibility and no prohibition against lobbying), and "twins" (501c4s with an affiliated 501c3 foundation that raises tax-deductible donations).[10] The scholarly work on these organizations has emphasized the traditional subjects of interest group research: advocacy tactics, lobbying effectiveness, and membership recruitment. The impact of the tax code receives scant attention.[11]

It may seem rather curious that interest group scholars show little interest in this nation's more than three-quarters of a million 501c3 nonprofits—a sector that is huge by any standard.[12] And all who work in the field would surely acknowledge the critical role that nonprofits play in American society. At first glance the answer may seem to lie in the ostensibly nonpolitical mission of so many nonprofits. For scholars, though, the primary mission of an organization is not what is important. The underlying mission of General Motors is to manufacture cars; yet its lobbying office in Washington, a minuscule part of the entire organization, is studied closely by those that work in the interest group field. Logically then, it should not make a difference to political scientists that the nonprofit raising money for breast cancer research is primarily engaged in a seemingly nonpolitical cause.

A more cogent explanation for this lack of attention is that the most influential interest group literature has concentrated on Washington politics.[13] It is in the local communities across America, not in Washington, where nonprofits are most important. Similarly, political scientists like to study power; they want to know who influences policy outcomes. As a result scholars are more likely to focus on the Business Roundtable or the AFL-CIO, than the neighborhood Community Development Corporation with its six employees.

Beyond this predisposition in the literature toward research on large, wealthy interest groups, those studying Washington lobbying have good reason to suspect that nonprofits are only of modest importance. The reality is that the research has cast a wide net across all sectors, thus not selecting out the groups to be studied. It fails to show much activity by 501c3 nonprofits. Leaving aside dedicated citizen advocacy groups, the

Table 2-1. *The Lobbying Universe*
Percent

| Type of lobby | Population of interest groups 1980 | | Participation 1979 |
	Organizations with own D.C. offices	Organizations having some form of D.C. representation	Proportion of congressional testimony
Corporations	21	52	22
Trade associations	32	20	29
Professional associations	15	8	12
Unions	3	2	4
Citizen groups	9	5	26
Nonprofits	6	3	7
Other/unknown	14	9	...
Total	100	99	100

Source: The data in columns one and two come from Kay Lehman Schlozman and John T. Tierney, *Organized Interests and American Democracy* (Harper and Row, 1986), p. 77. Their measurements of the make-up of the Washington interest group universe were derived from directories of organizations. For the statistical entries for "nonprofits" two of their categories, "civil rights/social welfare/poor" and "women/elderly/handicapped" have been combined. The percentages in column three represent the proportions of all interest group testimony offered in 1979 before congressional committees. In the original table from which this is taken, the category "nonprofits" was labeled as "other." Virtually all of the organizations that fell into this residual category, however, were nonprofits of one type or another. Jeffrey M. Berry, *The New Liberalism* (Brookings, 1999), p. 20.

other nonprofits have been found to be marginal players in Washington. In table 2-1, data from two separate works, each using a different methodology, lead to the same conclusion about nonprofits in the national political process. The first, a study by Kay Schlozman and John Tierney, utilized published directories to build a census of interest groups in Washington.[14] The authors used two alternative measurements. One counted only groups with their own offices in Washington, while the other combined those groups with organizations that employ lobbyists on retainer or are otherwise represented there. Both measures find that nonprofits constitute only a small slice of Washington's interest group community.

The second study, by Jeffrey Berry, documented which organizations participated in all the significant domestic social and domestic economic issues over three sessions of Congress. For each session of Congress, all those who testified on behalf of an interest group were categorized by the type of lobby they represented. After putting dedicated advocacy groups in a separate category, all other 501c3 or 501c4 nonprofits constituted only 7 percent of all those who testified before Congress in 1979. (This date is close to the time of Schlozman and Tierney's 1980 census).[15] Despite some imprecision in the two studies' coding, the bottom line remains the same: with the exception of dedicated citizen advocacy groups, nonprofits are a comparatively small part of the Washington interest group scene.

Representation

The preceding discussion may seem to put the cart before the horse. Why are nonprofits being defined as part of the interest group system in the first place? This designation lumps together community-based nonprofits—the vast majority of all nonprofits—into the same universe as the high-priced corporate lobbyists on K Street in Washington. It's mixing Gucci with sensible shoes. Out in the neighborhoods, the multiservice center does not consider itself an interest group. The organizers of the local soup kitchen do not think of themselves as lobbyists.

Although the neighborhood multiservice center may seem to have little in common with a Washington-based trade association, considering both these organizations interest groups requires no wild flights of conceptual fancy. The study of interest groups is the study of how various constituencies are *represented* in the political process. As already noted, interest group scholars believe that representation comes from an enormous variety of organizations, differing greatly not only in their substantive mission but in the scale of their operations, the level of government they focus on, and the institutions they lobby. In many ways this is a subfield without boundaries, summarily including any organization that has reason to talk to government and calling it an interest group.

"Representation" is a concept more typically associated with the role of legislators rather than interest groups. We elect legislators to stand in for us, to make decisions on our behalf, because we all cannot take part in the policymaking process. As the political theorist Hanna Pitkin put it, when we think of people in government representing us, we mean that their job "is to speak for, act for, look after the interests of their respective groups."[16] As Pitkin points out, this activity extends beyond legislators to others who stand in for those of us who cannot go to the state house or to the city council. In this sense nonprofits represent their constituents if they become active in the political process. Nonprofits "speak for," "act for," and "look after the interests" of those they are concerned about. And if an organization speaks for, acts for, or looks after the interests of constituents when it interacts with government, it is, by any definition of political science, an interest group.

Despite this logical certainty found in political science, many nonprofit leaders, like the executive director who regularly harasses her state legislator but denies involvement in the public policy process, would be baffled by a description of their organization as an interest group. In our study questionnaire, individual interviews with executive directors, and focus groups with directors and board members, we tried to understand just how nonprofit leaders do think of themselves when it comes to their relations with government.

Not surprisingly we found little consensus and a lot of confusion about the intended role, if any, of nonprofits in public affairs. Even when we did focus groups with the directors of social service organizations who had some involvement with government, we found little common ground. Some said their efforts were only educational in nature, transmitting good information to policymakers so they could make more intelligent decisions. Others freely acknowledged that they were trying to shape public policy, and some even used the word "lobby." Occasionally we even heard executive directors explicitly acknowledge their role as representatives. In a focus group in Minneapolis-St. Paul, the head of a women's group said, "I think it's easy for people to sit over on the Hill somewhere and make decisions about people's lives and never really have an opportunity to look into a woman's eyes who is struggling to make ends meet. . . . [We're giving] a voice to populations that are often not part of the discussion or are disenfranchised." Another panelist picked up on this theme and said his organization, which worked with the unemployed, helped them not only by giving them training but by "representing the reality of their lives" to those in government.

The Rules of the Market

Arguing that the government has seriously stacked the deck against the participation of nonprofits in the political process may seem surprising on many counts. The most basic "rule of the game" for interest groups is the First Amendment. Although it seemingly sanctifies lobbying because lobbying can be construed as "freedom of speech," the First Amendment also explicitly recognizes lobbying as a distinct freedom when it declares in its last clause that Americans have the right to "petition the Government for a redress of grievances." Antiquated as some of the language is in the

Constitution, there is no better definition of lobbying than "petitioning the government."

This charge may also seem surprising because nonprofits are revered while interest groups in general are considered the bane of American politics. Americans regard lobbies as selfish, unsavory, and impervious to the greater good. But the argument is that interest groups of all other types are treated better under the laws governing political participation than are 501c3 nonprofits. It is certainly not the public's preference that the law facilitates political participation by the Teamsters or the cement industry while discouraging it by Catholic Charities or the Boys and Girls Clubs. But that is the reality of the rules governing interest groups.

As discussed in chapter 1, nonprofits have become increasingly important in the administration of government services. Many of these organizations in health care and human services are an arm of government, carrying out its programs, living off its grants. As nonprofits have taken on more and more responsibility for administering government health and welfare programs, shouldn't the government have moved to put an end to their second-class political citizenship? The greater reliance on nonprofits should give government reason to rethink 501c3, but, inexplicably, recent efforts in Congress relating to the restrictions in the law have mostly been proposals to tighten the existing rules on lobbying by nonprofits.

Market Images

As economic thinking has pervaded the other social sciences, scholars have adapted its analytical tools to many problems not normally associated with economics. For example, interest group scholars have been influenced by economists to think of membership recruitment not so much as a process of people coming together to act on their collective interests but instead as a dynamic process of marketing by competing groups, each offering potential members a package of incentives, many of which have little to do with public policy. The idea of a marketplace is relevant not only to membership recruitment but to the shape of the interest group universe. Just like business markets, the interest group market has its own incentive system, regulatory framework, and barriers to entry.

To conceive of interest groups as operating in a regulated market is to understand that government sets rules making it easier or more difficult for private or nonprofit organizations to participate in public policymaking. No one has ever argued that interest group politics is practiced on a level playing field. Even pluralists like Robert Dahl recognized the inequities of wealth in interest group politics. Still, considerable theorizing in modern political science is a conscious refutation of pluralist thinking. Pluralism may be long dead, but interest group scholars delight in disinterring the body and performing additional autopsies.

Pluralism was not only a theory of government built around interest group activity, but it was a celebration of American democracy. In *Who Governs?* the most influential and controversial argument on behalf of pluralism, Robert Dahl concluded that "New Haven is an example of a democratic system, warts and all."[17] It took only a year before a resounding refutation of the theory appeared in the *American Political Science Review*, but the debate continued because it was difficult to let go of its basic premise: interest groups operate in an open market.[18] Groups arise as they are needed, as citizens come to understand that their interests are at stake in some emerging policy debate. Not all groups have the same resources—one of the "warts" of democracy—but what is critical in pluralist imagery is that the political system is wide open and small groups as well as large have access to policymakers who are willing to negotiate with them.

This conception of an open market for groups has its roots in the writings of James Madison and Alexis de Tocqueville.[19] Given the reverence for these compelling arguments for interest groups and associations, pluralism remains a lofty ideal. But if there isn't a freely operating market for interest groups of all types, does that mean that America isn't a democracy? This is exactly what the power elite theorists said: America is not a democracy but instead an oligarchy composed of powerful families and corporations.[20] In their mind the whole idea of interest group democracy is an illusion. This is a tough pill to swallow even for those who regard pluralism as far too optimistic.

A more penetrating and convincing critique of pluralism came from economist Mancur Olson. In the *Logic of Collective Action* he argued that voluntary associations are beset by the free rider problem, and that members of interest groups often join for reasons having nothing to do with the lobbying conducted by the organization.[21] Although Olson badly underestimated the degree to which Americans are willing to join voluntary associations for their lobbying—free riding be damned—his book has been enormously influential among scholars of American government. Olson's line of thinking has been adapted to a broad range of problems, and the collective action problem is at the heart of modern interest group research.

Political scientists have been so taken with the rigor of Olson's analysis that his more normative argument is often overlooked. The end point of his "logic" is that while some in American society are well represented because their organizations have either institutional support or strong incentives to offer potential members, many others, what he calls the "forgotten groups," are victims of the system. They "suffer in silence" because the costs of organizing outweigh the individual benefits.[22]

A third perspective utilized by interest group scholars, especially those who write about social movements, is political opportunity theory. It is also known as political process theory, but the idea is the same. New groups periodically challenge the existing status quo, but their success is highly dependent on the opportunity structure of the governmental process (whether that government is a democracy or not). Elites can, to a significant degree, manipulate those opportunities to make it easier or harder at any one time for challenging groups to move from contentious politics to being an accepted and integrated participant in the political process.

This theory has a great deal of currency in comparative politics where it has been used by scholars like Sidney Tarrow to explain the political development of various societies over time.[23] Its adaptation to American politics is more problematic. Doug McAdam uses political opportunity theory to explain why the civil rights movement declined after some important successes in the early 1960s.[24] Opportunities that arose out of the government's response to the civil rights protests began to sharply contract during the second half of the 1960s. The idea of opportunities to participate in the political system—opportunities that can expand or contract over time—has a clear relevance to the situation of 501c3 nonprofits. Yet unlike social movements, nonprofits are not really challenging the system; most are fairly conventional in their political orientation, and their general role in society is already embraced by political elites. Political process theory also assumes some mechanism of control by a coherent elite. Nonprofits are treated in such wildly different ways by the federal government and by local governments that clearly there is no one political opportunity structure.

These are not the only theories that have guided interest group research, but they have been central to the field for many years.[25] Directly or indirectly, they all place interest group participation within a market structure. For Dahl, the market is relatively open, allowing access to government for even those groups with modest resources. For Olson, the interest group system is characterized by market failure. Numerous constituencies are badly in need of representation by interest groups, but no organizations arise to provide that service. And for McAdam, the market is manipulated. Plenty of groups are participating at any one time (equilibrium), but others wishing to enter the marketplace face stiff barriers to entry. Sometimes these obstacles are relaxed because elites find it too costly to refuse entry to challengers. Subsequently, those elites will reduce access when they have the opportunity and it is to their advantage to do so.

Regulation

Each of these broad theories provides some insight into understanding the composition of the interest group universe. In the last analysis, though, they all fail to adequately explain the participation of nonprofits in public policymaking. This should come as no surprise since none of these theories were conceived with nonprofits in mind. Moreover, the sheer complexity, scope, and variety of the nonprofit sector are a challenge to any all-encompassing theory of interest groups. For whatever the reasons, nonprofits are generally disregarded in interest group theory.

An alternative perspective is to think of the interest group market not as an open market, a failed market, or a manipulated market, but instead as a regulated market. This is not a grand theory of interest groups; it makes no effort to explain anything beyond the role government plays in facilitating or inhibiting the participation of lobbying organizations. This framework emphasizes the ongoing bargaining and negotiation between government and the groups that are governed by the regulations. Regulation is a dynamic process, and adjustments in the rules are made frequently as government responds to requests from groups for easier access or from opponents of particular groups wanting to inhibit those lobbies' access.

This may all seem unnecessarily abstract. There is value, however, in trying to think systematically about all the ways in which government may help or hinder interest groups. Our democracy, for better or for worse, is heavily dependent on interest groups to aggregate like-minded citizens and to articulate their preferences before government. For purposes of analysis it is impossible to make an appropriate evaluation of the fairness of the regulations governing participation by nonprofits without a comparative framework. Just how does the regulation of nonprofits compare with the rules that govern other interest group sectors?

The regulation of interest groups is surprisingly pervasive, especially in light of what appears to be a rather unambiguous First Amendment right to lobby. Of course there are general limits to the right of free speech—one can't falsely cry "fire" in a crowded theater. The regulation of interest groups, however, goes far beyond such modest restrictions. The freedom to speak—to hand out leaflets in public spaces or to stand in a park on a soapbox and give a speech regardless if anyone is listening—is a qualitatively different exercise than the freedom to lobby. The basic difference is that free speech is about speech while lobbying is as much about who is listening as it is about who is talking. The targets of lobbying speech are members of the government and therein lies the rub. For many forms of lobbying, policymakers have to open the door before the group can commence its petitioning. Are those behind the door obligated to open it to all groups that seek an audience? Can those who get an audience bring gifts with them, like campaign contributions? If so, how much? Obviously, there have to be some rules.

In practical terms, there are at least four underlying rationales for government regulation of interest groups:

INTEGRITY AND ACCOUNTABILITY. If government did not regulate the participation of interest groups, the wealthiest organizations would have such undue influence that democracy would be threatened if not extinguished. Some critics claim that is the case now, that the wealthy "buy" policies from the government through their campaign donations. Campaign finance laws are the most obvious form of interest group regulation as the corrupting influence of money is a serious threat to a system of government that relies on private financing of elections. Over the years Congress has periodically taken steps to limit the funds that interest groups can give to candidates and parties, such as the ban on soft money contributions enacted by Congress in 2002.

Lobbyists in Washington are required to register if they are working the House or the Senate and file expense reports of their efforts.[26] Administrative agencies have various ex parte rules to govern against favoritism. The 1978 Ethics in Government Act prohibits contact between an ex-agency official and his or her former employer for a year and forbids them from ever lobbying on an issue they worked on. A similar moratorium also applies to former members of Congress. Other rules limit gifts and speaking fees. Whether it is sweetheart deals on various investment opportunities for representatives and senators or golf junkets under the guise of a speaking engagement, interest groups have tried their best to curry favor with legislators.

When it comes to such integrity and accountability issues, government is always playing catch-up, trying to devise politically acceptable ways of stopping some interest group activity that is causing embarrassment because of revelations in the press. Even so, an extensive array of campaign finance restrictions and ethics standards is in place on the federal level. Each state has its own restrictions as well. Critics mock these rules, seeing them as something like the little Dutch boy with his finger in the dike: no sooner do you stop one form of interest group money from getting to the politicians than another source sprouts. For the less cynical, these regulatory steps are seen as crucial to the integrity of the political system, and for that reason these restrictions on the First Amendment right to lobby are easily justified.

Conversely, government sometimes facilitates participation by interest groups so that lobbies may keep government accountable. The Data Quality Act, enacted in 2000, requires each agency of government to publish standards for the scientific and statistical information it bases its decisions on. Anyone has the right to point out errors in government databases and, if the charges are borne out, documents built around them must be withdrawn and, potentially, regulations may be rescinded. The Data Quality Act is widely seen as a great tool for business trade groups fighting regulations they oppose.[27]

PRESERVING ORDER. Government is sometimes called on to referee participation when it is impractical to let interest groups participate in any way they want. For example, what happens when more than one union wants to try to organize workers at a particular site? It is not in the public interest to let them fight it out without any clear rules of engagement. Even more basic is the right of the union to organize in the first place. The Wagner Act, protecting the rights of unions to organize workers, is a landmark in the regulation of interest groups.

Passage of the Wagner Act was hardly the last word in government's regulation of labor unions. The National Labor Relations Board referees the ongoing fight between labor and business over the rules of organizing campaigns. What kind of communication can management have with its workers during a unionization effort? What constitutes evidence of firings by management intended to intimidate union sympathizers? These rules have evolved incrementally over time as unions and corporations have challenged the status quo. The changing of the political guard between Republicans and Democrats in the White House is an incentive for challenge, depending on the political outlook of the president's appointments. Labor unions are further regulated by the Landrum-Griffin Act, which requires them to operate in a democratic fashion.[28]

Another critically important form of regulation is standing for litigation. A litigant cannot file suit unless that individual or organization meets the criteria for injury. But what constitutes injury or damage? This, too, changes over time as the courts modify the rules to make it easier or harder for interest groups or interest group sectors to file suit.[29] At one time a corporation or trade group could not litigate if its alleged injury was caused by business competition. The federal courts changed this rule and allowed suits in certain instances when the injury to one business or industry was caused by competition from another business or industry.[30]

INCORPORATION. The government often finds it is in its interest to draw interest groups more formally into the policymaking process. It may do this because it wants a forum to resolve disputes among interest groups, or because it wants to try to treat competing interest groups more equitably and it sets up a process to do that. A ubiquitous approach is the creation of advisory boards to agencies; the federal government has around 1,000 currently in operation.[31] Federal advisory boards must comply with the provisions of the Federal Advisory Committee Act of 1972, including a stipulation that they be fairly balanced in the views represented by the various members. Individuals are sometimes chosen to represent specific interest group constituencies, and the groups can sometimes influence who is chosen, by making recommendations to an agency or through the intervention of sympathetic legislators.[32]

Negotiated regulations are a means of government-sanctioned interest group bargaining. Guided by the Negotiated Rulemaking Act of 1990, agencies can select a small number of lobbies that represent all the interests that "will be significantly affected" by the regulation. For example, a negotiated regulation (or "reg-neg") on clean burning gasoline in smoggy cities was produced by a committee composed of representatives of the Sierra Club, the Natural Resources Defense Council, the American Petroleum Institute, the National Petroleum Refiners Association, and the Environmental Protection Agency. Once the interest groups agree on a rule, the agency issues it as government policy. This process has great benefit as it expedites policymaking and reduces challenges in the courts by getting the involved parties to commit themselves to the finished product.[33]

SUBSIDY AND PROMOTION. The intervention of the government into the interest group marketplace extends beyond setting rules to structure access for the lobbies that approach them. Government sometimes goes a step farther and helps to create interest groups where it sees a need, or in the language of regulation, where it senses that there has been market failure. A classic example is the Department of Agriculture's nurturing of farm groups in the early part of the twentieth century. The Smith-Lever Act created a grant program to further the education of farmers in their local areas and designated local farm groups as an appropriate recipient of such funds.

This was instrumental in creating county farm bureaus throughout the country, and this in turn led to the creation of the American Farm Bureau Federation.[34]

The government, when it believes that a sector is systematically under-represented, has sometimes acted to promote and support its participation. For a brief time the federal government used intervenor funding to pay the expenses of citizen groups wishing to participate in administrative rule-making. The imbalance of industry to all other interests was seen as especially egregious in agency policymaking, and the Federal Trade Commission and a few other agencies subsidized citizen groups during the late 1970s.[35] Citizen participation requirements, common in social programs, represent remediation efforts on the part of government, as well as a means of incorporation.

There are endless numbers of grant programs that provide support to interest groups. A large number are training grants that permit an organization to educate and prepare clients for certain kinds of tasks or jobs. Conservatives have long complained that these grants are a subsidy to liberal lobbies like labor unions or poor people's groups.[36] The grants to nonprofits to carry out services, while not intended to promote interest group advocacy, are certainly awarded with an eye toward building up the administrative capacity of service providers. As discussed in later chapters, this general support also works to strengthen the political capacity of nonprofits by helping them to grow and become more professional. Government needs a vibrant and successful nonprofit sector, and only the most naïve would think that grants do not help those nonprofits that want to become politically active. At the same time, this promotion of nonprofits is balanced by a much more insidious form of regulation, section 501c3 and its limits on lobbying.

Not a Level Playing Field

Despite the extensive and evident freedom to lobby in the American political system, this substantial array of federal regulatory standards prescribes both opportunities and restrictions for interest groups that are active in national politics. Other rules have been adopted by cities and states. Some are fairly innocuous (lobbying registration), while others (judicial standing) determine whether an interest group can participate at all in a particular arena. There is certainly no master plan that rationally sorts out these privileges, prohibitions, and rules of behavior. There is no orderly approach to balancing a new law or administrative rule for one institution against the existing rules for other arenas. Different sectors of the interest group community play by different rules, and when all the rules and regulations are considered together, they don't add up to a level playing field.

Policymaking for interest group participation is incremental, changing slowly over time as new problems emerge or old ones gain greater visibility. Like any regulated subject, interest groups search for ways to develop or exploit loopholes in existing regulatory standards. No sooner had the ink dried on President George W. Bush's signature on the law restricting soft money than efforts were under way to create organizations and means of channeling additional corporate and labor money into the party system.[37] And when an interest group sector succeeds in going around rules through practices not anticipated by regulators, pressure may build on policymakers to reregulate in that area.

Regulations on interest group participation are not dictated by a unified elite, operating out of our sight or under our radar. Instead, they are negotiated in mundane, everyday policymaking processes. As standards are negotiated, different interest group sectors come to the bargaining table with differences in resources and status. The anticipation of how those resources may be used can influence policymakers before they even begin to formally consider taking action. Since interest group regulations create advantages or obstacles for various interest group sectors, conservatives and liberals fight over them. For example, when labor bills come before Congress, conservatives will work to restrict union political activity and liberals will work to expand it. The political calculus is not much more complicated than answering the question "Whom does this help?"

One does not have to subscribe to an elitist view of American politics to acknowledge the advantages that business has in American politics. Although there are some significant restraints in the way it can use its wealth in the political process (such as campaign finance laws), business retains substantial means to enhance its access to policymakers. But unlike business (or even labor), there is little concern that nonprofits will use their wealth to unduly influence policymakers. Nonprofits do benefit from government rules that prescribe citizen participation so, overall, interest group regulation helps as well as hinders their efforts to represent their clients and members in the political system. Yet being able to conduct advocacy with local administrative agencies does not compensate for the sharp restriction on legislative lobbying. The development of the 501c3 regulatory standard will be described later, but it is important to emphasize that of all the regulatory standards that govern interest groups, few are as restrictive as the tax code's treatment of nonprofits.

Fear Factor

The experience of leaders of Washington-based organizations that promote nonprofits and offer training to nonprofit executives on government relations led to the creation of this book. Over the years as they traveled around the country they heard a familiar story from nonprofit directors who indicated that they were afraid of doing anything that could result in the loss of their tax deductibility. Although the nonprofit mavens from Washington knew that section 501c3 allowed much more advocacy than the rank-and-file executive directors believed, they realized that perception of the law could be far more influential than the letter of the law. Even though the evidence seemed persuasive to them, it was still anecdotal and the desire for more concrete, systematically gathered data led, somewhat circuitously, to the survey and other research endeavors reported here.

Four basic questions emerged to guide construction of our questionnaire and the basic strategy of inquiry for the interviews and focus groups. The beginning point was, quite simply, to determine if the tax code truly deters the participation of 501c3 nonprofits. Although the question is simple to phrase, answering it is not. As noted earlier, there are other reasons why nonprofits may choose not to get involved in the public policy process. There are also legal ways of getting around the limitations in 501c3. Consequently, there is no one test that can categorically answer this question. In chapters 3, 4, and 5, we examine the question from different perspectives. Cumulatively, these tests offer what we believe is a convincing answer.

A second and related question is to ask, if section 501c3 does influence the level of political activity by nonprofits, what are the consequences? As already emphasized, nonprofits are critical in providing social services to the poor, disabled, minorities, immigrants, and other vulnerable populations. With half of all nonprofits in health and social services, any adverse impact of the tax code on nonprofits is going to be damaging to the clients of these organizations.

Third, is there a differential impact of 501c3 on administrative lobbying as opposed to legislative lobbying? The limitation on lobbying by nonprofits applies only to legislative lobbying and grass-roots mobilization.

Nonprofits registered under 501c3 are free to lobby administrative agencies as much as they like.[38] This is particularly important to community-based nonprofits since so many of them administer government programs. Does the regulation of lobbying by nonprofits inhibit 501c3s in their relationship with agencies, even though the law was not intended to do so? Alternatively, if nonprofits correctly understand the law, do they use this freedom to lobby agencies for more grants, regulatory changes, or greater autonomy?

Fourth, what do politically effective nonprofits look like? Choosing to become politically active is the first step toward political effectiveness. But beyond that, what characterizes those nonprofits that have earned greater access to government? As more and more government-supported services have been subcontracted to nonprofit providers, the relationship between agencies and nonprofits has become more interdependent. Can specific attributes of nonprofits, such as resources, tactics, or organizational structure be linked to success in dealing with the government?

In the broadest sense, the goal is to document how and how often nonprofits interact with government. Such activity takes many forms, and these four lines of inquiry shaped our efforts to measure all the different ways nonprofits communicate with policymakers. The answers to these questions may not tell us everything we need to know, but they should provide a foundation for understanding how nonprofits represent their constituents before government. Nonprofits have a political role to play as interest groups, even if they are not always aware of it.

Observing Nonprofits

A guiding assumption from the outset was that there was no one method that could provide all the information we needed. Surveys are excellent instruments for gathering systematic data from a large number of subjects. At the same time, questionnaires must often depend on simple responses (checked boxes or circled numbers) since asking people to write out answers ensures a low return rate. Questionnaires do not allow the researchers to probe for depth or subtlety. Interviews with nonprofit leaders offer the opposite in advantages and disadvantages. Interviewers can pursue interesting topics or insights raised by the subject, asking follow-up questions and probing beyond superficial answers. This kind of interviewing is labor intensive, and the number of questions that can be asked is rather limited. Focus groups are a different approach to interviewing. They allow the researcher to observe and record the discussion and debate that ensues when people in the same profession are put into a room and given some broad questions to chew on. Focus groups are somewhat unpredictable, can go off on tangents, and are often dominated by a few aggressive participants while more reserved individuals fade into the background. Yet participants spark one another and initiate discussions about topics that the researcher had not thought to bring up. This study, recognizing the strengths and weaknesses of each of these approaches, has utilized all of them.[39]

Even though these three different methodologies were all used, most of the resources went into the mail survey. It is the most scientifically reliable source of data since the organizations included were drawn randomly and the sample size was quite large. From the outset, the interviews and focus groups were seen as means of supplementing the survey, by asking questions that could not be asked in the questionnaire and as a means of pursuing topics in more depth.

The survey sampled only those nonprofits large enough to file a tax return with the Internal Revenue Service. Nonprofits with at least $5,000 in annual income are required to register with the IRS. Only those 501c3s with at least $25,000 a year in income are, however, required to file a tax return.[40] A large proportion of all nonprofits fall below the $25,000 threshold, and many of these organizations even fall below the $5,000 minimum for registration. These smaller organizations are commonly ones run out of people's homes, such as Little Leagues and neighborhood associations. There is no national database for such organizations.[41] Consequently, the survey misses these small but numerous entities. Given the focus of this study on the public policymaking process and emphasis on health and social service providers, the exclusion of Little Leagues and PTAs and other tiny nonprofits should not undermine the study's validity. At the same time, we recognize the importance of small nonprofits in building community. As Putnam argues, they form the glue that bonds our communities.[42]

Unlike our personal Form 1040 income tax returns, a 501c3's Form 990 tax return must be made available to the public. Since taxpayers subsidize nonprofits through the deduction for charitable donations, it is entirely appropriate that citizens have the right to these financial records. For example, the 990 requires that nonprofit filers reveal how much of their funds go for fund-raising costs, a useful piece of information for a potential donor choosing among competing charities.[43] Each year the IRS provides scanned images of Form 990s to the National Center for Charitable Statistics (NCCS) at the Urban Institute, a Washington-based think tank. The NCCS gives these images to GuideStar, a nonprofit that creates an electronic database from them. Finally, the NCCS puts these data into a format that is usable by scholars.[44] By random selection, 2,738 nonprofits from around the country were chosen for inclusion in the study. (More specifically, we drew random samples of four different groupings of 990 filers, though for simplicity's sake we only use two of them in the presentation of data in the chapters that follow. See the appendix for further detail.) The return rate of completed questionnaires was 64 percent, extremely high for mail surveys of nonprofits. In most cases the surveys were sent to the executive director of each organization.

For technical reasons, hospitals and hospital systems as well as universities were removed from the survey database. Principally, they are egregious statistical outliers, and to include them would necessitate presenting separate statistical findings for samples with and without data from these very large organizations. All other kinds of health care nonprofits are included in the sample as are other types of educational organizations. Individual church congregations do not file Form 990 so they are not included, though other kinds of religion-related nonprofits are found in the samples.

The central challenge in constructing the questionnaire was the paradox illustrated by the story that begins this chapter. Embedded in the identity of being a nonprofit is that the organization is part of the third sector, performing a useful societal function outside the spheres of business or government. For nonprofit leaders it is all too easy to believe that contacts with government have little to do with politics or even public policymaking. To complicate matters further, the common understanding of section 501c3 makes many nonprofit leaders insistent that they don't "lobby." A main purpose of this study, though, was to find out just how much nonprofits do lobby. If the questionnaire appeared at an initial scan to be about lobbying, too many nonprofit executive directors would toss it in the wastebasket. However, to properly test the questions posed earlier, the questionnaire did have to accurately measure the political activity of the organizations selected for the study.

The approach taken was to ask about a variety of activities and to overlap questions so that we tested for particular forms of political behavior in different ways. The three items that used the term "lobbying" were part of lists of a variety of statements, so there was no reason for respondents to believe that we expected all nonprofits to engage in this activity.[45] Since political scientists define lobbying so liberally, regarding it as just about any activity undertaken with an eye toward eventually influencing policymakers' understanding of issues or their action on them, there was no need to rely only on the few questions that used this sensitive word. Because multiple questions were used to measure different forms of interaction with government, the chances that statistical results are artifacts of question wording are significantly reduced. The questionnaire is reprinted in the appendix (figure A-1).

The task of writing survey questions was made a bit easier by the knowledge that the questionnaire would be followed by a set of interviews with executive directors of nonprofits. These interviews were done with questionnaire respondents who filled in a box on the last page saying that they would be willing to be interviewed and supplying their phone number. Since respondents had to volunteer to be included, there is a self-selection bias in the resulting set of possible respondents, though it is hard to know if there is any meaningful difference between those who volunteered and those who did not. More than half of respondents filling out questionnaires offered to talk to us and, thus, they come from a broad section of the potential pool.

Approximately forty phone interviews were conducted from this pool of respondents by the two coauthors. The questioning was open ended, and the interviewers used only a small set of core questions, following their instincts once the subject began talking. These interviews were enormously valuable in teaching us about the day-to-day operations of nonprofits. Allowing nonprofit leaders the latitude to talk at length about what they did, and about how they think about their relationship with government, enriched our understanding of how government affairs fits into the broader work of these organizations. We quote liberally from these interviews in the text that follows. These leaders' words not only bring the subject matter to life, but their observations often confirmed patterns in the survey data, and we use their insights to provide context beyond the numbers from the tables.

Another set of around twenty-five interviews was done outside of the pool of participants in the survey. This second set was composed of people we sought out to talk about a specific subject that we needed more information on, such as practices within the tax-exempt section of the IRS. Interview subjects included current and former government officials, academics, executive directors of nonprofits, and some long-time observers of nonprofits who work for advocacy organizations in Washington. These individuals are also quoted extensively as their words make important points far more eloquently than we could.

Besides the interviews, seventeen focus groups were held with nonprofit executive directors and board members in a diverse set of cities across the country. Some were held with the leaders of organizations that were working with specific minorities, and other sessions drew on people from a specific policy field like health care. Additional information on the focus groups, as well as on the survey and interviews, is, again, in the appendix.

Conclusion

Nonprofit scholars focus on the uniqueness of third-sector organizations. There is certainly justification for this perspective. Although nonprofits may be businesslike in their operations, they are not businesses. Their incentive system is fundamentally different from an organization that must make a profit and then expand on that profit the next year. They are different from government agencies too. In thinking about how nonprofits interact with government, it is useful, however, to consider them against the larger universe of organizations that try to influence government.

As is true of other interest group sectors, the participation of nonprofits in the public policymaking process is regulated by the government. Despite the First Amendment the freedom to say what you want is not the freedom to interact with government in any way that you want. There is a surprisingly dense set of rules that governs how various types of interest groups can lobby the government. In this sense nonprofits are no different than labor unions or corporations. When the political regulation of nonprofits is examined against this larger array of rules for all types of private organizations, the restrictiveness of rules governing 501c3s is striking. If one did not know better, a review of all the regulations affecting interest group participation might lead to the conclusion that nonprofits are the lobbying organizations that are most threatening to our form of democracy.

The irony, of course, is that so many leaders of nonprofits do not regard themselves as working in anything remotely like an interest group. That they do not see the world in the way that political scientists do is understandable. Yet viewing 501c3 as simply part of the lot of nonprofits is unfortunate because it reinforces the notion that they should not be playing a role in trying to influence legislators. And if they shouldn't be lobbying legislatures, then it follows that they do not have a responsibility to represent their clients before government.

CHAPTER THREE

The Regulation
of Lobbying

W e had the following conversation with the executive
director of a statewide organization representing hospice providers:

We publish a newsletter but we never tell our people to urge a
vote.
*You don't tell them to contact their legislators on issues of impor-
tance to you?*
We tell them to contact their legislators but we *don't* tell them to
urge them to vote a certain way.

For an organization actively lobbying a state legislature, informing their
constituents about an important vote but refraining from telling them to
urge their legislators to vote a particular way certainly doesn't make sense
unless, of course, that organization is a public charity as defined by section
501c3 of the Internal Revenue code. If an organization tells its members to
tell legislators to vote a certain way, that constitutes *lobbying* because it is
an attempt to influence the passage or defeat of legislation. Telling the readers of the newsletter to contact their legislators but not giving them a
message to include can be construed instead as an activity aimed at *educating* members.

This may seem a rather dubious distinction, but under the logic of section 501c3, it is a distinction that matters. A beginning point in this analysis
is to ask why government policy distinguishes between lobbying and other

forms of communication with government. The ostensible answer—that government cares because it subsidizes nonprofits through the tax code— merely begs the question. No one thinks it is a bad idea for nonprofits to communicate with government, offering their first-hand knowledge of problems and program operations to those who write laws or administer them. But lobbying is something else entirely. Or is it?

The Dirty Word

The distinction between lobbying and other means of trying to influence government is an artifice of those who write laws and regulations. In contrast political scientists who study interest groups make no such distinction, believing that lobbying extends far beyond the attempt to sway legislators. Texts on interest groups define the term *lobbying* in a generic manner. "Lobbying is all-directional," says one.[1] Another states that lobbying is "attempting to influence government decisions."[2] And "When an interest group attempts to influence policymakers, it can be said to be engaging in *lobbying*."[3] Kay Schlozman and John T. Tierney go as far as to list twenty-seven different types of lobbying, with different tactics aimed at different institutions, including agencies, courts, and the media.[4] In short, the scholars who work in this area regard lobbying as an attempt to influence any part of government.

The reason why political scientists and policymakers conceive of lobbying differently is easy enough to summarize. Political scientists develop their definitions with an eye toward conceptual unity: grouping like behavior under the same term. Policymakers, including legislators, must contend instead with a complicated calculus when they consider lobbying. They know that lobbying is protected free speech, but they also know that Americans distrust legislators because they see them as easily susceptible to the persuasion of interest groups. Legislators are seen as more corruptible and less ethical than other policymakers because of their need for campaign contributions. Money taints legislators.

The public is not without reason in seeing the direct relationship between lobbies and legislators as more worrisome than other forms of lobbying. In spite of numerous reforms throughout our history, "interested money" has always found its way to receptive legislators. Whether it is nineteenth-century legislators riding the trains for free, courtesy of railroad lobbyists, or Newt Gingrich and Hillary Clinton taking huge advances on book contracts from large corporations with interests before Congress, the stories stain all members of Congress and all lobbies. Today, most of that stain emanates from campaign finance—from perfectly legal (and perfectly suspect) contributions to parties and candidates for office.

The drumbeat goes on, year after year, case after case. We read in our papers of legislators accused of toadying up to lobbies to gain their contributions. There are always reform bills in Congress aimed at reducing the influence of money over elections and lawmaking, but they are usually voted down. Investigative journalism uncovers scandals, stoking cynicism. The editorial cartoonists, the monologues by David Letterman and Jay Leno, the radio talk shows, all contribute to the simple notion that Congress is dirty. From their study of public opinion, John R. Hibbing and Elizabeth Theiss-Morse conclude, "People believe wholeheartedly that interest groups have too much influence over members of Congress. An astounding 86 percent of respondents believe Congress is too heavily influenced by interest groups."[5] Another survey finds that almost two-thirds of the public thinks interest groups are a threat to American democracy.[6]

Public Charities

But if the popular suspicion of lobbyists and legislators is understandable, why are nonprofits regulated with an intent to reduce their role in the legislative process? Isn't it in the public's interest to broaden the mix of interest groups before Congress, state legislatures, and city councils? Legislative bodies are lobbied relentlessly by corporations, trade associations, professional associations, and labor unions. It seems perverse that tax law discourages participation by groups like the hospice organization mentioned above. Nonprofits are uniformly admired, and no one speaks of the dangers of too much nonprofit influence in the political system. More lobbying by nonprofits would increase the representation of the disadvantaged and the dispossessed, those who are poor and those who are forgotten. Discouraging their participation in the political system is surely American politics at its most perverse.

The rationale for the regulation of nonprofits through 501c3 is relatively straightforward: they're public charities. Nonprofits that wish to come under its provisions must be "organized and operated exclusively for religious, charitable, scientific, testing for public safety, literary, or educational purposes."[7] If a nonprofit does in fact qualify as a public charity, it is able to offer donors a powerful incentive to contribute. For taxpayers with a marginal income tax rate of 35 percent, a $1,000 contribution to a tax-deductible nonprofit effectively costs them only $650.

In the language of economics, tax deductibility under 501c3 is a tax expenditure. In the language of English, it is a subsidy, plain and simple. If government chooses to spend money on a subsidy for nonprofits, it will have to take more revenues from other sources. If there were no subsidy for charitable donations, our marginal tax rate could be a bit lower. Alternatively, if there were no subsidy for nonprofits, government could spend more on various programs or create other subsidies. Indeed, one of the strongest arguments in defense of the subsidy is that nonprofits perform services that government would like to see offered. Government may even pay the nonprofits directly to perform that service, but it gets the added bonus of nonprofits attracting private money to support these activities too.[8]

The 501c3 subsidy is easy to defend. What's much more difficult is to define exactly what kind of organizations are eligible for that subsidy. Which nonprofit organizations are public charities and which are not? This is hardly a new issue. As Evelyn Brody and Joseph J. Cordes note, "Nonprofit organizations have long enjoyed a special relationship with the tax collector. At least since Joseph's proclamation of a land law in Egypt that 'Pharaoh should have the fifth part; except the land of priests only, which become not Pharaoh's' (Genesis 47:26), societies have acknowledged the presence of a nontaxable sector."[9]

The eligibility requirements for inclusion under 501c3 are liberal, though some nonprofits have been excluded because they violate "public policy." Such was the case for Bob Jones University, which allowed the enrollment of African Americans but whose stated policy was to expel "students who date outside of their own race." The Supreme Court held that the university did not abide by "common-law standards of charity" and upheld the revocation of its tax-exempt status by the Internal Revenue Service.[10] Organizations that have unrealistic aims or are based on unscientific claims may be denied 501c3 status. An organization claiming that aliens are among us could be denied tax deductibility.[11]

The rather broad eligibility limits for 501c3 status make it appear as though the regulation of nonprofits by government is rather light. Quite rightly the government has treaded carefully in defining the boundaries of eligibility and to its credit it has generally shied away from excluding organizations espousing unpopular political views. It has not been as cautious in going after political organizations that appear to be violating the limits on lobbying and have offended some strong political interests. In terms of its purpose, however, 501c3 is generous in allowing organizations of all stripes to qualify for the tax subsidy. In other words, an organization can stand for just about anything. Acting on those beliefs is another issue.

An Even Dirtier Word

Regulation of lobbying by nonprofits is firmly grounded in the belief that the subsidy granted through the tax code gives the government the authority to restrict such behavior. The Supreme Court said in *Regan v. Taxation with Representation* (1983) that "Deductible contributions are similar to cash grants" from the government. The Court held that in writing its tax laws Congress had clearly made a conscious decision not to subsidize lobbying by nonprofits. Moreover, as it had held earlier, "Congress is not required by the First Amendment to subsidize lobbying."[12]

The origins of the lobbying restriction on nonprofits are murky.[13] The 1917 tax legislation establishing the deduction for charitable donations included no lobbying restrictions. In 1919 the Treasury Department issued regulations that said that organizations "formed to disseminate controversial or partisan propaganda" were not educational and thus were not eligible for tax deductibility.[14] Armed with these grounds for denying tax deductibility, the Treasury Department did so on occasion and reminded all nonprofit organizations of its power to ruin them financially. One of the groups it rebuked was the American Birth Control League, which was organized to help married women prevent "uncontrolled procreation."[15] After losing its tax status the organization challenged the IRS ruling. A federal appeals court acknowledged that the organization was a bona fide charity but noted that its charter explicitly set forth a goal of enlisting legislators to change relevant laws on birth control. This important decision, *Slee v. Commissioner*, made it clear that no matter how worthy the goal, "agitating for the repeal of laws" could not be supported by taxpayer funds.[16] A few years later in 1934 Congress took action to strengthen the intent of the Treasury regulations, incorporating a section on the political activity of nonprofits into statute.[17] Tax deductibility was to be withheld from organizations where a "substantial part of the activities . . . is carrying on propaganda, or otherwise attempting, to influence legislation."[18] This language remains in place today. For a nonprofit to decide how much lobbying it can do, it has to figure out what amounts to "substantial" lobbying. Despite repeated requests from the nonprofits, the IRS refuses to define this standard.

What is striking about the development of 501c3 is the definition of lobbying as a form of "propaganda," a rather inflammatory word that suggests manipulative and dishonest communication. Nevertheless, propaganda is still today the definition of lobbying in the law governing nonprofits. Although this wording may reflect a harsher view of an earlier era, it all too accurately reflects widespread distrust of lobbyists and legislators. In theory existing tax law is designed to protect citizens from having their tax money used to subsidize lobbying. The taxpayer subsidy is for charitable purposes, and lobbying is not a charitable purpose. Rather lobbying is something akin to the distribution of propaganda. The law's intent is to severely limit legislative advocacy by nonprofits with tax deductibility. In practice, that policy is unworkable.

Inconsistency Mixed with Contradiction

Regulating nonprofits presents a difficult dilemma to government. On the one hand it needs to keep public support for charity and philanthropy from being undermined by overt lobbying by controversial and unpopular nonprofits. Americans do not have a sophisticated understanding of the relevant tax law, but similar to Justice Potter Stewart's definition of pornography, they know obnoxious lobbying when they see it. Those opposed to abortion do not want their tax dollars to support lobbying by prochoice groups. Those supporting choice would be incensed to have right-to-life organizations lobby with tax-deductible donations. It is surely no coincidence that many of the most visible cases of IRS action against nonprofits holding 501c3 status are highly ideological organizations lobbying in an open, if not flagrantly noticeable, fashion. The American Birth Control League would not have been singled out if its views were more in the mainstream of American values at the end of the 1920s. The right-wing Christian Echoes, run by the anticommunist zealot Rev. Billy James Hargis, lost its tax exemption because Hargis openly refused to be constrained by the limits on lobbying and the prohibition against involvement in political campaigns.[19] More recently, the Christian Coalition was denied tax-exempt status. It applied to be a 501c4 nonprofit, which allows unlimited lobbying, though contributions are not tax deductible. Its direct, overtly partisan involvement in support of Republicans running for Congress ran afoul of IRS restrictions because 501c4 does not allow partisan electioneering.[20]

On the other hand, while the IRS must be wary of the most objectionable organizations inciting their opponents by flaunting tax-subsidized lobbying, it must also be mindful of First Amendment freedoms. Unfortunately, Congress's criterion that public charities should not engage in propaganda-like lobbying is a standard ambiguous as it is provocative. The law doesn't say that public charities cannot speak out on public policy questions, only that they cannot lobby to a substantial degree. Distinguishing what is permissible free speech and what is appropriate regulation to protect the taxpayers' subsidy to nonprofits is more than a knotty theoretical problem. In the real world legislators need to interact with the leaders of nonprofits. Congress's intent in its laws on public charities was not to inhibit the executive director of a mental health facility from coming to Washington or the state capital and stopping by a legislator's office to talk about the need for new policies. Just the opposite: legislators want to talk to the leaders of nonprofits back in the district, learn from them, and, of course, have them go home and tell their friends and colleagues how much the legislator is concerned about the issues confronting the organization.

How have the IRS and Congress resolved this dilemma between restricting lobbying and facilitating lobbying? In short, the effective policy is to allow lobbying but to call it other things. This is not a matter of "don't ask, don't tell." Rather, the IRS and Congress have carved out so many exceptions to the admonishment on nonprofit lobbying that what's left as impermissible lobbying does not seem to cover much at all. Statutory provisions, regulations, Office of Management and Budget circulars, and IRS revenue rulings spell out exception after exception (along with an occasional prohibition) to create an illogical patchwork of policies on advocacy by 501c3 nonprofits.

Perhaps the largest loophole in the restriction against nonprofit lobbying is that communication for educational purposes is not considered lobbying.[21] As just discussed, the difference between educating legislators and lobbying legislators has no real meaning outside of the tax code. It is the same thing. But under the tax code, a nonprofit's communication with members or the public about public policy issues is not lobbying if, as in the case of the hospice organization, it doesn't specifically ask members to try to persuade legislators of a particular point of view. If requested by a legislator to testify or to offer advice, a nonprofit is not engaging in lobbying either. The other striking loophole is the exclusive focus on legislative lobbying. Since under federal law only advocacy before a legislature is considered suspect, lobbying the executive branch or filing a court suit is not considered lobbying. This means that while nonprofits are restricted in lobbying Congress on a proposed statute, it is perfectly legal for them to lobby an agency formulating regulations under that same law or to file a suit to invalidate it. Just to make matters more confusing, some states define lobbying in their own terms, usually for purposes of clarifying which organizations must register as lobbies with the state legislature. Registration per se does not prohibit lobbying, but because of 501c3 nonprofits will not be eager to register under state law since it is an acknowledgment that they lobby.[22]

The inconsistencies and contradictions under 501c3 are breathtaking—they're a logician's nightmare. Yet there is a certain pragmatism to this policy toward nonprofit advocacy because of the dilemma that government faces. The government's schizophrenic policy is simply the result of its trying to protect taxpayers who are subsidizing nonprofits and to allow unfettered communication between policymakers and nonprofits.

These inconsistencies and contradictions are only half of a crazy quilt of rules governing what nonprofits can and cannot do. The biggest inconsistency of all is that public charities can check a single box on a tax form and choose to be regulated by a second version of 501c3.

The Stealth Policy

Congress and the Internal Revenue service have actually created two separate policies to govern political advocacy by nonprofits with the 501c3 charity status. Besides the conventional 501c3 policy, tax-deductible nonprofits have the option of the "H" election, allowing them to ignore the "substantial" limitation on lobbying. One policy sharply restricts lobbying; the other allows for virtually unlimited lobbying.

This second, contradictory policy was part of the Tax Reform Act of 1976, an omnibus rewrite of many major provisions of the nation's tax laws. The new law affected estate and gift taxes and capital gains taxes and had serious implications for investors and for Wall Street.[23] Overshadowed by these momentous sections of the new law, the alternative to the conventional 501c3 rules received little attention by the press, and there is no available record as to why the "substantial" rule wasn't simply replaced by the new policy. What is evident is that Congress came to regard 501c3 as a problem, and its intent was to give nonprofits some guidelines on how much lobbying they could do so they wouldn't have to contend with the vagueness of the existing law. Congress was spurred on by continuing controversy over the IRS's treatment of nonprofits. Some prominent groups, most notably the Sierra Club, ran afoul of the lobbying rules and had their 501c3 status revoked. Since the Ford administration supported the proposed change, this part of the tax overhaul moved through Congress easily.[24]

In contrast to the ambiguity of the substantial criterion, the 501c3 H election is highly specific as to the quantity of lobbying that is permissible. It delineates two sliding scale formulas, one for the direct lobbying of legislators and one for grass-roots lobbying.[25] At the low end, nonprofits with budgets of up to $500,000 can spend 20 percent of all their expenditures on direct lobbying. An organization with a budget between $1.5 million and $17 million can spend $225,000 plus 5 percent of the budget over $1.5 million. The formulas for grass-roots lobbying allow for one-quarter of the spending on direct lobbying.[26] The new law also spelled out many of the exceptions to the definition of lobbying, giving statutory authority to distinctions that pretend that lobbying isn't lobbying. For example, a nonprofit can offer "technical assistance" to legislators as long as they are asked. In other words, a nonprofit could help draft a statute and not have that count as lobbying.[27]

Despite its detailed definitions and standards, the new H election apparently wasn't clear enough for the Internal Revenue Service. To call its pace in writing the regulations snail-like would be unfair to snails. It took fourteen years before regulations to implement the alternative to the substantial test were issued in final form. Since the Internal Revenue Service is not the most forthcoming or public of agencies in Washington, the reasons for this extraordinary delay have never been adequately explained. One longtime nonprofit leader recalled, "The deal on 501h was more ineptitude than anything else. There was very little pressure on IRS to do anything. And they didn't have the money." When the IRS finally issued draft regulations in 1986, it ignited opposition in the nonprofit community. Nonprofit leaders were outraged, believing that the proposed regulations would further restrict nonprofit lobbying, which was not the intent of Congress.[28] Conceptually, the IRS draft was logical, but nonprofit leaders opposed the proposed regulations' definition of certain kinds of communications as grass-roots lobbying. That would have placed such expenditures within the lower grass-roots lobbying cap.

After a few years of fighting with a coalition of groups led by Independent Sector, the bureaucrats at IRS responsible for the regulations raised the white flag and issued a new set of rules that were highly satisfactory to nonprofits.[29] Indeed, the nonprofits couldn't have realistically hoped for a more liberal set of regulations. One Treasury Department official said she was flabbergasted when she saw the new draft. "I just looked at the regulations and said [to a colleague], 'There's nothing left that's lobbying.'" She added that when some nonprofit heads came in to look at the new draft, they smiled and said, "We can live with this."

Figure 3-1. *IRS Form 5768*

Form **5768** (Rev. December 1996) Department of the Treasury Internal Revenue Service	Election/Revocation of Election by an Eligible Section 501(c)(3) Organization To Make Expenditures To Influence Legislation **(Under Section 501(h) of the Internal Revenue Code)**	For IRS Use Only ▶
Name of organization		Employer identification number
Number and street (or P.O. box no., if mail is not delivered to street address)		Room/suite
City, town or post office, and state	ZIP + 4	

1 Election—As an eligible organization, we hereby elect to have the provisions of section 501(h) of the Code, relating to expenditures to influence legislation, apply to our tax year ending..and all subsequent tax years until revoked.
(Month, day, and year)

Note: *This election must be signed and postmarked within the first taxable year to which it applies.*

2 Revocation—As an eligible organization, we hereby revoke our election to have the provisions of section 501(h) of the Code, relating to expenditures to influence legislation, apply to our tax year ending...
(Month, day, and year)

Note: *This revocation must be signed and postmarked before the first day of the tax year to which it applies.*

Under penalties of perjury, I declare that I am authorized to make this (check applicable box) ▶ ☐ election ☐ revocation on behalf of the above named organization.

_____ (Signature of officer or trustee)   _____ (Type or print name and title)   _____ (Date)

General Instructions

Section references are to the Internal Revenue Code.

Section 501(c)(3) states that an organization exempt under that section will lose its tax-exempt status and its qualification to receive deductible charitable contributions if a substantial part of its activities are carried on to influence legislation. Section 501(h), however, permits certain eligible 501(c)(3) organizations to elect to make limited expenditures to influence legislation. An organization making the election will, however, be subject to an excise tax under section 4911 if it spends more than the amounts permitted by that section. Also, the organization may lose its exempt status if its lobbying expenditures exceed the permitted amounts by more than 50% over a 4-year period. For any tax year in which an election under section 501(h) is in effect, an electing organization must report the actual and permitted amounts of its lobbying expenditures and grass roots expenditures (as defined in section 4911(c)) on its annual return required under section 6033. See Schedule A (Form 990). Each electing member of an affiliated group must report these amounts for both itself and the affiliated group as a whole.

To make or revoke the election, enter the ending date of the tax year to which the election or revocation applies in item 1 or 2, as applicable, and sign and date the form in the spaces provided.

Eligible Organizations.—A section 501(c)(3) organization is permitted to make the election if it is not a disqualified organization (see below) and is described in:

1. Section 170(b)(1)(A)(ii) (relating to educational institutions),

2. Section 170(b)(1)(A)(iii) (relating to hospitals and medical research organizations),

3. Section 170(b)(1)(A)(iv) (relating to organizations supporting government schools),

4. Section 170(b)(1)(A)(vi) (relating to organizations publicly supported by charitable contributions),

5. Section 509(a)(2) (relating to organizations publicly supported by admissions, sales, etc.), or

6. Section 509(a)(3) (relating to organizations supporting certain types of public charities other than those section 509(a)(3) organizations that support section 501(c)(4), (5), or (6) organizations).

Disqualified Organizations.—The following types of organizations are not permitted to make the election:

a. Section 170(b)(1)(A)(i) organizations (relating to churches),

b. An integrated auxiliary of a church or of a convention or association of churches, or

c. A member of an affiliated group of organizations if one or more members of such group is described in **a** or **b** of this paragraph.

Affiliated Organizations.—Organizations are members of an affiliated group of organizations only if **(1)** the governing instrument of one such organization requires it to be bound by the decisions of the other organization on legislative issues, or **(2)** the governing board of one such organization includes persons (i) who are specifically designated representatives of another such organization or are members of the governing board, officers, or paid executive staff members of such other organization, and (ii) who, by aggregating their votes, have sufficient voting power to cause or prevent action on legislative issues by the first such organization.

For more details, see section 4911 and section 501(h).

Note: *A private foundation (including a private operating foundation) is not an eligible organization.*

Where To File.—Mail Form 5768 to the Internal Revenue Service Center, Ogden, UT 84201-0027.

Cat. No. 12125M   Form **5768** (Rev. 12-96)

The IRS has made it remarkably easy for a nonprofit to take the H election. If a 501c3 wishes its lobbying to come under the expenditure test of the 1976 tax reform rather than the substantial rule, it only has to fill out the simplest of forms. IRS Form 5768 merely requires that someone fill in the address of the nonprofit, write in the tax year, check the H election box, and then sign it (figure 3-1). Yet while the form may be simple, the H alternative remains elusive at best. Most nonprofits have no idea that there is such a thing as the H election, and only about 2.5 percent of all 501c3s filing a tax return choose this path. If a nonprofit does not file this separate form, it is by default a conventional 501c3 subject to the vague substantial rule. There is no choice offered on the 990 tax return form.

Although some nonprofits do not need the additional protection of the expenditure test, nonprofits that are politically active benefit from it because they don't have to be concerned about violating the law. The expenditure limits are more than generous since only an outlay of money to support direct legislative lobbying counts against them. Unless an organization only does lobbying, it would take gross incompetence by an accountant to let his or her nonprofit client hit the expenditure limits. In practical terms it is difficult for an IRS auditor to contest a nonprofit's records of how its employees spend their time. The head of a facility for troubled youth who frequently interacts with government officials said, "Our attorney has explained to me that we can actually lobby up to a certain percentage of our budget . . . There's a lot more I can do before I would cross that line."

The only possible disadvantage to a 501c3 choosing the H election is that it may feel it needs to improve its accounting of lobbying expenditures.[30] Still, for an organization that is politically active, there is really no reason not to elect the H option. The IRS has been explicit in indicating that taking the election is not a reason for an audit. Just the opposite: the Internal Revenue Manual states, "Experience also suggests that organizations that have made the election are usually in compliance with the restrictions on legislative activities, so they do not appear to justify an effort to examine solely on this issue."[31] Despite the advantages the H election remains something of a stealth policy. Although some organizations that conduct training for nonprofits make an effort to educate the leaders of organizations about the advantages of the H election, there has not been much growth in the percentage of nonprofits choosing to come under the expenditure test.

Is Confusion a Problem?

More than a decade after the H election was implemented, most nonprofits remain woefully ignorant of the alternative to the substantial test. In the interviews conducted for this study, the executive directors of nonprofits who had not taken the election demonstrated that they knew little, if anything, about this option. The head of a statewide association spoke for many when asked why he hadn't taken the H election: "I'm completely ignorant of it," he said. But politically active nonprofits that don't choose the expenditure test option can usually figure out ways to cope with the lobbying restrictions under the conventional 501c3 standard. If that's the case, why should we be concerned about the complexity and confusion of the two contrary IRS policies on nonprofit lobbying? The fundamental issue is not an aesthetic preference for clear and concise tax law. The only concern is representation in the political system: does current tax policy hinder or facilitate participation of nonprofits in public policymaking? If the organizations manage to get their message across to government, no matter what the convoluted policy on lobbying is, maybe it's just a case of "no harm, no foul."

Poor Test Results

The first step in determining whether 501c3 makes a difference is to examine whether or not typical nonprofits understand what the tax code allows in political participation. That this part of the tax code is confusing should hardly be surprising. What part of the tax code is simple and straightforward? Yet the fact that the tax code is generally impenetrable does not mean that its complexity is not without consequences. Wealthy taxpayers, for example, hire attorneys and accountants to figure out ways of taking advantage of the tax code's complexity and loopholes. That exacerbates inequities in the application of taxes.

The survey we sent to nonprofits included a quiz about current government rules on political activity.[32] We prefaced the quiz by telling respondents, "There is a good deal of confusion about whether various activities by nonprofits relating to the policymaking process are permissible." Listed below were eight statements with a yes box and no box opposite each. Respondents were asked to read each one and then indicate whether it was permissible for their organization to engage in that activity. Table 3-1 lists the wording of each of the statements along with the percentage of respondents who checked the right answer. Since respondents checked either yes or no, guessing or flipping a coin would have, on average, yielded a correct response rate of 50 percent. Thus 50 percent is the appropriate baseline, not 0 percent, to measure the proportion of correct answers against.

As with many of the tables that follow, table 3-1 makes a comparison between H electors that list lobbying expenditures on their 990 tax return—presumably the most politically active type of tax-deductible nonprofits—and what we call conventional nonprofits—501c3s that are

Table 3-1. *(Mis)Understanding the Tax Code*

	Percent with correct answer		
Can your organization	Correct answer	H electors	Conventional 501c3s
Support or oppose federal legislation under current IRS regulations (n = 307/476)	Yes	92	54
Take a policy position without reference to a specific bill under current regulations (310/466)	Yes	96	61
Support or oppose federal regulations (303/477)	Yes	95	62
Lobby if part of your budget comes from federal funds (260/464)	Yes	74	32
Use government funds to lobby Congress (265/467)	No	92	93
Endorse a candidate for elected office (299/474)	No	90	84
Talk to elected public officials about public policy matters (313/488)	Yes	98	80
Sponsor a forum or candidate debate for elected office (290/472)	Yes	70	45

nonelectors and list no lobbying expenditures on their 990 tax return. We call these nonprofits "conventional" because 97 percent of all tax-deductible organizations fall into this category. H electors listing lobbying expenditures are around 0.5 percent of all 501c3s.[33] The differences between the two samples' knowledge of the law governing their participation is rather considerable. One would expect that the H electors would do well on this quiz given that there is a self-selection bias in choosing to take this option. And given that the tax code is so confusing and contradictory, one should not be surprised by the high level of ignorance displayed by the conventional 501c3s. Nevertheless, the differences between the two groups are striking. Since flipping a coin or guessing would yield a score of around 50 percent, it is distressing that only 54 percent of the conventional non-profits know that they have the right to take a stand on legislation before Congress. This is a basic freedom, and close to half of typical nonprofits believe they have been stripped of their right simply to say publicly that they support or oppose a bill before Congress. They do not do much better (61 percent) when asked if they are allowed to take a general policy position without reference to a specific bill. Many conventional nonprofits believe that when it comes to legislation, they must remain quiet. As an executive in one organization told us, "We're not allowed to lobby. We're not allowed to influence public policy." And another said firmly, "I have to wait until a legislator contacts us."

Even more startling is that only 32 percent of typical nonprofits believe they are allowed to lobby if they receive federal funds. One executive with an AIDS organization told us firmly that she couldn't "be involved in lobbying as a nonprofit because we receive government grants." She was so careful that when she faxed a message to a legislator, "I always do it as a voter, not as a staff person of the organization." The common misunderstanding of this part of the law means that many organizations believe their choice is between taking money from the government and having the right to speak out on issues that affect their clients.

The Law's Impact

Despite this depressing level of ignorance about 501c3, one cannot assume that misunderstanding the law deters participation in public policymaking. Even though they think the law is severely prohibitive, leaders of conventional nonprofits may believe that advocacy must be done anyway—that it is worth the risks. Or they may think the IRS will never come after them even if their nonprofit goes beyond what the law allows. Most plausibly, leaders may engage in lobbying by rationalizing that what they are doing is educational. If you believe that harassing your state legislator all the time does not constitute involvement in public policy, the law may not be much of a hindrance.

Determining whether 501c3 makes a real difference in organizational behavior is no easy task. The initial problem facing analysts is that not all nonprofits have reason to be involved with government. And if nonprofits have little stake in government programs or policies, there is less reason to be concerned with their ignorance or lack of political involvement. Hobby groups or YMCAs may not have much need to contact people in government. The Montauk Point Lighthouse Museum occasionally talks to people from the State Historic Society, but, generally speaking, it has had little cause to think through the complexities of 501c3. In contrast to the Montauk Lighthouse Museum, some 501c3s carry out programs of the government, and these nonprofits have a clear stake in public policy matters. If the misguided behavior of the executive of the AIDS organization just discussed is representative of such nonprofits, then the ignorance of 501c3 may have substantial consequences.

One possibility is that there is something of a rational sorting out among nonprofits about the tax status they choose. Organizations that need to have a lot of interaction with government may choose to take the H election. Those that forgo the H election may have little interest in talking to government and do not worry about crossing the substantial threshold.

There is no direct measure in the survey of an absolute need to interact with government, but there are two variables that serve as relatively good proxies. First, those answering the questionnaire were asked to estimate the amount of their organization's annual income that came from various sources. As a percentage of their entire budget, the politically sophisticated H electors received an average of 19.6 percent of their annual budget from government, not much different than the 22.1 percent for typical 501c3 nonprofits (table 3-2).[34] An organization receiving a significant percentage of its budget from government has a compelling reason to stay in close and continual contact with policymakers and their staffs. It has every reason to lobby for support and for an increase in funding. Such organizations risk their existence by not being aggressive in their relations with government. In this respect the two samples appear to have the same level of need.[35]

A second method of trying to determine if there is a rational sorting out of politically active and politically indifferent nonprofits into the two tax categories is to ask what these organizations' mission is. Fortunately the 990 tax returns can help. A group of scholars working with Independent Sector in the early 1980s created the National Taxonomy of Exempt Entities (or NTEE codes), which is now used by the Internal Revenue Service. Analysts can use these codes to identify the broad policy area that nonprofits work in because a primary NTEE designation is embedded in each 990 tax return.[36] The major NTEE categories are arts, culture, and humanities; education; environment and animals; health; human services; public benefit; and religion. Nonprofits in these categories constitute 87 percent of all 990 filers with the remaining 13 percent falling into a variety of other categories. (See figure 1-1 in chapter 1.) All these nonprofit sectors, with the possible exception of religion, have obvious ties to broad areas of public policy. Although not every nonprofit in each of these groupings has reason to be involved in public affairs, it is difficult to dismiss any of these sectors as marginally connected to the public policymaking process. Furthermore, close inspection of the organizational identity of respondents to the survey reveals that the $25,000 threshold for 990 filers filters out a large proportion of organizations like hobby clubs or Little Leagues that obviously have limited interest in public policymaking.

It seems safe to assume that nonprofits that administer government programs are likely to have a significant stake in public policy. Two NTEE

Table 3-2. *Similar Constituencies, Different Levels of Advocacy*

	Percent of nonprofits in policy area		Proportion of budget from government (percent)		Measures of advocacy, human service providers		
	Human services	*Health care*	*All*	*Human services*	*Mean scores*		
					Q.5***	*Q.6b****	*Q.6d****
H electors	25.6	19.7	19.6	29.0	2.9	2.4	2.8
Conventional nonprofits	37.4	10.8	22.1	33.4	1.9	.9	1.6

Q.5. For some nonprofits, there is a need to educate those in government so that policymakers will have a better understanding of the problems facing the community. How often does your organization undertake an effort to educate government officials at any level? (Experimental design question: "educate," "lobby," and "advocate" were each used in one-third of sample. Responses are aggregated here. Scale: "Never" = 1; "Once a month or less" = 2; "Two, three times a month" = 3; "Four or more times a month" = 4.)

Q.6b. Lobbying on behalf of or against a proposed bill or other policy pronouncement. Scale: 0-4.

Q.6d. Working in a planning or advisory group that includes government officials. Scale: 0-4.

***The differences in the mean scores are significant at the .000 level.

categories that would appear to contain high concentrations of 501c3s administering one or more governments are human services and health care. (As noted in chapter 2, since they are egregious statistical outliers in gross revenues and government support, hospitals and hospital systems were removed from our survey and thus are not included in this grouping of health-related nonprofits.)[37] When the two samples are compared, it turns out that 37 percent of conventional nonprofits are in human services and another 11 percent in health. This is only slightly higher than the aggregate total of the H electors who fall into these two categories. Health care organizations are a modestly higher proportion of the H electors, suggesting that there may be a greater self-selection bias in this sector. Nonprofits in these two areas receive a higher percentage of their budget from government than do nonprofits working in other policy areas. Clearly, the conventional nonprofits in human services and health have no less vital interests before legislative bodies than do the H electors in these same categories. By no means can we conclude that typical 501c3s working in these areas have no need to correctly understand the rules regulating their participation in the government. Just the opposite is true.

The H electors are not a true control group because these nonprofits actively choose this status. But since there is strong similarity between conventional 501c3s and the H electors around these variables of government support and organizational mission, a comparison between the two sets of organizations can still provide some measure of the impact of the two different regulatory standards for lobbying. Some care must be taken in measuring the activity of these two cohorts, however, because "lobbying" may be a red flag to those conventional 501c3s who believe it is prohibited or to be generally avoided. We approached this problem by using multiple indicators. The scores reported are for human service providers, not only because of the strong similarities of such nonprofits in the two cohorts, but also because this sector is the largest among all 501c3s large enough to file a tax return.

The results for three separate questions on advocacy, very differently worded, show a strong and consistent pattern. The full wording of the questions is shown at the bottom of table 3-2. One question deliberately used the red flag word, asking respondents how often they engaged in "lobbying on behalf of or against a proposed bill or other policy pronouncement." The differences are enormous, 2.4 for the H electors and just 0.9 for the conventional 501c3s. (A higher score indicates more public policy involvement.) Although the magnitude is striking, some difference was to be expected because of the concern that conventional nonprofits have about violating the IRS rules. Another question asked how often respondents worked "in a planning or advisory group that includes government officials." Although there is no prohibition in 501c3 against such work, large differences emerge here too: 2.8 versus 1.6. (These two questions used a five-point scale.) In a third question an experimental design format was utilized. The words "advocate," "lobby," and "educate" were alternately used in an otherwise identically worded statement about how often the nonprofits approach government. The third of the samples that received the "lobbying" version of the question reflected the red flag effect, but the broader pattern remained when all three versions of the surveys were aggregated within each cohort.[38] The mean for the aggregate of H electors is 2.9, while the conventional 501c3s score 1.9. This is a huge difference on just a four-point scale. There are more questions in the survey on advocacy, using different terms and focusing on different tactics. The pattern remains the same.

Whatever the imperfections of these questions and this comparison of human service providers, clearly the different regulatory standards have a strong impact on the public policy activity of nonprofits.[39] Although less rigorous and less precise, the interviews and focus groups revealed the same tendency. Some leaders said they were involved in the governmental process, pushing their clients' interests forward. Other executive directors, despite an obvious stake in governmental policy, professed a reluctance to become engaged in government relations because of 501c3.

As far as can be determined from the survey, interviews, and respondents' tax returns, there is no rational sorting out of nonprofits by mission, funding, or programs into a politically active set of H electors and a residual 501c3 set of organizations who have little reason to understand the tax code or be involved with government. The major difference between the two subsamples of human service providers examined is that the conventional 501c3s know less and do less. These differences cannot be explained by the semantics of question wording. The conventional nonprofit human service providers do not have less reason to lobby government. Like the H electors they receive significant budget support from government and administer programs from the same federal and state agencies.[40] Conventional nonprofits are, of course, in touch with government, but clearly they are less aggressive in their advocacy. The consequence of these differences between the H electors and conventional nonprofits is that clients who receive social services from the more sophisticated H electors receive more representation in the political process. It's not that these constituencies necessarily need more political representation than the same constituencies served by conventional 501c3s, but rather they benefit because the leadership of their nonprofits is more politically astute and more committed to changing the system for the better. In the final analysis, section 501c3 of our tax code makes a difference, a profound difference, in the degree to which some Americans are represented before government.

Conclusion

Although it is not the direct intent of the tax code to determine who is represented before government, it does affect the representation of interests. The intent of the lobbying provision of 501c3 is to protect the integrity of the tax deduction for charitable giving. This is a laudable goal, and there must be some protections. Unfortunately, the consequences of 501c3 on the mobilization of interests are severe. Health and human service nonprofits in particular have as their clients the most underrepresented segments of American society: frail elderly, mentally retarded children, the physically disabled, battered women, runaways, drug and alcohol addicts, immigrants, AIDS victims, poor pregnant women, institutionalized adults, and countless other constituencies that are too poor, unskilled, ignorant, incapacitated, or over-whelmed with their problems to organize on their own.

What possible public purpose does it serve to still the voices of those who work with clients like these? As for the goal of preventing tax-subsidized lobbying, the adoption of the H election meant that Congress—at least in 1976—was in favor of allowing significant tax-subsidized lobbying by non-profits. The H election facilitates lobbying just as the substantial test discourages it. But since only about 2.5 percent of tax-deductible nonprof-its take the H election, the substantial test under 501c3 is still, for all intents and purposes, the law governing the political activity of nonprofits.

No matter how the survey and tax data assembled for this study were sliced, contorted, and thrashed about, the bottom line remained the same: conventional 501c3 nonprofits look a lot like H electors—except when it comes to lobbying. Close to the same percentages of the two samples work in human services and health care combined and receive close to the same percentage of their income from government. What is disturbing is that such a large percentage of conventional 501c3 nonprofits misunderstand the tax code so badly that they believe that their tax-deductible status has stripped them of basic First Amendment freedoms. Too many nonprofits are intimidated by the ambiguous restrictions of 501c3. Ironically, their voice is quieted by a policy that the government abandoned in principle in 1976 but has maintained in practice.

Chilling
the Liberals

Not surprisingly, the federal government's contradictory policies regulating the political activity of nonprofits have produced contradictory results. As a group 501c3 nonprofits are clearly affected by the broad regulatory intent to minimize their political activity. At the same time some nonprofits view the expansive exceptions to the lobbying restrictions as a green light to participate in all but the most blatant political activity.

The share of nonprofits that has business connected with government but nonetheless is relatively inactive is far greater than the share of nonprofits highly involved in the policymaking process. Nevertheless, that active cohort is big enough to draw attention from government regulators. In any community in the United States there are nonprofits trying to push local government to do more. There are nonprofits criticizing government. And there are nonprofits trying to stop the best-laid plans of administrators and block the pet projects of legislators.

Unfortunately, if a nonprofit sufficiently irritates a policymaker, it may provoke a call to have its tax status reviewed. A government official's rationale in asking for an Internal Revenue Service (IRS) audit is always the same: under section 501c3 nonprofits are not allowed to do any substantial lobbying. If an organization is doing significant lobbying, then the call is for its advantageous tax status to be revoked. Although this can happen to any nonprofit with ideological leanings in any direction, in recent years it has been nonprofits with a liberal outlook that have had to look over their shoulder. Many conservative legislators, think tanks, and lobbying groups want to put a stop to tax-supported lobbying because it is a subsidy that favors the liberals.

Aggressive Nonprofits

Since local politics is not characterized by a dense network of interest groups, nonprofits easily stand out among all the organizations lobbying city hall. They are not obscured by the huge array of private lobbies, as is the case in national politics. Even in state politics, nonprofits are highly visible because they tend to have no organized opposition and because they are intertwined into program administration. In short, in state and local politics, the lobbying of politically active nonprofits is obvious to anyone following politics in that venue.

In a city or state the politically active nonprofits are a combination of conventional 501c3s, 501c3 H electors, and 501c4s. The survey's battery of questions about advocacy tactics can be utilized to gauge the dimension of the politically active strata of 501c3s. Table 4-1 reports the responses of conventional 501c3s that, again, are 97 percent of all tax-deductible nonprofits. The responses at the two highest numbers on the five-point scale have been aggregated and are defined as a high level of activity. Only 12 percent of the 501c3s score themselves above this threshold for lobbying legislators, and only 7 percent rate themselves at this level for testifying. For other forms of advocacy that are more cooperative in nature (and less dangerous in terms of 501c3), such as working in a planning group with government officials or talking to government officials about grants, the comparable figures average 24 percent.[1]

Even though the percentages of 501c3s that fall into the highly active cohort are modest, this calculation may mask the impact of these organizations in state and local politics. There are enough politically active 501c3s to be a strong and visible presence in any community. Even though the lobbying restrictions in the law significantly inhibit advocacy, clearly 501c3 status fails to deter a significant minority of nonprofits from ongoing involvement in the policymaking process.

Fuzzy Math

Politically active nonprofits have reason to fear the IRS because the infrequent audits of politically active 501c3s are still sufficient to alarm the nonprofit sector. How do organizations that are highly involved in the

Table 4-1. *Politically Active Nonprofits*

Activity	Percent of conventional 501c3s reporting a high level of activity[a]
Testifying at legislative or administrative hearings	6.9
Lobbying on behalf of or against a proposed bill or other policy pronouncement	12.1
Responding to requests for information from those in government	26.4
Working in a planning or advisory group that includes government officials	26.3
Meeting with government officials about the work we are doing	24.6
Encouraging members to write, call, fax, or e-mail policymakers	20.6
Releasing research reports to the media, public, or policymakers	11.2
Discussing obtaining grants or contracts with government officials	22.6
Interacting socially with government officials	20.1

Q.6. A variety of means of communicating and interacting with those in government are listed below. Please use the scale on the right to indicate how frequently, if at all, your organization engages in these activities. (By "your organization" we mean the executive director, other staff, volunteers, or members of the board.) In this scale, 0 means never, 1 is relatively infrequent interaction, and 4 is ongoing interaction.

Note: $N = 583$.

a. The percentages aggregate those marking 3 or 4 for each item.

policymaking process protect themselves against an audit, an audit that could provide evidence for a revocation of their eligibility for tax-deductible contributions? The interviews suggest that the leaders of active nonprofits have a rationale to explain why they are not violating the 501c3 prohibition or the H expenditure test. When they were asked if the tax code was a problem, virtually all respondents replied that they were not in violation of the lobbying limits. Take, for example, this leader of a nonprofit working for affordable housing. Asked about its work with government he offered the following description:

> At the local level we're viewed as a technical resource. At the state level we're viewed as advocates. We work a lot with the state legislature but even more with state agencies. Right now we're [extensively] engaged in the state budgetary process. We have pages and pages of initiatives we'd like the state to adopt, and actually we're doing pretty

well on it. There are also freestanding legislative issues that arise independent of the state budget. We have the staff on board who have the expertise in policy, who have the expertise in advocacy. We have someone who does grass-roots organizing to get our members to contact government. We hire contract lobbyists when we have multiple issues at the same time. At the national level, we work through national coalitions like the National Low Income Housing Coalition. . . . And we work with the National Coalition on Homelessness. We work with them on their advocacy agenda, talking to members of [our state congressional] delegation who are sympathetic to these issues.

This is an enormous amount of advocacy, and there were more advocacy efforts described in other parts of the interview. This organization does not operate any housing itself; when asked what the group's mission is, he said it was to be "an advocate" for low-income housing. And when asked how much his organization spent annually on lobbying, he said that it was usually below 5 percent. He added, "The IRS doesn't mind if you lobby as long as you keep your spending below 5 percent. We're a $1.7 million a year organization, so 5 percent of that is a lot of money. You can do a lot of lobbying with 5 percent of that."

The answer illustrates the confusion over 501c3 and the H expenditure test, as well as the illogical accounting encouraged by the IRS regulations governing nonprofits. There is no 5 percent limitation on lobbying expenditures.[2] As chapter 3 notes, the H election expenditure test is a limit of 20 percent of the first $500,000 of a nonprofit's budget that can be spent on lobbying. There is a sliding scale of what can be spent on lobbying above that.[3] We heard many other figures as well, but hardly anyone got the H expenditure limit right. Moreover, many of those who cited an expenditure limit were conventional 501c3s and were subject to the vague "substantial" standard rather than any specific expenditure test. The IRS has done such an inadequate job of publicizing and explaining the H election, and the 501c3 law is so vague, that it is certainly understandable that nonprofits are confused on this issue. The interviews and focus groups indicate that it is not just the IRS that is to blame, but it's also the fault of nonprofit leaders whose eyes glaze over when they meet with their accountant.

The accounting engaged in by this affordable housing nonprofit is representative of highly politically active nonprofits at the state and local levels. The housing nonprofit's raison d'être is to push policymakers to do more for low-income Americans. The idea that only 5 percent ($85,000) of this organization's budget is going toward lobbying legislators seems preposterous. The way nonprofits justify calling what appears to be lobbying expenditures something else is to account for only the salary spent for the time a representative of the organization is in a legislator's office. As the executive director of an environmental nonprofit put it, "Where we make a distinction is that all you do under the gold dome [at the statehouse] is lobbying . . . The rest of the time, our advocacy is 'advocacy' and not 'lobbying.'" The other activity that organizations will account for as lobbying are expenditures involved in sending letters and alerts aimed at trying to get members to urge legislators to vote a certain way. Generally, nonprofits ignore all the supporting work, all the research, all the work with coalitions, and all the networking that prepares them to meet with a legislator.[4]

Nonprofits can get away with such accounting because the IRS created the loopholes that they use, and the IRS has little interest in forcing nonprofits to use more accurate accounting practices. As already noted, an IRS agent is not in a good position to question the paper trail produced by a nonprofit during an audit. A nonprofit is not going to be vulnerable unless it becomes notorious and opponents not only complain, but also provide accounts of the alleged violator's lobbying efforts. Standard accounting software allows nonprofits to create documentation for audits.[5] One nonprofit executive said that its software "allows you to segregate every dollar that comes in and then show what that dollar was spent on." This kind of accounting is now common.

Shell Game

For conventional nonprofits with legislative lobbying that is too blatant to hide or who work on a cause that brings them into conflict with other interest groups, a further level of protection may seem advisable. A common tactic is to have two related organizations, one a 501c3 and, as its sibling, a non-tax-deductible 501c4. The executive director of a prochoice organization, clearly concerned about the possibility of a complaint to the IRS from a prolife group, explained the steps her nonprofit took to protect itself.

We begin with separate bank accounts. The appeals we send out are very clear as to whether they're for the c3 or the c4. We have clearly written job descriptions. We have clear time allocations. We have time sheets—everyone has to keep track of what they're working on and who they're working for. We literally bill out at the end of the year. We match the time allocation and the time sheets and if they don't correspond, we write a check. We have the same staff but they get two different paychecks. They get a c3 paycheck and a c4 paycheck. It's bookkeeping.

Only the donations to the 501c3 are tax deductible so money to support the c4 must come from sources willing to give without the benefit of tax deductibility (typically individual contributors). Since most of what supports legislative lobbying can be called something else, the vast bulk of money can go through the 501c3. "We do so much education work anyway, it's not difficult to charge things to the 501c3," said the executive director.

Just as a 501c3 might recognize the need to start a 501c4 to give it more flexibility and auditing coverage for its lobbying, the opposite dynamic is often at work too. An organization that started as a 501c4 because its goals were overtly political, could subsequently decide to start a 501c3 to take on tasks that easily fall outside of the IRS definition of lobbying. The manager of a civic organization initially chartered as a 501c4 said, "In the late 1970s, hard money was increasingly hard to come by. We founded the c3 to get soft money. Corporations and other entities were much more willing to give to a tax-deductible group. We have the same office, but there are two different boards."[6]

There are no available data on what percentage of 501c3s are tied to a 501c4. It may seem like an ideal solution to the problem faced by nonprofits that want to be politically active and need to raise a substantial amount of their budget through tax-deductible donations. The Supreme Court has also held that such combinations are permissible, so there is no question about their basic legality.[7] At the expense of some extra bookkeeping administrative costs, a nonprofit can have its (tax-deductible) cake and eat it too. Although such arrangements are not rare, there has been virtually no growth in the number of 501c4s during the past few decades while the number of 501c3s has skyrocketed.

Convenient as they may be, c3-c4 marriages make a mockery of the initial purpose of tax deductibility, which was to provide a tax incentive for public charities while restricting lobbying. Even before the Supreme Court indicated that such combinations are allowable, the IRS had never made any effort to crack down on c3-c4 marriages. Such arrangements are just one more gigantic loophole in the application of section 501c3. The prohibitions in 501c3 are intended to prevent nonprofits from engaging in the kind of activities conducted by 501c4s. C3-c4 combinations are perfectly legal charades that allow c3s to operate as active, aggressive lobbies. In the end, however, the biggest problem is that many nonprofits have no constituency capable of making individual donations to fund a 501c4 and, thus, believe they must remain cautious in their lobbying so that they do not violate the substantial rule.

Intimidation

Given the apparent ease with which a 501c3 nonprofit can engage in fantasy accounting or use a c4 organization to protect itself, our expressed concern about the freedom of nonprofits to lobby might seem excessive. If the problem is that nonprofits serve those who are chronically underrepresented in the political system and are afraid to lobby because of their tax status, the solution might seem clear from the preceding discussion. Organizations that do training of nonprofits and the trade associations for nonprofits in various policy fields, simply need to train executive directors and chief financial officers how to do the accounting necessary to keep the auditors at bay. Or, when feasible, 501c3 nonprofits could be strongly encouraged to set up a 501c4. Or they can become H electors. Any of these solutions would seem to take care of the problem.

Still, today, 501c3 nonprofits cannot ignore the IRS's occasional inclination to look into cases in which an organization is suspected of violating the prohibitions on lobbying. Although some nonprofits recognize that this is part of the game they play with the IRS and as long as they handle their accounting in the right way they're safe, others are not so confident. Tax deductibility is an absolute lifeline to 501c3s—they could never raise the amount of money they do without the tax incentive for their donors.[8] Consequently, many are not willing to take the risk, even if that risk is a tiny one, and they restrict their advocacy work instead of trying to game the tax code.

Is there a bona fide risk? Do nonprofits really have something to worry about in terms of being audited and, potentially, losing their tax deductibility? The interviews make it clear that the threat of audit is very real. Eighteen percent of the organizations we interviewed had experienced at least one audit by the IRS, other federal agency, or state bureaucracy in their past.[9] By the respondents' descriptions, these were audits aimed at uncovering political expenses and not just a general review of accounting and operations. Since politically active organizations were deliberately oversampled in the interviews, we cannot generalize to a population of all nonprofits. Yet it is the politically active that are most at risk from the IRS and administrative agencies. If audits occur often enough to be more than a chance occurrence or routine bureaucratic monitoring, it will surely have a chilling effect on nonprofits that have not been audited.

None of the interviewees whose organization was audited believed that the IRS or other agency chose them as part of a random review. All believed they were singled out for their political activity, and many were able to cite what they had, allegedly, done to incite the ire of opponents. A conservation group, which had infuriated a developer by its success in stopping a proposed real estate project, believed that an innocent newspaper error gave its opponents some ammunition:

> Some of our members spun off a new group and they became key players . . . on a bond issue and the paper was sloppy in its reporting. That group wasn't 501c3 but our board members who were with that group were identified as being from [our organization]. One of the attorneys on the other side turned us in to the IRS. It took us three years and $20,000 to defend ourselves.

The executive director of a housing group cited repeated efforts to uncover violations of the political prohibitions on nonprofits:

> Once somebody got mad at us and asked the Inspector General to look to see if federal funds were being used for lobbying. All grant agreements with the government strictly forbid that. We can't use any of our HUD funds to do any lobbying. When we get involved with local plans, we write out the plan and then send it to HUD and ask them to review it so that anything we then do has HUD approval. We have to raise private money to do lobbying. I don't know how many times the Inspector General has investigated us. We've had three IRS audits which looked at our lobbying. Each time we came out clean.

Another housing group with extensive government contracts claimed that it was the victim of revenge by a prominent U.S. senator. "We were called before Phil Gramm's committee. I think he thought . . . we'd support [his views]. Well, that wasn't true and he got irritated with us. He asked people to look into our lobbying."

In an interview an IRS official confirmed that when letters encouraging an audit of a particular 501c3 come into the tax-exempt division, those charges are considered. He refused to describe the decisionmaking process that leads to an audit except in the vaguest of terms. Under repeated questioning, two different officials refused to offer any guidelines as to what might prompt an audit.

The problem for nonprofits extends beyond the IRS. Any state or federal agency can conduct an audit to see if its money is being spent appropriately.[10] Nonprofit executives worry that political participation that antagonizes government officials responsible for the programs those nonprofits implement, invites an audit. The head of a nonprofit that works with homebound frail elderly said, "Take a position critical of the state agency and the next day you get an audit of your records." The head of a community development corporation said, "We're going to keep quiet about some things because it just isn't worth it. But on other things we're willing to take the risk where you're going to take a stand even though it means getting the auditor out."

These leaders were not worried that the audit will turn up anything because they are careful to do their accounting right. Rather, they're worried because such examinations are a warning shot across the bow. The next shot would be the direct hit: a termination of program funding. And there are more government eyes looking over their shoulder. Even though 501c3 is a disincentive for nonprofits to register under state lobbying rules, some feel they must file as lobbyists at their statehouses or run afoul of the law. This requires the filing of reports as to what they've done in their lobbying. As just noted by the director of the housing nonprofit that was audited by the IRS three times, nonprofits have to be careful with the contracts they sign as to what they are permitted to do in terms of communication with government. If they accept federal grants they are also regulated by a set of OMB regulations and by individual agency rules.

There is no way for us to verify any of these individual charges that we have recounted from our interviews or focus groups. But whether the executive directors' charges about retribution are completely accurate is less important than their perceptions. The belief that opponents can activate an audit at the IRS, or that angry state officials will audit their books, is enough to make them think about the wisdom of speaking out. Those offering services to needy populations would be remiss if they ignored the risks involved in alienating policymakers. As one nonprofit head put it, "You have to decide where to draw the line where you're willing to risk your money."

Challenge from the Left

For the executive directors of nonprofits the threat of retribution by the IRS and state agency officials is all too real. Given all the loopholes of 501c3 or the option of marrying a 501c3 to a 501c4, there are straightforward and reliable ways to create clean financial statements to protect against a revocation of tax deductibility. Yet there is no such protection against an angry agency administrator (or his overseer at the state legislature) who is upset about a nonprofit that has embarrassed or challenged him. For a nonprofit losing a key grant may mean cutting services, laying off workers, a loss of face, and another nonprofit gaining that same grant.

This uneasiness builds on more than the nonprofits' own experience with an audit or a case involving another nonprofit working in their policy area. There is also a strong historical context, one that reverberates through the nonprofit world. This is not the abstraction of academics trying to tie the grand sweep of history to a more immediate example. Rather, our interviewees made the connection. We heard about the attack on legal services as "an example of government going after the critics." We even heard about the revocation of the Sierra Club's c3 tax status, even though it happened thirty-five years earlier. The relevance was clear: if the IRS can go after a popular national organization like the Sierra Club, think how easy it would be for them to bust a small nonprofit like ours.

Sistine Chapel

The history that leads today's nonprofit directors to see their own vulnerability against a broader backdrop of national policy does, in fact, begin with the Sierra Club's fight with the IRS in 1966. By this time the court case involving the American Birth Control League had long faded from memory, and there was little controversy over section 501c3. There was no real concern about the impact of 501c3 because politically active nonprofits and citizen advocacy groups were few and far between. The tax-deductible nonprofits that were around were docile. The interest group literature on politics in the 1950s found little activity by citizen lobbies, and nonprofits were generally ignored.[11] It was the lull before the storm.

The Sierra Club is one of the nation's most venerated citizens' group. It was started in 1892 by the legendary John Muir, and it reflected the turn of the century concern about conservationism. In the mid-1960s it was led by David Brower, a man of vision but also a headstrong leader who didn't suffer fools gladly.[12] When Congress began to seriously consider a proposal to build two dams on the Colorado River, Brower was aghast and committed the Sierra Club to fighting the projects with all the resources at its disposal. If the dams were built, part of the Grand Canyon would be turned into a 500-foot deep lake. The proposed dams were part of a broader, long-term effort to bring water from the Northwest to the Southwest. The day before a House subcommittee was prepared to vote, the Sierra Club placed full-page ads in the *New York Times*, the *Washington Post*, and a few other papers, excoriating Congress for this environmental blasphemy. The Department of Interior defended the lake as a means of bringing the canyon walls closer to the tourists who would be able to take a boat out on it. In its ad the Sierra Club ridiculed this "benefit" of the lake, sarcastically replying, "Should we flood the Sistine Chapel, so tourists can float nearer the ceiling?"[13]

As part of the ad, there was a form readers could clip and send to the subcommittee's chair, Wayne Aspinall (D-Colo.). Aspinall, a crusty congressional baron of that era, was incensed by this public affront to his leadership. Aspinall's anger was widely held to be the reason why the IRS, an agency not known for impulsiveness, reacted with lightning speed. At 4:00 p.m. the day after the ads appeared, a federal marshal hand-delivered a letter to the Sierra Club's San Francisco office informing the organization that it was under investigation for possibly violating the prohibition against substantial lobbying. More ominous was that the IRS suspended the organization's tax deductibility status while the case was under investigation. The IRS acknowledged that this was the first time it had suspended a non-profit's tax deductibility while it was investigating the case.[14]

The Sierra Club's 501c3 status was ultimately revoked by the IRS. Ironically, the organization won for losing. The dams were never built, and the organization's stature grew. Moreover, in the aftermath of the initial IRS warning letter, the membership grew significantly, from 38,000 to 47,000 in the space of a couple of months. Donations, even though they were no longer tax deductible, grew too as sympathizers were provoked by the IRS's action to show their support. The organization also had a dormant Sierra Club Foundation that had 501c3 status, so while the Sierra Club itself became a 501c4, it could use its c3 foundation for tax-deductible donations. Today it has 550,000 members and an annual budget of $43 million.[15] Over time, few citizen groups have prospered to the degree the Sierra Club has.

Nevertheless, the broader impact of the IRS's actions were chilling. The immediate retribution and the suspension of tax deductibility while the investigation was being conducted were extraordinary actions. Congress, through the IRS, threw the gauntlet down. The IRS could have easily determined that the Sierra Club had not crossed the "substantial" line since the ads cost the organization around $10,000 while its budget that year was around $1.5 million. Instead, the IRS said, in effect, "We may enforce 501c3 rather selectively, but if you're the one caught, the consequences are serious."

Containing the Left

Although the IRS reacted in an excessively harsh and vindictive manner by its immediate revocation of the Sierra Club's tax deductibility, there is certainly an argument to be made that it responded in line with the spirit of the tax law governing public charities. The Sierra Club had made it clear to all that it was prepared for a sustained fight over the Grand Canyon dams. It was raising money for the fight, and its ads were part of a larger lobbying strategy that involved mobilizing the grassroots and direct lobbying of legislators. It was certainly reasonable for the IRS to consider the Sierra Club's advocacy as substantial. But without any operative definition of what constituted "substantial" lobbying, the IRS left itself open to charges that it was acting on behalf of Aspinall and not in defense of section 501c3. Indeed, the arbitrary nature of what the IRS did to the Sierra Club led to the movement for an explicit standard; later that would lead to the section of the 1976 tax act that created the H election and the expenditure test.

The capricious nature of the IRS action against the Sierra Club should not obscure the larger issue that confronted the government during this period. For those in Washington, it may have seemed that the government was being challenged on all fronts by liberal organizations demanding change. The IRS decision was not so much idiosyncratic as it was symptomatic of policymakers trying to figure out to what degree they wanted to facilitate the participation of liberal groups who seemed fundamentally hostile to the conventional practices of government. The antiwar movement was in full swing by this time, and the Democratic Party seemed incapable of containing its rage. The civil rights movement had brought about change but not tranquility.

Aspinall and other policymakers who saw the Sierra Club as a real threat were absolutely right. It was not just one organization saying "I dare you" to Congress and the IRS. It was part of a burgeoning public interest movement keen not only on changing policy but reforming the policymaking process as well. Environmental groups wanted to break up the cozy arrangements among congressional committees and agencies that excluded organizations like themselves from any role in policymaking.

Although 1966 was early in the development of the modern public interest movement, it was certainly clear that these groups were not going to play by the same rules that other Washington lobbies followed. Ralph Nader had already published *Unsafe at Any Speed*, and he gained considerable notoriety for his consumer advocacy. Public interest groups began suing the government with regularity. The IRS itself faced more challenges after the

Sierra Club decision.[16] New organizations, with clear political goals, were applying for tax deductibility. In 1970, in its letter of approval to the Natural Resources Defense Council's application for 501c3 status, the IRS attached an unexpected stipulation that the NRDC would need to gain prior approval for any litigation it wanted to file. The NRDC quickly filed suit since there is no explicit prohibition against litigation in the laws governing public charities.

Shortly after its decision on the NRDC the IRS suspended all applications for tax deductibility from new public interest groups, saying that it wanted to formulate some clear eligibility standards. Liberals saw the heavy hand of the Nixon administration, which correctly regarded these new organizations as dedicated and resourceful opponents. The outpouring of criticism toward the IRS's actions led to a retreat later that year, with the agency declaring that prior approval of litigation by a 501c3 was not, in fact, required.[17] The hostility of the IRS toward the public interest movement continued however. The Center for Corporate Responsibility's application for tax deductibility languished for two and a half years. When a *Washington Post* reporter publicized the IRS's refusal to issue the approval, the agency finally acted and rejected the application. The organization, which had antagonized business with shareholder actions, had made enemies at the White House too. When a judge ruled against the IRS in the organization's subsequent court suit, it said that the White House's refusal to release documents relating to the case was an admission that it tried to improperly influence the IRS.[18]

The actions of Congress, the IRS, and the White House against these public interest organizations reflected their concern over the challenge they presented and their uncertainty over what to do. These groups wanted to participate in policymaking in a meaningful way, not just testify before committees or have an occasional grip and grin in a legislator's office. Their participation was not a neutral factor; bringing them into congressional policymaking, opening up the rulemaking process, broadening the rules of standing in the federal courts, all tipped policymaking leftward. How far leftward no one in government knew, and this uncertainty added to the apprehension.

With one hand the federal government waved new groups on in and said "become part of the process," while it held up the other hand and said "stop, go no further." At the same time the IRS was taking action against the Sierra Club, the War on Poverty was putting into place its maximum feasible participation rules. After a federal appeals court greatly expanded the rules of standing for public interest law firms, the IRS tried to put an end to the tax exemption for these same organizations. There was no coherent response to these challenges because there was no one section of government that could produce a comprehensive policy on the participation of citizen groups. At the very least, though, the political parties were quick to sort themselves out on these issues. During the Johnson years the Democrats were split with an old guard fighting liberal reformers. This conflict would reach its climax at the 1968 Democratic convention in Chicago. Once Richard Nixon became president, it became easy for the Democrats to resolve their differences over the participation of these new challenging groups in American politics. All these groups, from the local nonprofits participating in Community Action Programs, to national citizen groups like the NRDC, were fighting the Republicans and, therefore, were allies. As liberals took power in the national party, the Democrats' ambivalence toward expanded participation vanished. The Republicans' position hardened.

Conservative Outrage

Republicans knew, just as the Democrats did, that facilitating the participation of nonprofits and citizen lobbies in government worked to the Republicans' disadvantage. The Nixon White House saw all too well that the more public interest law firms like the NRDC that were around, the more trouble they would cause conservatives. At the local level, expanded participation was a means of giving liberals more leverage in acquiring federal money and a greater role in the delivery of social services.

For conservative politicians, there was more than political expediency at stake. Their political calculations were anchored to a simple belief: that the government should not be in the business of providing financial support to nonprofits so that they can participate in public policymaking. For conservatives this is a fundamental matter of equity. Government was not simply making it easier for local nonprofits and national citizen groups to participate through expanded standing in the courts and greater opportunities to become involved in administrative rulemaking. Rather, the government was providing financial support to these organizations. Beyond the subsidy provided by tax deductibility of donations to 501c3s are direct government outlays to nonprofits. Particularly galling to conservatives is that some of this direct financial support goes to liberal advocacy groups, organizations that conservatives believe are masquerading as public charities.

This financial support comes in the form of grants and contracts, and it generates outrage by conservatives in Washington who see the federal government as a financial spigot for their political opponents. During the 1980s conservative think tanks repeatedly compiled lists of what they regarded as subsidies to the left. Why was the NOW Legal Defense Fund receiving money from the Department of Education to run television spots promoting gender equity? What was the reason Jesse Jackson's PUSH was getting job training funds from the Labor Department? Was there anyone who believed that an organization associated with Jesse Jackson was a neutral player in the political process, just working to train the unskilled? Was there an explanation why the Citizen/Labor Energy Coalition, with people like Tom Hayden on its board, was receiving grant after grant from the federal government? Since when did the labor movement need taxpayer support?[19]

In theory both the tax subsidy through 501c3 and the financial support that comes from government grants and contracts to carry out services for various departments and agencies, are available to all nonprofits regardless of their political outlook. There are some conservative nonprofits that qualify for 501c3, but they are a relatively small percentage compared to the liberal ones. The locally based social service providers that predominate among all nonprofits are in the best position to compete for government grants. Many grant programs were created with local social service nonprofits in mind. Because they are in the business of offering social services, these nonprofits tend to favor an expansive government with generous programs for the poor and disadvantaged. In other words, their outlook on domestic policy is decidedly liberal. There is no conservative analogue to these organizations on the local level, and this is surely one of the reasons President George W. Bush pushed his faith-based initiative to identify federal grant programs that could be directed to churches or church-related c3s.

The conservatives' attack on what they regarded as subsidies to the left is grounded on what they see as a bedrock principle of personal freedom. Their grievance is that government uses its power to coerce taxpayers to support political organizations even if those citizens do not back those organizations' point of view. The tracts produced by conservative think tanks on this subject like to cite Thomas Jefferson's dictum "To compel a man to furnish funds for the propagation of ideas he disbelieves and abhors is sinful and tyrannical."[20] Liberals would not want their taxes to support organizations sponsored by Jerry Falwell or Pat Robertson, so why should conservatives pay taxes to support Jesse Jackson's or Tom Hayden's groups?

As former senator Phil Gramm put it, the liberal groups are acting as "advocates for the existing welfare bureaucracy, and while they may have a right to do it, they don't have a right to do it with taxpayers' money."[21]

Liberals have an easy rejoinder to this: tyranny is being poor and having no one to represent you in the political process. Yet this rationale is hardly convincing to conservatives. In their view liberals who want to support work on behalf of the poor can raise the money among themselves. Political fund-raising is the free market of political ideas.[22] Moreover, some of the liberal nonprofits, like environmental lobbies, weren't working for the poor but for middle-class suburbanites. Conservatives wanted to know why they had to provide tax money to government so that government could fund advocacy groups who would then turn around and sue the government. Where is the justice in that?

Defund the Left

Conservatives have been interested in more than a philosophical debate over what they regard as tax-supported lobbying. Periodically, conservative lobbies and members of Congress have worked to try to reduce the federal support to organizations they think of as advocacy groups rather than public charities. It has been a difficult mountain for conservatives to climb, and they have acted only when electoral fortunes shone on the Republicans, notably after Richard Nixon's and Ronald Reagan's elections and after the Republicans' sweep of the 1994 congressional elections.

The failure of the Nixon administration to win its battles against citizen groups with tax-deductible status did not deter the Reagan administration. Nixon's domestic policy was imaginative and relatively liberal for a Republican; it was hardly a template that Reagan was interested in following. Reagan himself set a tone for his administration when he called public interest lawyers "ideological ambulance chasers."[23] Conservatives at the Cato Institute and the Heritage Foundation embarked on a serious effort to document the abuses and prepare the intellectual groundwork to "defund the left."[24]

The administration believed that its cuts in domestic spending would have a secondary impact on the liberal community's advocacy groups. Since the administration thought that nonprofit advocacy groups were biologically dependent on government domestic spending, cutting that spending down would starve many of these organizations, leaving them emaciated if not dead. This was surely the administration's greatest failure in trying to contain the left. The initial cuts were significant, but the 1981 recession,

Democratic gains in the 1982 election, and lack of public support for wholesale termination of programs moderated the administration's budget-cutting efforts. The administration's attack on the welfare state and environmentalism only worked to mobilize the liberals. Liberal public interest groups became the loyal opposition, and having the Reagan administration in office helped them to raise more money from individual donors.[25] Interior Secretary James Watt and Environmental Protection Agency head Anne Gorsuch were probably the best fund-raisers the environmental movement ever had.

A more pointed effort to defund nonprofits was initiated at the Office of Management and Budget by its counsel, Michael Horowitz. Horowitz's goal was to prevent nonprofits that were receiving federal grants from lobbying government. He reflected the widespread belief among conservatives that nonprofits took some of the money they got in the forms of grants and paid for lobbying with it. And that lobbying, he believed, was aimed at acquiring even more government grants. Horowitz's vehicle was an innocuous and deadly dull bureaucratic document called "Cost Principles for Nonprofit Organizations."[26] Published at the end of the Carter administration, it set forth accounting rules for cost sharing—how much overhead could be charged to federal grants. Horowitz took these guidelines and fashioned new regulations that forbade any cost sharing from federal grants for facilities or staff involved in lobbying.[27] Instead of the exceptionally narrow definition of 501c3, lobbying was defined in commonsense terms as attempts to influence government decisions at any branch. Under the guise of accounting rules, Horowitz's plan was a sweeping policy proposal that would have essentially forced every 501c3 receiving grants to start a separate organization to do lobbying. Gary Bass of OMB Watch, an advocacy group for nonprofits, said the new rules meant "You couldn't use a copier purchased with federal grant dollars for any purpose related to lobbying."[28]

Nonprofits regarded OMB's proposed rules, contained in Circular A-122, as nothing short of a declaration of war against them. These restrictions would have fundamentally altered the administration and organization of 501c3s. Public charities receiving grants would not be able to engage in advocacy. All advocacy would have to come through other nonprofit organizations that took no federal money. The intense reaction by the nonprofit community was manifested in legislative lobbying and in letters to OMB and the White House.[29] The problem for the administration was that it was easy for conservative ideologues to talk about why the government should not be giving money to Jesse Jackson, but it was another thing for members of Congress to come up with a cogent answer when constituents back in the district were asking why the government was attacking nonprofits. Legislators were hearing from people who sat on the boards of the United Way or volunteered with the local Meals on Wheels. Horowitz's proposal became an embarrassment for the administration, and Reagan's chief of staff, James Baker, instructed Horowitz to withdraw the rules. As Horowitz recalled, Baker confronted him in the hallway of the Executive Office Building and said, "The leader of the free world has come to me and said that all he has been hearing about is this business of A-122."[30]

The administration enjoyed at least one victory against advocacy groups, emasculating a number of citizen participation programs in federal agency proceedings.[31] These programs, a legacy of the maximum feasible participation requirement of the War on Poverty, had been instituted widely throughout the federal government, and they were designed to give citizens a role in agency planning and administrative rulemaking. Few worked as intended because bureaucrats had little incentive to make them work.[32] Since the citizen participation programs of this era were generally ineffective, liberals in Congress made a prudent choice in not making them one of their priorities as they fought the Reagan administration's domestic program.

The citizen participation programs were not tied to financial support for these groups, so even this victory did nothing to pull federal money away from nonprofits. By the end of his administration even Reagan's allies were calling the effort to defund the left a failure. "Not a single one of the Administration's proposals for defunding its sworn enemies has been fully implemented," concluded one conservative analyst.[33]

Hunt Them Down

After the Republicans' stunning success in the 1994 congressional elections, conservatives were once again emboldened to try to defund liberal nonprofits. Conservative think tanks, magazines, and GOP legislators began working together to build a coalition capable of passing a law that would restrict these organizations' advocacy. Virginia Thomas, the wife of Supreme Court Justice Clarence Thomas and an aide to House Majority Leader Dick Armey, coordinated the initial effort. The goal, once again, was to stop federal funding from going to nonprofits that used the money to lobby the government. Said Grover Norquist, the head of Americans for Tax Reform and a close ally of Speaker Newt Gingrich, "We will hunt [these liberal groups] down one by one and extinguish their funding sources."[34]

Conservatives quickly coalesced around a rider to an appropriations bill sponsored by Republican representatives Ernest Istook, David McIntosh, and Robert Ehrlich.[35] Istook and his colleagues recognized that federal grants provided support for lobbying even though no federal money was directly allocated to lobbying. The conservative critics understood that since lobbying with federal dollars is generally illegal, nonprofits took care in the way they allocated expenditures in their accounting statements. In a weary replay of the A-122 regulations, Istook and his colleagues tried to find ways to stop nonprofits from using their grants to build an infrastructure that supported lobbying. The key charge was that federal grants amounted to "welfare for lobbyists": nonprofits kept themselves alive by using grant money to lobby for more grant money.

The Istook amendment took various forms. In its initial, and harshest, incarnation it broadly expanded the definition of lobbying beyond the existing 501c3 rules and limited all advocacy by an organization to 5 percent of its budget. For nonprofits with a budget over $1 million, an additional 1 percent could be spent on lobbying. Grantees could not pass money on to an organization that did lobby. By broadening the definition of lobbying beyond the narrow, if ambiguous, 501c3 standards, the Istook amendment would have made nonprofits receiving federal grants much more hesitant to lobby. Conservative think tanks and magazines produced a series of studies documenting how much federal money was going to individual organizations.[36] Their favorite example was the National Council of Senior Citizens, which received 96 percent of its budget from the government.[37] Also flogged were United Cerebral Palsy (81 percent of its budget) and the Association for Retarded Citizens (66 percent).[38]

The nonprofit community in Washington again mobilized organizations from around the country. What Istook proposed was of cataclysmic importance to nonprofits. The head of a statewide mental retardation organization described the Istook attack as "one of our darkest days. We all had to drop everything and fight it; otherwise we might not have stayed alive." Istook's bill went through three more iterations, softening the approach at each stage to try to gather more support.[39] The bills foundered for the same reason A-122 flopped. The approach Horowitz and Istook used may have been intended to stop Jesse Jackson and national environmental lobbies from receiving government grants, but their net would have caught food banks, YMCAs, and centers for retarded citizens too. When congressmen were approached by the leaders of these organizations, the legislators had little interest in lecturing them about "welfare for lobbyists." Leaders of nonprofits are highly respected in their communities, and legislators want to take credit for helping them *get* grants, not take them away.

As the issue developed, it became increasingly clear that the choice for Republican legislators was being on the side of the Red Cross back in the district or on the side of the Heritage Foundation in Washington. For most it was an easy decision.

Was Istook Right?

Despite the failure of Istook and his allies to get their bill through the Congress, it gave a real scare to nonprofits. That he resurrected an argument made by Horowitz in the early 1980s was a sobering lesson about the endurance of conservative anger over government financial support of liberal nonprofits. While Istook lost the political battle, the charge he made still rankles liberals (because they think he is wrong) and conservatives (because they think he is right). Since efforts to defund liberal nonprofits may arise again, it is worth taking a look at the conservatives' charges to see if they are valid.

Before trying to test the accuracy of the accusations made by Horowitz, Istook, and other conservatives, let us specify the different charges that emerge repeatedly in their proposed legislation and in their publications. The first is that grant money is fungible. Typically a nonprofit gets a grant to provide services of some kind. Portions of that money can be used to pay for new staff and to provide overhead support for the entire organization. None of that money will be expressly used for lobbying—careful accounting ensures that direct lobbying expenses are paid from other funds. Nevertheless, grant money that provides for staff and overhead can easily free up other monies so that staff can do other kinds of work, including lobbying. Second, Horowitz and Istook claimed that the definition of lobbying in 501c3 is so narrow that it allows nonprofits to lobby freely in spite of the original intent of the tax deduction for public charities. Third, there is the "welfare for lobbyists" allegation that nonprofits use the funds they receive from government to lobby for more funds from government.

As is already evident, the interviews with nonprofit leaders support the first two of these contentions. There is little question that grant money helps build the infrastructure of nonprofits and, in turn, growth in staff and infrastructure facilitates political work. And, as emphasized throughout, the operative definition of lobbying in section 501c3 is so ridden with inconsistencies and ambiguities that it legally allows for a good deal of lobbying by those nonprofits that understand the law.

It is the third charge, that nonprofit lobbyists become parasitic, attaching themselves to the host and then draining it, that is the most controversial and, if true, the most damaging. The first two charges, while valid, are not terribly harmful to nonprofits—only the most rabid conservatives are going to get upset about nonprofits building up their infrastructure. But is it true that nonprofits use federal grant money to lobby for more federal grant money? In this view nonprofits are entrepreneurial businesses, trying to expand their share of the federal largesse. The charge is one of excess—of a government that provides funding to organizations who will then waste the government's money by using it to lobby for more government money. The broader implication of this allegation is that the federal government becomes more bloated as pressure builds on it for more and more funds for nonprofits. This accusation is the heart of the Istook indictment: these organizations are not serving the public good, as befits nonprofits with tax deductibility, but simply serving themselves.

The survey and the tax returns of each respondent organization can shed light on this charge. A first step is to look at the responses to a survey question that asked, "Turning from barriers to inducements, what factors motivate your organization to become involved in the public policymaking process?" One of the items then listed was "opportunities to obtain government funding." Respondents circled a number from zero to four, with zero indicating that factor had "no influence" and four indicating that the influence was "high." If the Istook thesis is right, the nonprofits that are primarily advocacy organizations should score relatively high on this question. Nonprofits with a strong advocacy orientation, like environmental groups or public interest law firms, are the 501c3 organizations that conservatives have singled out for lobbying with tax dollars for more federal funds.[40] Again the National Taxonomy of Exempt Entities (NTEE) classification system can be used to facilitate a comparison of 501c3s working in different fields. The two NTEE sectors where the organizations would seem to have the most explicit orientation toward advocacy are the categories of "environment/animals" and "public, society benefit." The environment/animals category is self-explanatory, and public, society benefit includes those nonprofits that work to reform government, engage in advocacy on issues like civil rights, or are oriented toward social action.[41] Unlike many nonprofits, few of the organizations in these categories have clients to serve, and thus their lobbying for grant money cannot be defended on grounds that they are seeking money for the services they provide. Rather they work to benefit a broader public.

A useful comparison for these two groupings is "human services" and "health," which as noted earlier are the two NTEE categories that best iso-

Table 4-2. *Grant Seeking*

Type of nonprofit	Government funding as a motivating factor, mean scores	
	H electors[a]	Conventional nonprofits[a]
Environment/animals (*n* = 57/20)	1.1	1.6
Public, societal benefit (41/32)	1.0	1.6
Health (60/52)	2.0	2.2
Human services (80/184)	1.6	2.2
Arts, culture, and humanities (--/60)	[b]	2.5
Mean, all categories (306/479)	1.4	2.0

Q.16. Turning from barriers to inducements, what factors motivate your organization to become involved in the public policymaking process? The scores here are for the first item listed, "opportunities to obtain government funding." Scale is 0–4 for "significance of motivating factors," with 0 representing "no influence" and 4 representing "high."

a. Statistical significance: for the H electors, when health groups are compared with environmental nonprofits and then to public, societal-benefit nonprofits, the differences in the means for both comparisons are statistically significant at .05. When the human services nonprofits are compared with environmental nonprofits and then to public, societal-benefit nonprofits, the differences in the means for both comparisons are statistically significant at .05. When the tests are repeated for conventional nonprofits, the mean differences do not reach statistical significance at .05.

b. Insufficient number of cases.

late social service providers. The data here are further disaggregated by dividing the survey responses by tax status, thus separating out the H electors from the conventional 501c3 nonprofits. For purposes of testing the Istook thesis, we have separated out the most politically active nonprofits by their tax filings, and then from that grouping we have taken out the most overtly political NTEE categories. In short, we have separated out the most political of the most political nonprofits.

The results may seem surprising, and they certainly cast doubt on the Istook thesis. The H electors working on environmental policy or for a broad social goal like civil rights were the organizations we selected out as the most political of the most political. Our results show that these organizations display the lowest mean scores for becoming involved in the policymaking process as an incentive to obtain more government funds (table 4-2). Health and human service nonprofits are more likely to regard the possibility of more government funds as an inducement for lobbying. Among all nonprofits, it turns out that art and culture organizations find this inducement the strongest. Thus, by the logic of the Istook thesis, opera companies and local humanities councils are the greatest threat to the integrity of government grant making.

Table 4-3. *Reasons for Nonprofits to Lobby*

	Mean scores	
Reasons	H electors	Conventional nonprofits
Opportunities to obtain government funding (N = 306/479)	1.5	2.0
Protecting government programs that serve our clients, constituents, or community (313/485)	3.3	2.5
Promoting government programs that support our mission (311/490)	3.6	2.7
Raising public awareness of important issues (310/493)	3.5	2.5
Defending nonprofits' advocacy rights (299/472)	1.9	1.8

The same question on the survey listed four other incentives for organizations to become more involved in the policymaking process. The comparison of the mean scores is revealing and again undercuts the logic behind the Istook amendment. For the more politically minded H electors, obtaining government funds is not nearly as strong an incentive as protecting government programs, promoting government programs that support the nonprofit's mission, or raising public awareness of important issues (table 4-3). Those three incentives have a mean score roughly two points higher than that of obtaining government funds, a substantial difference on a five-point scale. The differences are not as great among the conventional nonprofits, but the pattern is otherwise the same.

To crosscheck these findings a third test was to see if there is a relationship between the percentage of each nonprofit's budget that comes from government and the amount of lobbying they do. The Istook thesis suggests that nonprofits that derive a larger percentage of their budget from the government should be more active in lobbying the government. Again we select out the H electors to give us a cohort of highly active lobbies. For the H electors there is no statistically significant relationship ($r = -.01$) between income from government and the amount of lobbying, a clear refutation of the Istook thesis.[42] For conventional nonprofits, there is a significant correlation ($r = .28, p = .000$), so this provides some support for Istook's case. A final judgment on this relationship must await the application of some statistical controls, weighing all the variables discussed against one another.

Figure 4-1. *Government-Initiated Contact and Lobbying Levels*

Percent of nonprofits at two highest lobbying levels

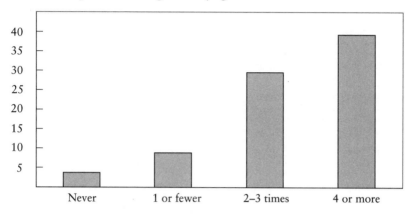

Level of government-initiated contact, per month

Q.4. In some cases contact with those in government comes about at the initiative of the policymakers themselves. How often on average would you say that people in government approach the executive director, staff, or members of the board to discuss matters of mutual interest?

Note: Conventional nonprofits, *n* = 551.

Before conducting the statistical analysis that compares the different competing explanations of nonprofit lobbying, one more variable had to be included. A major finding that emerges in this study is that there is a strong, cooperative relationship between nonprofits and local government. Government frequently has reason to approach nonprofits to request information or to ask for their participation in some phase of policymaking or grant writing.

Although the fuller explanation of these dynamics must wait until chapter 6, the basic finding can be integrated into this analysis. One of the variables from the survey is the frequency of government-initiated contact. Respondents were asked to estimate the number of times each month people in government approached the nonprofit "to discuss matters of mutual interest." When that variable is crosstabulated with the respondent's estimate of the amount of lobbying his or her organization does, a striking pattern emerges. As figure 4-1 illustrates, a nonprofit's level of lobbying is strongly related to the frequency with which government approaches it.

Table 4-4. *Predictors of Propensity to Lobby*

Variable estimate (standard error)	Significant at:
Level of contact with nonprofits initiated by government .625 (.111)	.000
Opportunity to raise public awareness of important issues .323 (.108)	.003
To defend nonprofits' advocacy rights .200 (.079)	.011
To protect government programs that serve clients, constituents or community .209 (.110)	.057
To promote government policies that support our mission .270 (.123)	.028
Opportunity to obtain government funding −.009622 (.077)	Not significant, .210
Percentage of annual budget from government .0002161 (.003)	Not significant, .499
Pseudo R^2 .351	

Note: The dependent variable is lobbying level (Q.6b). Estimates are ordinal regression coefficients. Analysis is for conventional 501c3 nonprofits; n = 430.

As with the correlation showing a relationship between the level of government income and lobbying level among conventional nonprofits, this relationship between government-initiated contact and lobbying must be subjected to statistical controls to see if it is spurious. Multivariate analysis was used to weigh the relative impact of government-initiated contact, income from government, and the five incentives to lobby listed in table 4-3 against the propensity of conventional nonprofits to lobby. (These calculations were only done for conventional nonprofits since the Istook thesis was already disproved above for the H electors.) Table 4-4 shows that government-initiated contact is the most powerful predictor and that the relationship depicted in figure 4-1 is not spurious. Rather the relationship is as strong as that bar chart suggests. Of the five inducements to lobby listed in the question on incentives to lobby, three show statistically significant relationships, and one is significant at .06. Contrary to Istook, the only inducement that is clearly insignificant is the opportunity to obtain more government funding. Also throwing cold water on the Istook thesis is that the percentage of the nonprofit's income derived from government is not related to lobbying levels either.[43]

Through this set of different statistical tests, the Istook thesis repeatedly falls short.[44] For the most politically active nonprofits—the H electors—and for the conventional nonprofits most oriented toward advocacy, the evidence flatly contradicts the conservatives' charge that a certain subset of 501c3s is motivated to lobby by the opportunity to get more grant money. For conventional nonprofits as a whole, the hint of a moderate relationship between the percentage of their income from government and lobbying washes out when controls are applied. Not only is the Istook thesis incorrect, it appears that Representative Istook and his colleagues had the relationship backward. The nonprofits that lobby the most are the nonprofits that government approaches the most.

Conclusion

Although the Istook amendment never came close to passage, it had an impact nevertheless. It was one more case of a visible effort in Washington to curtail the political activity of 501c3 nonprofits. Since the IRS's lightning quick strike against the Sierra Club in 1966, nonprofits have felt a heightened sense of vulnerability to government action aimed at terminating their tax deductibility. The debate in Congress over the Istook amendment scared the nonprofit sector anew—it lost for winning. As Paul Light concluded, "Ironically, the sector has mostly protected its lobbying and organizing freedom by not using it."[45]

It has not been a systematic effort on the part of Washington—anything but. Rather, the attempt to intimidate nonprofits has been erratic and episodic, though the broadest attempts have emerged after a Republican election victory. Yet it is not just conservatives in Washington who have threatened 501c3s. State-level bureaucrats use the power to audit how agency grant funds are being expended to go after nonprofits that have angered them for some reason. The enormous power of the IRS to revoke tax deductibility and the power of state agencies to end their grants to organizations puts individual nonprofits at risk if they choose to lobby openly. The IRS also discourages lobbying by nonprofits indirectly because foundations, worried about protecting their own tax status, commonly forbid any lobbying supported by funds granted to 501c3s.[46]

As haphazard as these government actions against nonprofits are, they constitute an insidious form of regulation. Like other types of government regulation, enforcement of the rules need only be sporadic to have the desired effect of changing behavior. Unlike most other forms of regulation, however, the regulation of lobbying by nonprofits is based on law and practice that are wholly contradictory. As a result some nonprofits ignore 501c3 and lobby extensively, while others feel that it is too risky.

It's unlikely that the contradictions will be worked out soon because both law and practice reflect the bitter differences between conservatives and liberals over political activity by 501c3 nonprofits. The nonprofit world belongs to the liberals. It incorporates advocacy groups and social service providers. Those constitute hundreds of thousands of organizations around the country, and they are all supported by tax dollars through the 501c3 subsidy. Many of them receive grant money as well.

Although conservatives are correct in recognizing the political imbalance in government support, their attempts to eliminate or at least reduce the federal money going to nonprofits have been clumsy and ill conceived. It is easy to select out examples of unpopular organizations receiving large federal grants, but fashioning a policy to deal with alleged abuses of lobbying with federal dollars is something else entirely. Conservatives have proposed policies that would harm mental retardation centers, homeless shelters, and drug rehabilitation programs. Conservatives would argue that these are not the organizations they are going after but, in fact, the reforms they have proposed apply equally to all 501c3s. The conservative critics have never offered a realistic plan whereby nonprofits that have business before the government will still be able to freely talk to legislators without losing their tax deductibility.

Liberals have passionately defended the right of nonprofits to lobby the government. In their eyes the "market" has failed to provide representation for many disadvantaged and marginalized constituencies. Who is going to represent these people if not nonprofits? Whereas Istook sees nonprofits as advocacy organizations endlessly lobbying the government for more and more money, liberals see nonprofits as social service providers with a mission all citizens should support. If those social service nonprofits approach government and ask for more money to better serve their clients, liberals ask, "What's wrong with that?"

CHAPTER FIVE

Different
Standard,
Different
Behavior

This tale of government restrictions and even occasional hostility toward nonprofits may seem rather puzzling in light of the real reverence toward nonprofits in our culture and history. Americans see nonprofits as compassionate and generous. Nonprofits facilitate voluntarism; they tackle the problems that government cannot solve and business cannot make a profit from. Nonprofits enrich our lives in every possible way. And yet in official policy and actual practice, the federal government discourages nonprofits from interacting with the legislators that ostensibly represent these nonprofits' clients.

Just as puzzling, perhaps, is that the scholarly literature largely ignores this rather serious problem, focusing instead on the partnerships that exist between agencies and nonprofit social service providers. "Partnerships" evokes something positive, something cooperative. This literature on government-nonprofit partnerships is not misguided—such partnerships exist in abundance despite the limitations imposed by 501c3. These contradictory impulses of government exist side by side because American politics does not take place in a single arena with a single set of regulations. Rather, multiple venues and opportunities exist for access to government. By turning away from Washington and away from legislative lobbying and, instead, examining local politics and administrative lobbying, it is easy to derive a much different impression of the relationship between the government and the so-called independent sector.

No Opponents

To step away from Washington is to view interest groups, and especially nonprofits, in an entirely different light. Especially striking is that in their role as advocates, most nonprofits have no active opposition. At the state and local level nonprofits working on behalf of their constituents generally encounter few, if any, other organizations offering policymakers an opposing point of view. Asked about organizations working against his Oregon-based nonprofit, the executive director thought for a while and then replied simply, "I don't know of any group right now that is working against us."

For some nonprofits there is no opposition because they work in areas that are not politically contentious. Museums, for example, have only occasional reason to talk to those in government, and when they do they do not have to worry about entering into a conflictual arena. "It's tough to talk negatively about libraries," said the head of one statewide association in New England. For such nonprofits, operating in an uncontroversial area that only involves government at the periphery, the lack of opposition makes it all the easier for them to approach policymakers when they need to talk about funding or a regulatory matter. These nonprofits have every reason to believe that policymakers value their work, are happy to talk to them, and are not going to hear a disparaging word about them from opponents.

Yet most nonprofits work in policy areas that by any colloquial or scholarly definition are *political*. Human service providers, the largest sector of the nonprofit world, operate in environments that are highly regulated, extensively funded by government, and elicit significant government oversight. Many of these nonprofits rarely encounter organized opposition either. The services they provide to the poor, disabled, unemployed, and homeless are universally embraced. No one organizes to work against helping the frail elderly. This is not say that these groups do not face any barriers. Some face competition from for-profit providers in the same industry. A broader problem is that budget realities and public opinion constrain government funding, a lifeline to so many nonprofit human service and health care providers. Another hurdle is the limited capacity of government. As the head of a child care organization put it, "We have no opponents. Our problem instead is getting people to pay attention."

There are, of course, some nonprofits, that work in conflictual arenas— environmental groups for example. They must contend with business groups that oppose land use controls, antipollution measures, and other environmental objectives. The legislators and administrators they approach cannot ignore these opposing advocates and must try to find the middle ground among competing positions. Important and effective as some of the liberal citizen groups have been, these dedicated advocacy organizations are a relatively small proportion of all nonprofits. Environmental organizations of all types are about 4 percent of all 501c3s, and those ambiguously classified by the NTEE as "public, societal benefit" (which includes some highly political groups like civil rights organizations) constitute just another 7 percent.

This lack of organized opposition to nonprofits reflects a much larger pattern: interest group activity of any kind is generally low in urban political systems. Paul Peterson goes as far as to call local politics "groupless politics."[1] To oversimplify a vast literature in political science, it is difficult for would-be leaders to organize lobbies composed of individuals because of the collective action problem.[2] People have little incentive to join for the public policy benefits that may come from an organization's lobbying. If the lobbying yields a collective good (like clean air), individuals can share in it regardless of whether they are members of an organization that worked on the issue. Instead they can be "free riders." Some may still join because of ideological commitment, but others require some benefit that is derived exclusively from membership. This problem is most severe for local groups. Without the resources and economies of scale that accrue to larger organizations, small groups at the community level may not be able to offer much in the way of selective benefits.[3] Although local groups offer members the chance to socialize with other like-minded citizens, this can also be a disincentive as individuals may not want to be involved in an organization that expects them to go to meetings and participate in lobbying campaigns.

"Groupless" may be a bit hyperbolic as there are always a few unions, a downtown business association, and some civic groups active in cities. Still, freestanding organizations, whose primary purpose is to lobby government, are relatively sparse in local politics. It costs a lot to hire a staff, rent an office, put out a newsletter, and pay the fund-raising costs that are dictated by the need to pay those expenses. Institutions and trade associations do most of the lobbying in local politics. At the local level 501c3s and 501c4s constitute a higher proportion of all organizations engaging in government relations than is the case in Washington politics.

The differences between local and national politics are remarkable. Washington politics is characterized by extraordinarily dense networks of lobbies.[4] In any policy area there are competing interest groups, and policymakers are usually faced with two or three coalitions of lobbies, each antagonistic toward the other. Policymakers wanting to move proposals forward need to mediate among opposing factions in the hopes of finding an acceptable compromise. But interest group politics in Fresno or Chattanooga is different. Cities are not overrun with competing groups.

Although no one argues that city politics is the same as Washington politics, what we know about interest groups comes largely from studies of national politics.[5] Unfortunately, this literature is a poor guide to understanding advocacy in city politics. And, as chapter 2 points out, Washington-oriented research on interest groups generally ignores nonprofits.

Principal among institutions that lobby city government are the largest corporations, neighboring cities, hospitals, universities, and various other (nonmembership) nonprofits.[6] What these "lobbies" have in common is not just that they are organized for something other than politics, but that they have a steady and substantial source of funding even though they have no membership as such. It is not difficult for large institutions to absorb the cost of a vice president for public affairs or some equivalent because it is a small item in their overall budget. Harvard University is not organized as a lobby, and it is certainly not a voluntary association, but it has an office for public affairs headed by a high-ranking vice president. It is a major force in the politics of Cambridge and Boston. Such institution-based lobbying is also found in Washington, though it is usually manifested in separate lobbying offices set apart from the larger organization headquartered somewhere else.

Another major source of lobbying by nonprofits at the state and local level comes from the trade associations for health and human service providers. These umbrella groups, many of which are 501c4s, provide many services to their constituent organizations, including government relations. Trade groups for providers in areas such as mental retardation, community health, family planning, substance abuse, and nursing home care, are active and effective advocates for their industries before state and local governments. Even though the trade group or other type of umbrella organization leading a coalition may not be a 501c3, it is still hampered by the law on public charities because it is difficult for them to enlist their constituent organizations in grass-roots or legislative lobbying campaigns. This is a significant difference between trade groups for 501c3s and business trade groups.

In contrast to the low density of voluntary membership organizations that lobby city governments is the high density of nonprofits. They are everywhere. Research by Kirsten Grønbjerg and Laurie Paarlberg shows that in Indiana there are an average of fifty-seven nonprofits per 10,000 in population. This figure is for all types of nonprofits, not just 501c3s, but includes only those that are registered with the Internal Revenue Service. After adding Indiana's incorporated nonprofits that are registered with the state and religious congregations, Grønbjerg and Paarlberg concluded that IRS registrations only account for 60 percent of the nonprofits eventually identified in their research. Adding these organizations means that a more accurate estimate is about 100 nonprofits per 10,000 population.[7] That's a nonprofit for every 100 individuals. As they point out, however, their calculations do not take into account small nonprofits that do not register with either the state or the IRS. Hence, the true density of nonprofits is higher still.

A research team at Northwestern University, using a different methodology, confirms the high density of nonprofits in American communities. The team closely examined the Grand Boulevard neighborhood on Chicago's South Side. This is an extremely poor neighborhood of 36,000 residents, where 82 percent of the children grow up in families living below the poverty line. A block-by-block inventory revealed 319 nonprofits that they identify as "face-to-face organizations," where volunteers do the bulk of the work. About 100 of these nonprofits were churches or religious groups.[8] It is unclear how many more nonprofits would have been included if a more expansive definition had been used, but it is remarkable that such a poor neighborhood supports such a rich variety of organizations. The concentration of nonprofits tends to be higher in wealthier communities, so this neighborhood could be at the low end in density.[9]

The nature of interest group politics in local communities offers nonprofits (of all sizes, membership and nonmembership alike) an enormous opportunity. Relatively thin lobbying networks and few opponents give local nonprofits with the right political instincts a chance to exert real influence. In comparison to interest groups in Washington, the lack of opposition gives nonprofits at least four important advantages in lobbying city hall and state agencies:

First, little in the way of resources has to be devoted to getting a foot in the door, as the doors to city government and state agencies are already open.

Second, in comparison to their federal counterparts, city and state administrative agencies that deal with social service and health care providers do not have to worry as much about showing favoritism and do not have to safeguard their proceedings with as thick a cover of ex parte rules.[10]

Third, without substantial opposition or competition, partnerships with government are possible, if not imperative.

Fourth, policy initiatives are not typically stymied by lobbying groups pushing for diametrically opposed objectives. Initiatives may fail, but they will fail for other reasons.

In comparison to national politics, these are profound differences. In Washington, most groups struggle just to get heard above the din of competing interests. In local politics, the typical human service or health-related nonprofit has an ongoing conversation with government agency policymakers and does not have to worry about being heard. There is no prohibition in 501c3 against lobbying administrative agencies. There are some state laws that define direct advocacy in administrative rulemaking proceedings as lobbying.[11] This doesn't make it illegal—in the same way as lobbying is not illegal under 501c3. More important, such state rules do not seem to be much of an inhibition since formal rulemaking is not usually the target of nonprofits working on public policy. As long as they stick to the administrative side of state and local government, nonprofits would seem to be home free—free to lobby all they want.

Returned Phone Calls

Nonprofits at the state and local level have their share of frustrations with government, but access to policymakers is not one of them. Government is wide open. The relationship between nonprofits and government is multifaceted, and individual nonprofits interact with government officials in endless ways. The head of an agency devoted to child care issues offered this overview of her organization's relationship with government:

> We have a lot of interaction with the state Department of Education. We're on the phone with them every day. We do training and do conferences with them too. Local government, well, we're very involved there too. Right now I'm very involved on the committee that is doing the strategic plan for Proposition 10 cigarette money. I'm on the local child care planning council. Every county in California has one. I'm in touch with members of the city government. Our Board is focused [more and more] on advocacy. We're like a government agency because of our contracting . . . We work with our local representatives on legislation we want introduced. We had a piece introduced recently, with other child care providers, that is going through the state legislature.

Table 5-1. *Nonprofits' Interaction with Government*

	Meet frequently with government officials	Government officials interested in hearing our views
Arts, culture, humanities (*n* = 63/55)	20.6	52.7
Education (65/52)	18.4	46.2
Environment, animals (22/21)	36.3	66.7
Health (59/56)	35.6	57.1
Human services (211/190)	27.9	58.4
Public, societal benefit (39/35)	28.2	68.6

Conventional 501c3 nonprofits:

Q.6. A variety of means of communicating and interacting with those in government are listed below. Please use the scale on the right to indicate how frequently, if at all, your organization engages in these activities. (By "your organization" we mean the executive director, other staff, volunteers, or members of the board.) In this scale, 0 means never, 1 is relatively infrequent interaction, and 4 is ongoing interaction.
Meeting with government officials about the work we are doing   0   1   2   3   4
(The percentages aggregate those marking 3 or 4 for each item.)

Q.7. Thinking generally about those in government that your organization deals with, please select the description below that typically describes those officials' attitudes.
❏ Not really interested in hearing our views
❏ Sometimes interested in what we have to say
❏ Usually interested in what we have to say
❏ Interested in what we have to say and interested in actively working with us to achieve a common goal
(The percentages aggregate those marking "usually interested" and "interested . . . and interested in actively working with us.")

Later she added with a laugh, "I get my phone calls returned."

She is not the only nonprofit executive who gets her phone calls returned. Every indication from the survey, interviews, and focus groups is that the leaders of nonprofits find it relatively easy to gain access to policymakers. Most of this access comes at the administrative level, not because of the inaccessibility of legislators and their staffers but because nonprofits approach agencies more frequently. Beyond the chilling effect of 501c3 on legislative advocacy, some nonprofits have more reason to talk to agency policymakers because of the grants and contracts they hold and the partnerships they are involved in.

Table 5-1 offers summary statistics that reflect the openness of government to nonprofits.[12] For nonprofits in five of the six major policy areas, more than half believe that government is usually interested in hearing their views or, even beyond that, is interested in actively working with them. These data also show that a significant percentage of conventional non-profits meet with policymakers on an ongoing basis. These numbers, which range roughly from one-fifth to one-third of the nonprofits, may not seem high in the abstract but, again, all respondents are included and, thus, these data encompass many nonprofits that have little or no reason to interact with government on a regular basis. For example, 40 percent of arts groups say they never meet with government officials. Organizations like the Los Angeles Philharmonic or the Southeastern Minnesota Arts Council may not meet very often with policymakers, but the larger story is that most nonprofits believe government officials are happy to meet with them if approached.

Tactics

Political scientists studying interest groups have paid considerable attention to the tactics used by all types of lobbies in trying to influence government. The general purpose is to try to isolate those tactics that seem to work best in moving policymakers to enact or maintain policies preferred by an advocacy group or coalition. Part of this is a search for the Holy Grail of lobbying—what's the true key to influence?—and part is an effort to understand how various interest group sectors differ in their approach to influencing government.

The Holy Grail remains elusive, but research has shown that lobbies that utilize a variety of tactics certainly possess an advantage in the political process.[13] Although there are many commonalities, various interest group sectors stress different tactics. Business and labor rely heavily on campaign contributions to supplement their direct lobbying. National citizen groups have effectively utilized research to attract attention and to establish credibility.

As discussed in chapter 4 our survey asked respondents how often they utilized nine different advocacy tactics.[14] (Here the data are organized and presented differently than in table 4-1.) Most items refer to government or policymakers in general, but some reasonable inferences can be made about what branch of government the tactic is usually directed toward. Testifying, lobbying, and encouraging members to write are more suggestive of legislative than administrative advocacy. In table 5-2, these three are arranged together along with "releasing research reports," as they constitute the most aggressive advocacy tactics. (Releasing research results can be aggressive, as they are often aimed at embarrassing some part of government by showing

Table 5-2. *Confrontation or Cooperation?*

Tactic	Frequency, mean scores	
	H electors	Conventional nonprofits
More legislative, more aggressive		
Testifying at hearings	2.2	.7
Lobbying on a bill or policy	2.5	.9
Encouraging members to write, call	2.6	1.2
Releasing research reports to media, public, policymakers	1.9	.8
Average	2.3	.9
More administrative, less aggressive		
Meeting with government officials	2.8	1.4
Working in a planning or advisory group	2.7	1.4
Responding to requests for information	2.5	1.5
Discussing grants	1.7	1.3
Socializing with government officials	1.8	1.4
Average	2.3	1.4

Note: For the full wording of each of the tactics listed, see table 4-1 or the appendix. (Q.6).The averages are the mean of the aggregate scores for each tactic, not the mean of all responses. The n for each subsample is 320 for the H electors and 583 for the conventional nonprofits. The aggregate responses to each tactic are a tiny bit smaller.

how ineffective it is at dealing with a particular problem.) The other tactics are less confrontational and include more cooperative forms of interaction. The garden variety nonprofit shows a strong tendency to rely on administrative advocacy and the more cooperative tactics associated with that strategy.

There is no stronger evidence of the impact of 501c3 status on the political behavior of nonprofits. The conventional wisdom on interest groups is that effective lobbies must be ready to lobby all institutions with whatever tactics are most appropriate. The H electors demonstrate this truism, showing an equal propensity toward legislative and administrative advocacy. On a five-point scale, the utilization rate for H electors averages 2.3 for both clusters of tactics. In stark contrast, the conventional nonprofits' use of legislative tactics is considerably less than the frequency rate for administrative advocacy (0.9 versus 1.4). All things being equal, there is no reason why conventional nonprofits would have a decided preference for administrative advocacy while H electors would show no such proclivity. Recall from table 3-2 that H electors do not seem much different from conventional nonprofits outside of their level of activism. The difference, of course, is that for conventional nonprofits lobbying administrative agencies is perceived as much safer than lobbying legislatures.

Relationships

In the interviews and focus groups we didn't hear advocacy discussed in the context of "tactics." Not surprisingly, these real-world leaders use a different vocabulary than academics. More to the point, though, nonprofit leaders conceive of their interaction with government from a completely different perspective. A social service agency head spoke for many executive directors when she told us, "It's all about relationships."

Ironically, over time interest group scholars have placed less and less emphasis on personal relationships and have gravitated toward other perspectives for understanding interest group access to government. In an earlier era, personal relationships were seen as key to success in lobbying in Washington. A legendary lobbyist like Charls Walker could get things done because he had cultivated a friendship with the Speaker or the right committee chair.[15] That may still be possible for a few heavy hitters, but there are too many lobbyists and too many interest groups in Washington today and lobbying is not so easy. The interest group scholars who study national politics search for more systematic explanations for success, such as campaign contributions, the nature of the organization's membership, and the context under which particular tactics have the most impact.

On the state and local level, however, research shows that personal relationships still seem to count a great deal.[16] It's a matter of scale, and the typical bureaucracy in the typical city is highly penetrable by any lobby. City bureaucracies tend to be small, and most are actively interested in developing partnerships with client groups. Local agencies can find efficiencies by teaming up with nonprofits. Congressional committees and federal administrative agencies simply do not need interest groups as partners. They surely prefer cooperation from lobbies, but the conflictual environment enveloping Washington interest group politics makes real partnerships difficult. Which of the hundreds of competing health care lobbies in Washington is the Centers for Medicare and Medicaid Services in the Department of Health and Human Services going to partner with?

It is only human nature that given the opportunity, people in an organization are going to try to develop personal relationships with their counterparts in the organizations they do business with. Individuals who get to know one another as their organizations interact on a repeated basis are going to develop more trust and understanding of each other. Bigger projects—bigger deals—are facilitated by experience and trust. It is also more efficient; people who are used to dealing with one another can cut to the chase more quickly in negotiations. They are also more comfortable in acknowledging the true nature of their organization's capacity, what they can and cannot do well.

The interviews and focus groups revealed a consistent strategic approach: the goal of most nonprofit leaders who work with government is to create a set of relationships that enhances the place of their organization *within* the governmental process. The keys are to understand what governmental bureaucracies want from nonprofits, build those capacities into one's own organization, and develop personal relationships with the policymakers who make the decisions affecting the nonprofit.

The most elemental part of this strategy was summed up by the head of a social services nonprofit who says she tells her managers that part of their job is to "get out and meet with people in government." In human-scale cities and in small states, this is easy. One Vermont-based nonprofit head said the people in government "are our neighbors. We see them in the super-market." But the strategy is not all that different in the big cities. The head of an Orthodox Jewish human service agency in New York City told us that getting the right grants was a matter of politics, and politics is a matter of "who you know." Another director told us, "I'm a political animal. I tell my people when you go into a room, don't sit down. Work the room. You have to let people get to know you."

The strategy of the politically attuned leaders goes beyond making it their business to nurture relationships with the administrators who fund their grants or write the regulations for their programs. Optimally, there are a web of relationships between the nonprofit and its board of directors and a range of administrators and legislators who have responsibility over programs of concern. The most obvious step is to load the board of directors with men and women of status—individuals who are professionally respected or socially connected to those in government. Research does show that non-profit boards are full of high-status individuals. It is prestigious to sit on boards, not only on the ones for symphonies and museums and arts coun-cils but also for the social service agencies that deal with impoverished and marginalized constituencies. As Melissa Middleton points out, there are also professional incentives to serve because "Philanthropic work has become a career expectation for managers seeking to advance within corporations."[17]

Boards are used in different ways.[18] The head of a nonprofit serving trou-bled youth said he liked "to bring in agency directors to speak to our board.

The board is not shy. And they're persons with resources. The state agency heads will suck up to them because they're people with high standing in the community." A health nonprofit that is funded almost exclusively by government surely helped itself by making its congressman's local office head the chairman of its board. A small library association didn't leave anything to chance by giving each of its board members a city council "buddy."

Besides their boards, 40 percent of nonprofits also have at least one advisory council. Typically they are composed of elites who confer additional status on the organization. Most, according to Judith Saidel, are engaged in "political advocacy activities" and play a major role by acting to "open doors and facilitate staff access to public policy makers."[19]

The relationships between nonprofit executives and board members and policymakers amount to much more than an oiling of the machinery of government. The strategy of nonprofits is to use their expertise to build ongoing relationships with those in government. As officials interact with nonprofit leaders, they will come to appreciate their knowledge of issues and policies and come to respect them for the way they administer government-sponsored programs. As trust builds, the nonprofit hopes it will be increasingly integrated into the governmental process, and be able to work alongside of policymakers. Thus nonprofit leaders do not think so much of tactics of advocacy as they do of ways to insinuate themselves inside government.

Partnerships

A strong, if not dominant, theme in the literature on nonprofits emphasizes the growth of partnerships between government and nonprofit social service providers.[20] There is every reason for this focus. As discussed in chapter 1, the revolution in welfare in this country has devolved much of the administration of social services onto nonprofits. There is nothing that nonprofits do that is as important as caring for those who need services. Appropriately, scholars have focused on the quality of the administration of services and on the cost effectiveness of contracting services to nonprofits.[21] The concern here is about a question that has received insufficient attention: how do the partnerships between government and social service providers influence the ability of nonprofits to carry out their advocacy role?

Do Grants Buy Silence?

Researchers focus on partnerships because the increasing dependence of government on nonprofits has made nonprofits increasingly dependent on government. This interdependence troubles some scholars because they do not see such partnerships as relationships of equals. The concern is that dependence on government for a sizable part of their budget forces nonprofits to be too compliant, too ready to do what funding agencies want. Is a family planning organization that receives most of its money from government going to be a vigorous champion of women's interests on contentious issues before its funding agency?

This is a crucial question. If the price of government grants is stilling the voice of nonprofits, are those nonprofits truly serving the best interests of their constituents? We have already seen that government regulation through the tax code has quieted nonprofits before Congress and state legislatures. Since 501c3 does not restrict administrative advocacy, it may be that government instead uses its financial largesse as a way of keeping nonprofits from being overly aggressive or demanding in their dealings with agencies.

It is surely not government's explicit intent to use grants as a means of gagging nonprofits or as a way of pushing them toward programs that everyone supports. But is it an unintentional byproduct? Scholars are not of one mind. Jennifer Alexander and her colleagues argue that social service nonprofits forgo helping the most needy and instead focus on programs where they can show the most progress to government funders. Moreover, they claim that the growth of government funding of nonprofits has "substantially diminished their capacity to be political."[22] But Lester Salamon argues that the expansion of government funding has allowed nonprofits to make "a stronger commitment" to the poor and the disenfranchised.[23]

The survey allows us to examine this question. Unfortunately, determining the impact of government funding on advocacy before administrative agencies is a much more difficult problem than measuring the impact of 501c3 on legislative lobbying. Section 501c3 could be shown to reduce contact between nonprofits and legislators. But nonprofits holding contracts from government have to talk to their funding agencies at least occasionally. Consequently, the greater contact between conventional nonprofits and administrative agencies demonstrated in table 5-2 does not mean that providers are as aggressive in their administrative advocacy as they might like.

A first step in addressing this question is to "follow the money." Is access linked to grants? For conventional nonprofits the survey demonstrates that the percentage of an organizations's budget from government is correlated ($r = .37$, $p = .000$) with its frequency of meeting with government officials.

The more money nonprofits get from government, the more they talk to government. The survey cannot tell us what goes on in those meetings or how aggressive those nonprofits are. However, an indirect measure of the advocacy orientation of nonprofits that talk to administrators is the relationship between administrative and legislative lobbying. We assume that legislative lobbying by conventional nonprofits is a rough indicator of aggressiveness since such behavior entails risk under 501c3. The correlation between the frequency of meeting with government officials (mostly administrators) and lobbying (mostly legislators) is robust ($r = .55$, $p = .000$). After controlling for the proportion of the respondents' budgets that comes from government, that relationship is much the same ($r = .49$, $p = .000$). In short, grants and contracts are not drawing the least politically aggressive nonprofits into government while pushing away the organizations most likely to want to lobby government.

The limitations of a questionnaire to fully answer such a nuanced question are all too obvious. The interviews were an opportunity to ask nonprofit leaders in a more direct way about their relationship with funding agencies. It was clear from their responses that the aggressiveness of their advocacy was significantly tempered by their need to win and retain contracts. Asked if government grants made her less aggressive in lobbying agencies, the director of a health care nonprofit told us bluntly, "I want to be a good grantee. I want to be a good grantee because I want to continue to be funded." Survival dictates that the nonprofits' internal procedures, staffing, and resource allocation reflect the demands and expectations placed on them by funding agencies.[24] Yet what we also heard from interviewees was while their behavior was tempered by government funding, they were willing to speak up when they thought it was necessary. The head of a community development corporation told us, "You have to decide where to draw the line where you're willing to risk your money. We're going to keep quiet about some things because it just isn't worth it. But on other things we're willing to take the risk . . . to take a stand."

This is brave talk, and we have no way of evaluating just how often nonprofits consciously risk grant support by openly criticizing administrators. As discussed earlier, some nonprofit interviewees cited instances of retribution in the form of audits by state agencies. The risk is real and cannot be far from the minds of nonprofit leaders as they decide how aggressive to be in their advocacy.

Our summary analysis from the interviews is that nonprofits with government contracts did their best to avoid confrontations with funding agencies. At the same time they were not willing to sell their souls to the devil. As with the CDC director, there were limits to what nonprofit leaders were willing to do to be "a good grantee." We also came away from our interviews believing that the relationships between nonprofits and their funding agencies were genuinely cooperative and that only infrequently did nonprofits feel they had to choose between their conscience and their funding. If the downside of these relationships was a tempering of the nonprofits' advocacy, the upside was the tremendous opportunity they had to talk to agency administrators.

Planning Is Advocacy

In describing partnerships between government and nonprofits, politicians and social scientists tend to adopt language and concepts from the business world. Nonprofits are conceived of as vendors, hired by government to deliver a specified service at a specified price. Should the vendor perform poorly, it can be replaced by another. In business if FedEx doesn't do the job, then off with its head and call in UPS.

Nonprofits are comfortable with the business analogy. It compliments them as it evokes efficiency and competence on the part of the vendors. When Hill House in Pittsburgh took on the job of helping individuals moving off welfare and into the job world, its success spoke well of both the nonprofit and the Allegheny County's welfare bureaucracy. Sophisticated evaluation research demonstrates Hill House and other vendors in the program have been effective in helping participants make the transition to the work world.[25]

The vendor analogy, unfortunately, is not terribly apt. Yes, nonprofits delivering social services are judged as vendors and can be terminated if they do not do a satisfactory job. Yet the relationship between nonprofits and government is not like the relationship between a business and another company it contracted with to deliver a service. Consider this account from the director of a social service agency talking about "implementation":

> The way we operate is through task groups. They're made up of a couple of center directors and some mid-level agency managers in state government. The purpose is to work together with government as new program initiatives are being rolled out. We want to make sure that the contracts we enter into are the best they can be. We want to make sure that we deliver services to families in the best possible way. On a lot of policy issues we operate in this fashion with the task

groups. I'll give you an example. The TANF grant [that our state received] from the feds had some additional money for teens and young parents who have dropped out of school. Now we've had a lot of experience with that population. So we proposed that a community-based planning process be initiated so communities could think about how to use that money. In this way, we would avoid a one-size-fits-all approach. The state bought it so we did this planning for each of 12 regions. And it worked well. The implementation worked well.

This nonprofit hardly seems like a vendor. It helped to design the program it then proceeded to carry out. Whereas FedEx may deliver packages for an insurance company, it doesn't help it design life insurance policies. But nonprofits work collaboratively with government to imagine, plan, problem solve, design, and then implement programs. Maybe one of the reasons why the welfare-to-work program in Pittsburgh is successful is because nonprofits were involved in planning and designing it.[26] This type of relationship is better conceived of as "coproduction" or "joint production" of public policy. Social scientists have recognized that government does sometimes collaborate in the design of policy, though the prototypical relationship is often seen as one between a government agency and a technical advisory board from industry. The broader literature on public-private partnerships emphasizes the wide range of procedures used by government to devolve responsibility onto private sector and nonprofit organizations.[27] Still, the general image in the literature is that nonprofits take on responsibility at the end stage of the public policymaking process. In reality nonprofit social service providers are commonly involved many stages upstream, working with agency administrators, if not at the beginning of a new or newly revised program, long before the RFP (Request for Proposals) is published.

When one thinks of "collaboration" or "co-production" or "public-private partnership," it is easy to believe that "lobbying" falls outside of the process. The two processes do not seem to go together. Lobbying is generally viewed as one party's aggressive persuasion of another. Collaboration involves negotiation, to be sure, but the notion of a partnership negates the view of one party aggressively targeting the other. But for an interest group, partnering is a form of lobbying. Indeed, it is the kind of lobbying that every lobbyist in Washington dreams of (but few experience). To work collaboratively is a chance to shape policies and programs and that is what lobbyists want to do: influence programs and policies.

The relationship of nonprofits to agencies might seem to be a conflict of interest for businesses in an analogous position. For example, we do not expect that consulting firms competing for a government agency contract are going to be involved in developing the standards and processes underlying the projects to be put out for bid. If the consulting company worked on a task force, like the social service agency above, and helped to develop a program that favored itself, that would be regarded as an inappropriate (if not illegal) form of self-dealing. Yet this complaint rarely surfaces against nonprofits. It is not just that nonprofits wear a white hat and embody the totem of civil society. They are not accused of conflicts of interest because agencies sanctify their roles in the administrative process.

Intertwined and Interdependent

Public-private partnerships are lauded because they are seen as highly efficient, because they tap the imagination of the private sector and, conversely, because they are a means of escaping government's arthritic bureaucratic procedures. Each side brings different strengths and different resources.[28] In the case of nonprofit social service and health care providers, partnerships with government go far beyond efficiency or even sharing resources, though those are important. Over time agencies and providers can become dependent on each other. Service providers need funding and new projects to keep the organization alive and robust. Less obviously, agencies need nonprofits for political support.[29] They not only need nonprofits to remind state legislators of the wonderful programs that serve constituents back in the district, but agencies also need successful demonstrations of the programs they have been entrusted with.

An interviewee, "Sally O'Brien," told us a story that amply illustrates this dynamic. The Department of Public Health in her state needed a means of providing dental coverage because the dentists in private practice there generally refused to take Medicaid patients owing to the low reimbursement rate. The agency held hearings around the state on its proposal to create some dental clinics and "Mary Jones," an assistant commissioner of public health, saw O'Brien at one of these. Jones told her that "you really have to start a dental clinic in 'Lakeville.' It's a high need area." O'Brien expressed skepticism as she knew considerable financial risk was involved. There was no assurance that the state's grant would cover the full cost of dental services, and she knew that the social services center in Lakeville could be jeopardized by a program for the poor that was not fully supported.

Eight months later, Jones's agency put out an RFP that had been fashioned in collaboration with relevant nonprofits like O'Brien's. Despite the risks she saw, O'Brien began to fashion a proposal, one that she knew would get funded because of Jones's backing. When O'Brien went to her board for approval, they "were worried we'd lose our shirt. . . .When I told [Jones] that I was getting grief from my Board, she offered to come to a Board meeting. When she came to the Board they asked tough questions. She said, 'We're committed to the program.'" The board, with some reluctance, eventually agreed and the dental clinic was up and running nine months later. O'Brien added, "When [Jones] came to our open house she took me aside and said, 'This is a great example of the State Department of Public Health partnering with Lakeville.'"

When asked why the state agency was so aggressive in seeking out a grant application from her center, O'Brien's opinion was that the agency could not afford to fail. It was under pressure to solve the Medicaid mess, and it needed to demonstrate that it could deal with an increasingly embarrassing problem. The State Department of Public Health had a long history with the Lakeville Center, and the center operated a number of programs funded through its auspices. Jones had to rely on the service providers she knew could move the new program forward quickly and successfully.

Over the years as welfare moved more toward providing services, while at the same time pressures to trim the size of government grew, state and local agencies began to adapt their form to fit these changes.[30] Most broadly, it is sometimes hard to disentangle where social service agencies stop and nonprofit partners begin. As one nonprofit head said of government, "In many ways we're joined at the hip." As new services are developed while the agency maintains its same size (or even shrinks), nonprofits are drawn closer into the web of bureaucracy. Procedures are developed by agencies that help them manage their relationships with nonprofits. Like any agency of government, social service bureaucracies want to minimize conflict with their constituent groups. A nonprofit director in a southern state described how steady conflict over funding was ameliorated by a change in procedures:

> It used to be that the funding [for social services] came from recommendations from committees in the county and the two cities. But it was fraught with infighting among the politicians and among the nonprofits. The committees that were set up would finally come to a consensus and then their recommendations would be changed by the politicians. Drove everyone nuts. [The nonprofits worked] to change

this. [We] went to the County Commission and said, "Let us in the door; let us help work this out." I helped draft a compact that said that the decisions would be made by these committees and the recommendations would be followed. The county and the cities would defer to the committees' recommendations. I mean they didn't have to do that by law, but they would follow them. This way the nonprofits would have a voice. I would say that this stopped 95-98 percent of the fighting.

The penetration of nonprofits into the budgetary and policymaking process takes many forms. A hospice director said he wrote the regulations for a state agency needing rules for the use of drugs to chemically restrain agitated patients. The staff of a statewide trade group in the health field described a series of forty meetings with Medicaid administrators over a draft set of politically sensitive regulations. The director of a residential facility for troubled adolescents listed committee after committee he sat on, including one that made the decisions allocating grant money for juvenile justice programs and another that made policy decisions for the state on its mental health facilities. "[Technically] we make recommendations to the director directly—there's no one between him and us. He has so far enacted all of our recommendations."

These examples, and many others that could be offered, may exaggerate the prowess of the nonprofits since agency administrators were not interviewed for their version of events. Nevertheless, over and over again we heard of accommodations, of working arrangements between nonprofits and the agencies that administer the relevant programs. Fundamental decisions about funding and the broad outlines of social policy lie far beyond the reach of nonprofit executives. But at that next level of decisionmaking, about the specifics of public policy and the allocation of funds within the sector, the directors of nonprofits are real players. And that participation is, in a very real sense, advocacy.

Citizen Participation

One of the most conspicuous characteristics of social policy on the state and local level is the citizen participation requirements built into program operations. These federal and state mandates have contributed to the collaborative relationships that have emerged over time between nonprofits and agencies. Although widely discredited in the wake of the conflict that engulfed many Community Action Programs as they tried to implement the "maximum feasible participation" provision of the Economic Opportunity Act of 1964, citizen participation programs have flourished.[31]

Just how important citizen participation has been in promoting a collaborative ethic in local politics is difficult to judge. Some of those interviewed for this study were quite dismissive of these programs. As one HHS administrator told us, "If a state commissioner of mental health wants control, then the planning council may not do more than meet just once a year." We heard the same point of view from the other end of the process. The head of a Community Development Corporation said, "The citizen participation mandates as in CDBG (Community Development Block Grant) . . . essentially do nothing." Yet both these interviewees, one a federal government policymaker and the other the leader of a community nonprofit, then gave us extensive detail about the close collaboration between nonprofits and government.

Despite the many failures and disappointments that activists and policymakers can cite from personal experience, citizen participation requirements push nonprofits and government closer together. The legacy of close to forty years of expanded citizen participation is a dense thicket of laws and regulations that requires specific types of boards and procedures to ensure public involvement. Citizen participation provisions can be highly detailed. For example, the Massachusetts law requiring the Department of Mental Health to "provide for and cooperate with citizen advisory boards" gives boards responsibility for educating the public about the needs of those with mental illness, regularly receiving and reviewing reports on the department's programs, and making recommendations to the commissioner of mental health.[32] This broad set of tasks necessarily involves the nonprofits represented on the board.

The laws and regulations are full of vague mandates as well. But over time requirements tend to accumulate as agencies respond to demands before them and new processes emerge. Nonprofits understand the requirements and use them to their advantage. The director of a housing organization noted in an interview that the city agency that they usually dealt with had a strong incentive to work with them: "Should they contract with us, they can satisfy federal HUD requirements to fulfill a planning process requirement."

The basis in law also gives agency opponents an opportunity to sue if procedures are not followed. Despite the cost of litigation, citizen advocacy groups remain a threat to agencies that anger them. In this day and age, it's also more difficult for agencies to put on the "dog and pony" shows that sometimes passed for citizen participation in the 1960s. The people who sit on agency boards are community leaders and cannot be easily dismissed with just an opportunity to occasionally hear agency leaders describe new policies. Again, using Massachusetts as an example, the citizen participation requirements for policymaking relating to managed care organizations specify that membership on the advisory board include representatives of the Massachusetts Hospital Association, the Massachusetts Nurses Association, the Massachusetts Medical Society, Associated Industries of Massachusetts (a leading business association), and a number of nonprofit consumer groups. These are not organizations that are easily ignored. Although they would exert some influence outside of citizen participation programs, the advisory board adds leverage for all who are included. This is especially true of the nonprofit consumer groups who have more difficulty organizing and maintaining themselves. Their role on the board gives them stature and provides incentives for policymakers to cultivate them.

Citizen participation mandates have enhanced both the status of nonprofits encompassing high levels of technical expertise and those groups representing minorities. City bureaucracies are often tiny and have little in the way of resources. These agencies with advisory boards have every reason to reach out to those nonprofits that have the most experience in implementing that bureaucracy's programs or have the most respect in the community. One means of political incorporation is to put such neighborhood groups on an advisory council. When the law requires representatives of the community to be included in policymaking, the "community" is usually understood to mean minority constituencies if there are significant minorities in the catchment area. The federal program funding community health centers requires that the governing board have a majority of members from the community.[33]

Although the primary impact of citizen participation mandates has been to give state and local agencies incentives to work with community groups, it is also the case that public involvement regulations encourage nonprofits to work with one another. Some government grants are awarded to nonprofits for the purpose of pulling together their community to work together on a particular problem like AIDS or teen pregnancy. The nonprofit holding the grant will have already lined up its collaborators as part of the application process. The head of a family services center told us that

When the legislature created the funding stream for these family centers they mandated that there be ongoing public involvement . . . [so] community development is one of our jobs too. It's our job to work with other parts of our community: citizen groups, state agencies, the private sector. To dig into our community. To work collaboratively with other parts of the community. To figure out together how we can best make services available.

Increasingly, citizen participation is not about the participation of individual citizens or activists. The easiest and most productive way for city hall to work with the neighborhoods is to collaborate with the nonprofits that operate there. It is these nonprofits that have been the main beneficiaries of laws and regulations requiring government to incorporate members of the community into public policymaking. In today's cities, citizen participation is really nonprofit participation.

Benefits to City Hall

The value of nonprofits to agency administrators is clear: agencies need nonprofits to carry out programs and to provide political support to those agencies. Just as nonprofits are vulnerable to an environment they cannot control, the same is true for city and state agencies. Recessions, changes in administrations, emergencies, and swings in public opinion can all lead to cutbacks in any one agency's programs. More than anything else, though, budgeting is a competitive process, and agencies need to be aggressive just to stay even. Establishing partnerships with nonprofits that allow these organizations to participate in planning is an acceptable price to pay for the political support they can provide.

What may be less apparent is the value of nonprofits to elected officials. The literature on nonprofits generally ignores the role of nonprofits in electoral politics. Since 501c3s cannot be directly involved in partisan campaigns, it may not seem a very fruitful avenue of social science research. The political value of nonprofits to mayors and city councilors comes from what they can do for them between elections. To be re-elected, urban leaders must develop a record of accomplishment, encourage investment, maintain tranquility, and nurture optimism about the future of the city. They need the business and the nonprofit sectors to help them achieve those goals.[34]

City politics and the relationship of nonprofits to top elected and appointed leaders of local governments is a broad and complex subject.

Here we look at just two areas: the role of nonprofits in the politics of economic development and the role of nonprofits in representing ethnic immigrants who reside in our cities.

Growth Politics

Urban politics is about many things but, preeminently, it is about expanding the economic base of the city.[35] Increasing revenue and expanding the supply of jobs for city residents depend on investment from the business sector. At the top of any mayor's agenda is a list of projects that he or she wants to push through, and typically they will include proposals initiated by business interests, civic leaders, and city officials. Such projects might include plans for new office buildings, housing complexes, combined commercial and housing developments, industrial parks, shopping arcades, convention centers, sports stadiums, highways, or airport, seaport, hospital, and university expansions. Diverse as these projects are they all involve the "politics of growth." Proposals to literally build up the city involve difficult political negotiations because no proposal comes without costs to some sector of the city. Some residents will see such projects as damaging to their existing neighborhood or business, but others will see the proposals as an opportunity to redirect private sector or city resources to better help disadvantaged communities. Such demands may take the form of residential requirements for construction jobs, linkage payments, and additional, civic-oriented facilities for commercial development projects. Everything is negotiable. And everything is potentially contentious.

Social scientists have studied the politics of growth since the 1950s, when a combination of suburban flight, inner-city deterioration, and newly available federal aid led to broad-scale urban renewal efforts. Mayors working with city business leaders began to develop attractive commercial projects that would replace dilapidated housing or abandoned factories. Awakened by the civil rights movement and catalyzed by proposals to rebuild city neighborhoods, community groups became increasingly active in opposing city hall's plans. During the 1960s and 1970s, repeated conflicts occurred between downtown and neighborhood. Even in a city with a black mayor, like Atlanta's Maynard Jackson, conflict erupted when a proposed new highway was perceived as an assault on the neighborhoods it would traverse.[36]

Reduction in the conflict surrounding growth issues has come about for several reasons. Continuing demographic change, with minorities constituting ever-increasing proportions of the population, has fundamentally altered city politics.[37] With the election of more minorities as mayors and city councilors, neighborhoods have become increasingly incorporated into the process of government.[38] Conflict is inefficient (as well as unpleasant) and mechanisms for involving the neighborhoods, collaborating with them, and empowering them, became an appealing alternative to conflict that slowed projects down and delayed the political and commercial payoff to politicians and developers.[39] In her comparative study of growth politics in Chicago and Pittsburgh, Barbara Ferman found that an ethos of collaboration developed in Pittsburgh, which in turn brought about peaceful negotiations between city hall, developers, and neighborhood groups. In contrast ward politicians in Chicago rejected collaboration with community-based organizations and conflict continued to plague growth politics there.[40] Whether the policy-makers' goal is cold-blooded co-optation or public-spirited sensitivity to neighborhood preferences, more and more cities have developed means of institutionalizing cooperation in development politics.

As instruments for collaboration evolved, nonprofits emerged as the big winners. Developers and city hall do not negotiate with the "community," or the "people." They negotiate with nonprofits. It's easy for city hall to identify the organizations whose expertise, professionalism, and physical location give them legitimacy to speak on behalf of their neighborhood even though no one formally elected them to do so. In Pittsburgh, Ferman traces the institutionalization of neighborhood influence to the creation of the Pittsburgh Partnership for Neighborhood Development (PPND), the Allegheny Council for the Improvement of Our Neighborhoods (ACTION-Housing, Inc.), and a network of neighborhood-based Community Development Corporations.[41] There are 2,000 CDCs across the United States, and they constitute a major instrument of community representation in city politics.[42]

The relationships of nonprofits to city hall varies widely, but among the closest are the ties of city leaders to what might be called "super nonprof-its"—organizations sanctioned by city hall to develop a coalition of leaders from government, the private sector, and nonprofits, including foundations, service providers, and advocacy groups. The underlying strategy is simple: put all the stakeholders at the table and work toward a consensus. The sta-tus of such super nonprofits derives from the members appointed and the commitment of the city to stand by its recommendations. The following conversation with one such nonprofit, charged with regional planning for a large metropolitan area in the Midwest, is illustrative. Its task was to develop a plan for a watershed, a delicate political task since the affected area crossed so many political boundaries:

Now two years ago, the Nature Conservancy came to us and said, "We've got to get involved to save this." So we set up a task force, which I chair. The watershed affects six counties. The members [of the task force] include environmental groups, nonprofits, town councils, and mayors. We have meetings every two months or so. Out of those meetings came a consensus for a study of the state of the art on storm water, a best practices study. We now have that partly together and we've been talking to the Army Corps of Engineers about budget and scope, trying to work things out [about the next stage of the project].

You're more involved on public policy questions in comparison to the other nonprofits that filled out our survey. How come?

Because we're an association of governments. We're an activist organization. We're part of the solution but we're more than a public agency.

Are you a government agency or are you a nonprofit?

We're both.

The organization is not technically "both"—it's a 501c3 nonprofit. Yet its relationship with city halls is so close and its mission on behalf of government is so clear, it's certainly reasonable for this executive director to see his organization as having a foot in both sectors. These super nonprofits, if they are structured properly and effectively led, can be of enormous help to city hall as it tries to navigate the landmine of conflicting political interests. In contrast, a unilateral decision by the downtown business association to push for a favored project is not going to be seen as legitimate by neighborhood groups. A decision by a super nonprofit with neighborhood representatives on it stands a much better chance of being seen as representing the city's best interests.

The more typical, rank-and-file nonprofits in the neighborhoods can also provide considerable help to mayors and city councilors. In this day and age, few cities have political machines. Few cities have decentralized administrative structures (such as St. Paul's District Council system or District Coalition Boards in Portland, Oregon). What cities do have are nonprofits everywhere, and nonprofits are the vehicles through which city hall brings money into the neighborhoods. Nonprofits cannot participate in the campaigns for mayor or the city council, but they have other ways of telegraphing their political support. The mayor gets to come to the ribbon cuttings, have the local newspapers take her picture in front of a social service provider, and be the featured speaker at neighborhood functions sponsored by nonprofits. Nonprofit leaders value their relationships with city hall, and they are not shy about spreading the word about who their friends are downtown.

If a common theme runs through contemporary city politics, it is that city hall does everything it can to make residents believe their neighborhoods are *partners* with the mayor's office. The neighborhoods are still where the votes are and, thus, neighborhoods are to be cultivated as much as possible. Moreover, neighborhoods, partly through the growth of nonprofits, are much more politically savvy than they were when the Community Action Program and Model Cities were first launched and conflict easily triumphed over good intentions. Nonprofits are the bargaining agents for neighborhoods, and city hall is usually happy to bargain because the political rewards are high.

Diversity Nation

The civil rights revolution and the empowerment of African American and Hispanic advocacy organizations in city politics are well documented and well understood. Less understood is the role nonprofits play today in linking city government and city services to the other minorities in America.[43] Cities, especially large cities, are home to a rainbow of different ethnic groups. Recent immigration patterns have brought nationalities to our cities that were not present in significant numbers just twenty years ago. Some of these ethnicities might fall into "black" or "Hispanic" on a census form, but they have relatively little in common with the broader group of Americans falling into those categories. Cities like Los Angeles or New York seem to incorporate just about every ethnic group that has made its way to the United States. Other cities have dealt with a recent influx of just a single ethnic group. Small cities in California's Central Valley now need to offer specialized services to Hmongs. In a short period, Minneapolis found itself home to 15,000 Somalis.

Nonprofits have long served the needs of immigrant communities, so what they do today is not remarkably different from what they did 100 years ago. What is different though is that the revolution in welfare has led to a much broader array of services. Some of these services are available to clients whether they are citizens or not. Although some newly arrived ethnics will form advocacy organizations, there are great barriers to organizing a group to take action. Besides the lack of discretionary income to support an advocacy group, many of the new ethnic groups come from countries where there was no democracy and government was feared. Some (unknown) percentage of immigrants is here illegally, and illegal immigrants are probably the surest bet not to join a political organization. The language barrier is also an immense obstacle to organizing.

Nonprofits are a highly efficient means for city hall and state agencies to establish political relationships with the new ethnic populations. That is, beyond their capacity to deliver services and their effectiveness in reaching hard-to-reach residents, health and social service nonprofits become the political link between the city and these special populations. The city governments have real challenges in working with the new ethnic groups, not the least of which is the array of languages spoken in all of their neighborhoods. New ethnic groups tend to be geographically concentrated, and the health and social service nonprofits in their neighborhoods offer doctors, nurses, outreach workers, social workers, and receptionists who speak the language of the community. Besides Spanish-speaking employees, city hall might have only a few people, working as liaison with that ethnic group, who speak one of the other languages of the polyglot metropolis.

The real political advantage is that the leadership of neighborhood-based service centers ties the new ethnic neighborhoods to city hall. This is not old-fashioned patronage politics where votes are traded for resources, but there is an exchange of sorts. Nonprofit leaders cultivate the relationships they build with city and state agencies, which facilitate the awarding of grants and their individual participation in policy planning. This is no different from the general relationship between nonprofit providers and government just described. Still, it is important to stress that in neighborhoods with concentrations of recent ethnics, there are fewer competing channels of communication to city hall. The neighborhood-based health and service centers are the hub of a wide variety of government programs. In a focus group with leaders of nonprofits serving various Asian populations in Boston, one executive director listed several shortcomings at Boston City Hall but then mentioned almost in passing that her multiservice center currently held twenty-five different government grants and contracts.

Even though neighborhood-based nonprofits may not be government agencies, clients may still see them as linked to city government.[44] That can only work to the advantage of elected officials, but this relationship also facilitates advocacy on behalf of constituencies that otherwise receive little representation. An agency director of a mental health facility told us of the sharp growth in the Hispanic population in her southern city, a city that had almost no Hispanics just a decade ago. City hall, though not unsympathetic to minorities, was slow to respond to the needs of these recent arrivals. The nonprofit not only got more grants, but soon it initiated a Latino mental health coalition. Said its executive director, "The largest [government] social service agency here has no translators, no bilingual services. So we're documenting the need. We talk to the heads of departments, the country commissioners."

The entrée that these nonprofits have with their funders at city and state agencies also gives them the opportunity to educate officials about the unique culture of their constituents and of the misunderstandings and stereotypes that harm them. In the same focus group for Asian American nonprofits just mentioned, one executive director said, "When I first started telling those in Boston and at the state 'we have needs,' they [were still in the mind-set of] 'the Chinese take care of their own.'" She paused and then added, "We don't have needs?" Educating policymakers is something that all interest groups do, whether they are talking about steel imports, agricultural price supports, or the frail elderly of Boston's Chinatown. But unlike steel manufacturers or farmers, residents of Boston's Chinatown have not been terribly successful in organizing on their own. Those who have money and English language skills quickly move to the suburbs. Chinatown's new immigrants and elderly need their health care and social service providers to advocate for them.

Conclusion

The perversity of government's contradictory impulses toward 501c3 nonprofits is vividly demonstrated by the relationship of nonprofits to administrative agencies. The data demonstrate that conventional nonprofits lobby legislatures less frequently than administrative agencies not because they are inherently uninterested in influencing government, but because they are responding to the regulations that push them away from the legislative arena. The heavy involvement of conventional nonprofits in the administrative process makes it clear that these organizations are focused on public policy issues that affect them.

Government's regulation of nonprofits reflects, in large part, the differing needs of Congress and city hall. Years ago when the prohibition against legislative involvement by public charities was established, Congress was hardly giving up needed help. Today, with thousands of lobbies active in Washington, there is still no sense by Congress that, if it is to make more intelligent public policy decisions, it needs more involvement by nonprofits. Indeed, as discussed earlier, many conservative Republicans want to make 501c3 even more restrictive.

City hall views nonprofit organizations differently. Local government could not function without nonprofits to carry out the health and social service programs that the federal and state government fund through grants to the municipalities. But nonprofits are not mere vendors, offering cost-efficient services under an agency contract. Rather, they are partners with agencies who commonly work collaboratively in the planning process. There are so many opportunities to get involved that the executive director of a human services or health care nonprofit who is not a member of government task forces, advisory committees, and informal working groups, probably isn't doing a very good job.[45] Nonprofits can also provide critical political support to agencies, mayors, and city councilors. In short, nonprofits are incorporated into local government because they enhance the performance of government and the status of office holders.

CHAPTER SIX

Politically Effective Nonprofits

After the passage of the law "ending welfare as we know it" in 1996, welfare bureaucracies around the country began new programs under Temporary Assistance for Needy Families (TANF) to prepare welfare recipients for life with a much shallower safety net.[1] In one large metropolitan area in the Midwest, with many counties and local bureaucracies running their own individual TANF programs, an obvious need arose to compare experiences and share lessons of success and failure. Convening the initial meeting and then running an ongoing advisory committee wasn't a government agency but a nonprofit, "Metro Planning." It may seem odd that government could not manage to organize this effort on its own, but in many ways Metro Planning was the obvious choice to pull things together. The organization's focus was regional, and it had worked with virtually all of the agencies and nonprofits involved. It had years of experience in the field of welfare and a highly respected research capacity, and it had administered numerous grants in welfare, including a large recent grant to train nonprofit service providers to understand what TANF required. Indeed, local governments called on Metro Planning all the time.

By any standard Metro Planning is a highly politically effective nonprofit. It has the ear of government, and government is eager to collaborate with it. Yet there are many nonprofits that would like to play the same role but have much more limited interaction with local or state agencies. In short, not all the nonprofits that would like to partner with government get an invitation to the party. The variation we have observed in the political activity of nonprofits surely reflects, in part, the degree to which they are welcomed into the policymaking process. Is there a type of nonprofit that government favors by offering enhanced access to policymakers?

For scholars this is a variation of the Holy Grail question: what makes interest groups effective? Are there strategies an interest group can use for lobbying that will give it more influence in the policymaking process? Are organizational resources more important than particular advocacy tactics aimed at convincing legislators or administrators to do the right thing?

From the perspective of nonprofits, the fundamental question is how to allocate scarce resources. How can they gain the confidence of the agencies that administer the programs that concern them? Since not all the nonprofits working in a policy area have a seat at the table where programs are designed and advantages are gained for winning grants, what is the best way for a nonprofit to get that precious invitation?

Resources and Capacity

For a government policymaker who is trying to decide how much, if any, time to spend with representatives of an organization wishing to influence policy, the bottom line question is "what can you do for me?" It is exactly this question that makes interest group politics so controversial. For journalists and other analysts, the obvious answer is campaign contributions. In studying legislatures at least, the starting point in trying to understand the relationship between lobbyists and policymakers is to ask if contributions from political action committees or members of a lobby constitute the value that is exchanged for access.

For 501c3 nonprofits this may seem irrelevant since, by law, they cannot make campaign contributions. Moreover, as already noted, in city politics access to government comes much easier than at the federal level, and city agencies need the cooperation of nonprofits. Yet the question of value exchanged to policymakers for access is still central to understanding nonprofits. If cities abound with nonprofits and there is not enough room at any one agency's conference table for all of them, how do officials determine which of them have the most potential for helping that agency deliver its services, enhance its status, or protect its budget?

Several different organizational attributes of nonprofits may be of value to policymakers, and our data allow an analysis of many of them. These variables are weighed against one another to determine which ones have the greatest impact on the interaction between nonprofits and those in government. Our survey and the organizations' 990 tax returns, which we examined as part of the study, contain information on the raw resources of the nonprofits and on various organizational capacities that require the conversion (or investment) of those resources.

Wealth and Power

The beginning point in understanding an organization's political abilities is to ask simply, if a bit crudely, "How much do they have?" What are the resources at an organization's disposal, and how much does it have of each one? Although some nonprofits surely make better strategic use of their available resources, it may be that strategy only affects their political performance at the margins. One does not have to be a cynic to believe that the organizations that have the most in resources have the most access to policymakers. It makes perfect sense to expect that the United Way, with its substantial resources, is going to be of more interest to government than a small neighborhood nonprofit operating on a shoestring.

Some of the thinking on interest group effectiveness points toward the size of a group's membership. Years ago, V. O. Key wrote, "Numbers alone may carry weight; the more completely an organization encompasses its potential membership, the greater is its moral authority when it claims to speak for an interest in society."[2] This conclusion seems intuitive: more is better when it comes to interest group membership. The scale may be more modest for state and local groups since their potential membership is much smaller than a national organization, but the dynamic at work should be the same. Indeed, it is plausible that in the less dense interest group communities of local politics, it may take a smaller proportion of the potential membership to cross the threshold where the organization's size becomes an asset.

In a similar vein, the wealth of an organization is commonly thought to be a key to lobbying success. It is often assumed that the wealthiest lobbies have the most access, the most status inside Washington, and the most political punch. It's important not to caricature this argument. Although some journalists see a simple relation between money and policy outcomes, most political scientists see the relationship as more complicated and regard the evidence, at least on contributions from political action committees, as inconclusive.[3] Interest group scholars are more comfortable in arguing that access to policymakers is critical to influence and that financial resources is one of the factors that leads to access.[4]

Nonprofits may seem to be an unlikely set of organizations for testing the effects of wealth, but the typical nonprofit is a medium-sized organization, not a tiny hole-in-the-wall operation. The nonprofits in our survey have an average annual revenue of $1.2 million. The largest 10 percent average almost twice that figure. Nonprofits come in all shapes and sizes, and this variation allows for a testing of the relationship between wealth and influence. Conceivably, wealth is a proxy for status, with larger organizations presumably attaining more respect in their communities.

Nonprofits also offer an interesting test of this thesis because, unlike administrative agencies in Washington, local governments must depend on nonprofits to operate their programs. In this view wealth may not be so much a proxy for status as it is for stability. The larger the nonprofit, the less likely it is to fail. Since wealth, as measured by a nonprofit's budget, may already reflect government investment in the organization, as manifested in grants and contracts, this variable could reflect the ongoing confidence of agencies in their partners.

Converting Resources

Another view is that the relationship with government is not so much a function of a nonprofit's resources as it is what it does with those resources. It is helpful to conceive of a nonprofit's *organizational capacity*. Rather than thinking of a nonprofit as a political group using its resources to push arguments forward, envisage an organization making hard decisions on how to allocate scarce resources. Those decisions determine the capacity of an organization to achieve its goals.

This concept is also useful for thinking about the way administrators view nonprofits as potential partners. As they consider which nonprofits to consult, which nonprofits to ask for political help, and which nonprofits to give grants and contracts to, they consider the relative capacities of the organizations that would like to fill those roles. For the nonprofits that concern us most—social service agencies and health care providers—administrators must first and foremost judge each organization's capacity to deliver services. Is the mental health clinic effective in treating its patients, sensitive and humane in dealing with its vulnerable population, efficient in dealing with its caseload, stable in administration, and innovative in programming?

The literature on interest groups is of little help in trying to understand how nonprofits make internal investment decisions. Scholars tend to treat interest group *organizations* as rather unidimensional black boxes, and little attention is paid to decisions about structure, process, and budgeting. And comparatively little research tries to understand the evolution of lobbying capacity within the context of organizational development. For lots of different types of organizations, the development of a lobbying staff and the commitment of funds for advocacy come about as they grow, face a crisis, or need to revitalize themselves. As Elisabeth Clemens points out, interest groups are "arenas in which preferences and values are discovered."[5]

For nonprofit service providers, taking precious resources away from the provision of that service to its needy clients is a critical juncture in its organizational development. This decision is about more than just how to spend the organization's money. It is also about staff time and identity. Take "East Hill Family Center," which provides mental retardation services to its urban constituency. "In 20 years we've gone from a group of parents to a $3 million a year organization," said the executive director with pride. Politically speaking, those parents were a relatively unsophisticated lot at the beginning, consumed with the difficulty of finding a satisfactory placement for their children. When they realized that the state would give them some funding, they made a formal request but ended up with a particularly poor reimbursement rate. The director attributes this response to an initial meeting with state administrators who asked what the organization would do if it didn't get a grant. "We said, 'We'll probably do it anyway.'" Acknowledging that this was hardly a strong bargaining position, she added, "What did we know? We're parents."

Over time East Hill's director gradually came to understand that lobbying agencies and the state legislature was an important part of her job. She cited Medicaid waivers, help from the governor, and grants from the legislature as proof of her efforts. But as soon as she listed these victories she acknowledged that the money was relatively modest, especially in comparison to more politically active nonprofits offering the same kinds of services to disabled children. Without any prompting, she raised the question of why the organization continued to get only modest support from the state: "Why not? Well, it's because I'm just the parent of a disabled child. I'm more interested in programs for the children."

Like a business corporation, a nonprofit's capacity reflects its investment strategy.[6] Corporations select areas in which they believe they can have the greatest return on investment and then allocate their resources accordingly. Decisions inside the corporation reflect its culture, formal processes, and informal bargaining. Making a major push into a new area is risky, and proponents must overcome considerable opposition from those with other priorities and from traditionalists who want to stick to the knitting. As nonprofits like East Hill learn over time that it can be costly not to invest in advocacy, they must try to figure out how to add government relations to the work of their already overloaded staff. Resources to hire someone new may not be available, so the increased responsibility will be a net addition to workload of the existing staff. More important, it is the mission of the nonprofit that catalyzes the passion and commitment of the staff, and that mission is rarely politics. Thus advocacy is often seen as a distraction, an extra burden, to those to whom it is assigned. The leaders' dilemma is that there is much more potential for broad-scale change from new government policies than from the work that the nonprofit does.

The result is that nonprofit leaders struggle with this problem as their organization grows or goes through periodic reassessments of priorities.[7] Asked why his organization was not more politically active, the executive director of a relatively large nonprofit working on behalf of immigrants said, "Our goal is to protect and support our clientele." Yet he also recognized that his organization was applying Band-Aids and that it couldn't ignore the underlying political problems. As the nonprofit grew, it became more involved in public policy, eventually hiring its own lobbyist. Still, he remained conflicted because advocacy remained a small part of his organization's work. "Our strategy is to get others to act: religious groups, human rights groups, labor," he said somewhat defensively.

Every dollar for advocacy is a dollar taken away from someone badly in need of services, a vulnerable individual for whom the nonprofit is a lifeline. Thus, for many nonprofits, the initial question is not what political capacities to invest in but whether to convert any resources at all into advocacy.

Is Information Power?

Few nonprofits fully resolve this dilemma, but pragmatism usually dictates a compromise. The availability of funding through grants and contracts is, of course, a strong incentive for the development of a government relations capacity. There is no shortage of other reasons to be involved in public policymaking. As an organization becomes involved in the political process, it may restructure itself to create a new position or office or formally assign new tasks to staffers. It may develop a better communications network with donors or members. It may look for particular skills when hiring new staffers. It may appoint people with better connections to its board of directors. It may do all of the above.

The survey data collected for this study facilitate analysis of four of the most important organizational capacities believed linked to the effectiveness of interest groups. The first two are the most basic forms of lobbying: the direct lobbying of policymakers by group representatives and the mobilization of members to write letters or phone their legislators. The third is a simple structural component: does the organization designate someone as responsible for government relations? Fourth is the role of expertise. These qualities do not exhaust the possibilities—the ability to influence public opinion, for example, is beyond the scope of this research—but they address critical capacities of interest groups.

Asking about the first of these qualities, the capacity to engage in the direct lobbying of policymakers, may seem puzzling. By definition, isn't that what lobbies do, meet with people in government and try to persuade them of the organization's point of view? There is actually considerable variation on this score.

Many Washington corporate offices are small listening posts, and these companies depend instead on their trade associations to do much of the direct lobbying. Many of Microsoft's early losses in Congress have been attributed to a penchant "for keeping its distance from politics."[8] Conservative citizen groups have not placed much emphasis on direct lobbying, and this decision has reduced their capacity for influence. Thus, although almost all interest groups do it at some point, there is substantial variation in the resources, personnel, and organizational structure devoted to direct lobbying.

This type of variation is more obvious for outside lobbying. Policymakers are concerned—if not obsessive—about constituency opinion, and political scientists have long recognized that a lobbyist's work is enhanced by an active membership willing to contact policymakers when asked. We also know that this tactic must be used on a limited basis because of resource limitations, the danger of membership fatigue, and policy contexts that may be unsuitable for such an approach.[9] For community-based nonprofits mobilization might be more elite driven than in national politics. In the local arena notables on the board might use their contacts to press the organization's case forward with city hall. As such, the requirements for resources, equipment, and staffing are far more modest than what is needed at the national level.

Is there anyone in the organization who is designated as responsible for government relations? For nonprofits at the local level, this commitment represents an important threshold. Once someone is given that job, he or she can lay greater claim on organizational resources. The typical nonprofit is not initially designed with any significant advocacy effort in mind, and government relations are subsequently built into nonprofit organizations in a variety of ways, often slighting this area in favor of seemingly more pressing needs.

Finally, how much does the research capacity of the organization contribute to its effectiveness? Although all interest group organizations are knowledgeable about the issues they work on, the hypothesis that the research capacity of nonprofits is integral to their effectiveness is especially intriguing. The three capacities just listed all suggest some degree of "political muscle." Nonprofits may be more comfortable developing their information capacity rather than more overtly political attributes. An organization's information capacity offers a means of distinguishing itself from the field, and a long-term focus may lead to recognition of a nonprofit as the leading authority on an issue.[10] Information is not a commodity, like personal computers or two by fours, easily acquired from a variety of vendors who compete on price. Each product is unique, and the emphasis that individual organizations place on research is also highly variable. Organizations not only have to make decisions about what kind of people to hire and how much money to put into research, but they must also decide how to package the product, disseminate it, and move it internally with the least friction.

Earlier research on national citizen groups demonstrated that the information capacity of the liberal groups was a key to their status, access, and influence.[11] These groups invested substantial resources in hiring Ph.D.'s and other policy experts and allowing them to work on the same issues over the years, enabling them to become players in the cycles of policymaking that may extend over decades. No one would mistake these advocates for the high-priced lobbyists on "K" Street, but they have something else to sell instead of access, and they have found a large market of journalists and policymakers who are ready buyers.

Some of the information that groups provide may be political intelligence, but far more often it is technical in nature and concerns programs and policies. Since the average number of professional staffers for conventional 501c3s in the sample is twenty-four, nonprofits certainly have the personnel available to build a high level of policy expertise into the organization if it is deemed a priority.

At the same time, there is reason to be skeptical of the idea that information is power. Research on national politics suggests that people in government are afflicted with information overload. Part of the conventional wisdom in Washington is that research studies must be boiled down to a one- or two-page memo attached to the front of the report. No lobby-ist expects a policymaker or staffer to read a whole study. Research studies are also commonly seen as biased. Policymakers know what side the inter-est group is on. Has an interest group ever lobbied legislators or bureaucrats with a study that doesn't support its point of view?

Being Effective

Many of our judgments about the political system are based on our assess-ment of the influence of different interest groups. Most of us tend to be concerned about the power of the organized interests on the other side of the political fence. But while our blood may boil when we think about "powerful" business interests, the "undue influence of labor," or the "con-trol" of the American Association of Retired Persons (AARP) over Congress, moving from colloquial language to real measurement proves maddeningly difficult. There is no generally accepted methodology for measuring an interest group's influence. Asking interviewees about their prowess with policymakers is an invitation to exaggeration. Asking dis-passionate observers about various organizations is to ask about reputation. *Fortune* magazine uses this approach to rank its "Power 25" in Washing-ton—a methodology that makes political scientists want to reach for the poison.[12]

To test the competing hypotheses just outlined, the different resources and capacities must be linked to some common measure. Our focus is on "effectiveness," which is a narrower concept than interest group power or influence. This allows for realistic measurement because effectiveness can be tied to tangible organizational goals and clear mechanisms of interaction between groups and government. By contrast, assessing interest group power requires the analyst to move beyond an examination of advocacy or interaction to broad societal values. In theory such values, nurtured by dominant interests, create political biases that push policymakers toward particular actions (or inaction) on issues before government.[13] In short, the methodological difficulties of measuring power are substantial, if not intractable.

In general terms effectiveness is the degree to which a goal is accom-plished. But what does that mean when we talk about advocacy? The theoretical assumption that guided this research is that *the optimum rela-tionship of an interest group with government is to jointly produce public policy*. This is surely the goal of most nonprofits that want to influence policy: to develop a cooperative relationship with government and work together to resolve public policy issues. Accordingly, policymakers and non-profits have responsibilities that overlap and connect, requiring ongoing interaction. To a limited degree the joint production of public policy can be found in national politics: a set of interest groups is favored by the administration in power or in control of Congress, and these groups are invited to help fashion statutes or regulations. In the heady days of the Contract with America in 1995, Republican congressional leaders gave Hunton and Williams, a law firm allied with electrical utilities, the task of drafting deregulatory measures.[14] But this kind of relationship in Washington is highly episodic and dependent on an interest group's allies in government being firmly in charge and facing weak political opposition. In state and local politics, however, the needs of agencies create a different opportunity structure for organized interests.

The joint production of public policy is more than the sharing of resources. As noted earlier, the incorporation of nonprofits into administrative policymaking often takes place at the planning stage. At its most elemental level, letting the nonprofits participate in agency planning is a means of reality checking. Nonprofits are "our eyes and ears on the street," said one community development bureaucrat. People implementing the agency's programs have a well-grounded perspective on what works and what doesn't. Short-circuiting problems before they happen is to every agency's advantage. In general joint production also enhances the "feedback loop"—the flow of information back to the agency about program performance. As emphasized already, partnering with nonprofits helps agencies build political support. Nonprofits that have a stake in a relationship with an agency become that agency's promoter. The director of a statewide association noted that he agreed with the state's commissioner of mental health "on 90 percent of the issues . . . [but] the Division of Mental Health is not powerful enough to make change on its own." His organization worked with the division to promote policies before the legislature and other parts of the executive branch.

It is important not to exaggerate the nature of this relationship. Joint production does not mean "equal partners." Even in the best of relationships, nonprofits are in the subservient position. Partnering has a cost to agencies. All bureaucracies are sensitive about their autonomy and guard against encroachments from any source. Still, both sides have enormous incentives to partner, and it is a fact of life in an agency's policy formulation and in the delivery of social services.

To enable us to measure effectiveness and the underlying notion of joint production of public policy, the survey asked, "How often on average would you say that people in government approach the executive director, staff, or members of the board to discuss matters of mutual interest?" The value of asking about government-initiated contact is that it taps the degree of an ongoing relationship. Analysts can be much more confident that something meaningful is going on if the focus is on contact initiated by policymakers. Asking officials of lobbies instead about the frequency of group-initiated contact says nothing about whether anyone is listening at the other end. Recent interest group scholarship is clear on just how difficult it is to get anyone in the national government to pay attention. Moreover, as John P. Heinz and his colleagues emphasize, much of what lobbyists do is not designed to persuade policymakers but merely to find out what is going on.[15]

For interest groups government-initiated contact is by far the least expensive "tactic." If time, money, and other organizational resources don't have to be spent trying to obtain meetings with policymakers or mobilizing constituents to write or e-mail, those scarce resources can be used for the other endeavors, including the substantive programs of the organization. The early literature on lobbying stressed the importance of building relationships between lobbyists and policymakers, but, as already discussed, this dynamic receives less attention in the literature today. The large number of interest groups in Washington makes it more difficult for lobbies to build influence based on personal relationships. In the smaller arenas of city and state politics, such relationships are still common. In the end, the joint production of public policy is dependent on officials' trust and respect toward the leaders of nonprofits. As chapter 5 explains, nonprofits place a high premium on developing relationships and regard it as the heart of their government relations work.

Structure Matters

Multivariate analysis, weighing the impact of each of the resource and capacity variables on the level of government-initiated contact, should reveal any underlying relationships between the allocation of scarce resources within nonprofits and their effectiveness in promoting partnerships with agencies. With the exception of one variable the data used here come from the survey. The membership figure for each nonprofit is the respondent's estimate of the number of individuals who belong to the organization.[16] Two measures of an organization's wealth are used. The first is yearly revenue as listed on the organization's 990 tax return. Since some nonprofits are pass-throughs for government funds that are subsequently distributed to other nonprofits, budget figures for such organizations may exaggerate their available resources. Consequently, the number of full-time, professional staffers listed on the survey is utilized as an alternative measure of an organization's wealth.

Each nonprofit's capacity to engage in direct lobbying and grass-roots mobilization is calculated from the battery of questions on advocacy tactics. The five-point scale is a measure of frequency of use for each tactic and does not tell us directly about the depth or quality of the advocacy. Each survey respondent was also asked if there was anyone in the organization who was responsible for government relations. As a means of estimating the technical expertise of the nonprofits, respondents were asked to rate the capacity of their organization to conduct research.

An alternative hypothesis is that government-initiated contact is a function not so much of resources or capacities but of agency oversight. In this view government agencies need to monitor their grants, and those nonprofits more dependent on government financing should receive a disproportionate amount of attention. The percentage of each nonprofit's yearly income derived from government sources is taken from survey respondents' estimates.

The patterns found in the regression analysis for conventional 501c3s and for the more politically active H electors are in most respects similar (table 6-1).[17] The resource variables are all unrelated to the frequency of government-initiated contact. Neither size (both membership and staff) nor wealth (yearly income) lead nonprofits to a close, ongoing relationship with policymakers. In short, the larger organizations do not attract more interest from policymakers or create more reasons for interaction.

Two of the variables tap the structural design of the nonprofit. A nonprofit cannot make a decision to be wealthy or have lots of members, but it can make a decision to allocate resources to enhance its research capacity or to designate someone to be responsible for government relations. If a nonprofit does not see government relations as a top priority, it might not see any reason to build this functionality into the design of the organization. Not surprisingly, the H electors are much more likely to have formally designated one or more persons as responsible for government relations. Indeed, virtually all of them do so, and the lack of statistical significance shown in table 6-1 for H electors must be discounted because of the lack of

Table 6-1. *The Impact of Resources and Capacities on Government-Initiated Contact*

Independent variables	H electors	Conventional nonprofits
Membership size	–.00000/(.000)	–.00000/(.000)
Full-time professional staff	.00031/(.010)	–.00011/(.001)
Yearly revenue	–.00000/(.000)	–.00000/(.000)
Percent of income from government	.00059/(.006)	.00025/(.006)
Anyone responsible for government relations	.474/(.568)	1.028/(402)*
Capacity to conduct research	.532/(.145)***	.332/(.160)*
Lobbying on proposed bill or policy (frequency)	.258/(.155)	.556/(.232)*
Mobilization of membership (frequency)	.106/(.157)	.255/(.195)
Psuedo R^2	.141	.315

Note: Estimates are ordinal regression coefficients with the standard errors in parentheses. For H electors, $n = 154$; for conventional nonprofits, $n = 134$.
  *Significant at .05 level.
  *** Significant at .000 level.

variation in those cases. The conventional nonprofits do not demonstrate the same strong tendency to put someone in charge of government relations, but it seems that those that do are rewarded with much more in calls and requests from government. Since we cannot determine how these relationships begin, it is at least conceivable that it is the contact from government that leads nonprofits to formalize or expand government relations within the organization.

The other structural variable, the organization's capacity to conduct research, also demonstrates a strong relationship with the frequency of government-initiated contact. Some calls and requests from government may be requests for political support or are oversight related. The interviews, however, indicate strongly that the nonprofit's research and data appear to be key to the interaction initiated by government. Figure 6-1 illustrates the strength of the bivariate relationship (shown for the sample of conventional nonprofits). Conventional nonprofits with the highest research capacity are more than four times as likely to be contacted at a frequent rate—at least two times a month—than those at the lowest research capacity rating. The relationship between these two variables for the more politically active H electors is even stronger. Eighty percent of the H electors with the highest research capacity are frequently consulted. Sixty-three percent are contacted

Figure 6-1. *The Impact of Research Capacity*

Percent of nonprofits reporting frequent government-initiated contact

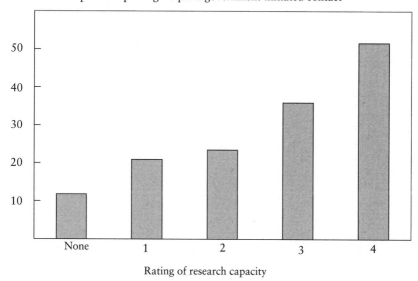

Rating of research capacity

Q.17. How would you describe the capacity of your organization to conduct and disseminate research? [Respondents ranked "conduct" and "disseminate" separately on the same five-point scale.] "Frequent" contact initiated by government was defined as the two highest categories, "two, three times a month" and "four or more times a month."
Note: Conventional 501c3 nonprofits, *n* = 530.

four times a month or more. If nonprofits have information at their disposal, the government seems to have a very strong interest in acquiring it.

As noted earlier, mobilization—the conversion of resources into lobbying—is at the heart of political scientists' explanation of lobbying effectiveness. The tactic "encouraging members to write, call, fax, or e-mail policymakers" comes closest to tapping our common view of mobilization by interest groups. Some caution, however, is warranted, because even allowing for the differences in scale, mobilization by nonprofits may not require the same proportion of resources as is the case in national politics. As just mentioned, a nonprofit dealing with its city government may feel (with justification) that a few phone calls from board members are sufficient to get their point across. The results for this mobilization variable are not significant. Possibly, the impact of mobilization could be much greater in influencing actual decisions or in raising the salience of issues than in stimulating agency contact. It might also be true that if this measure revealed something about depth or quality of mobilization, the results could be different.

The direct lobbying variable shows mixed results. For the H electors there is no statistically significant relationship between lobbying and government-initiated contact. For the conventional nonprofits, lobbying frequency does seem to matter as more frequent direct advocacy on bills and policy pronouncements is linked to greater attentiveness by government.[18] It seems intuitive that active lobbying would generate a government response. As with external mobilization, it might be a more powerful predictor of policy responsiveness than of government-initiated contact.

Finally, the contrary idea that government-initiated contact is a measure not of effectiveness but instead reflects oversight is dispelled by the data. The proportion of income derived from government is clearly unrelated to the frequency of contact by policymakers. Surely, officials do gather information on how their programs are doing, but this is not what drives the overall contact higher or lower. Rather, they are after something else. The interviews reinforce the statistics here: data and research are the coins of the realm.

The Value of Information

Political scientists have long recognized the value of information to interest groups. One of the first was Lester Milbrath who described lobbying as a communications process in his 1963 work, *The Washington Lobbyists*.[19] Over the years scholars have emphasized the role of information in interest group advocacy.[20] John Mark Hansen argues that interest groups try to gain a competitive advantage with their information. That is, their goal is to provide information that is superior to that of competing sources (such as other groups, parties, think tanks, and universities).[21] Advantages can be gained by producing information that is easily acquired (brought right to the office); easily digestible (can be quickly understood by key policymakers); unique (no one else has the information); noteworthy (others will take notice when it is made public); and high quality (not easily discredited on the grounds of bias or lack of rigor). It is difficult for an interest group to deliver information that meets all of these criteria, but the closer it can come to meeting these objectives, the more likely it is that its information will be well received by its target.

Washington lobbyists regard information as a means of entrée. They use it as a reason to ask for an appointment; then they use the study they bring with them as the starting point in their conversation with policymakers or staffers. After outlining the (ostensibly) new findings of their study and explaining the implications for the matter at hand, they will leave a copy of the report along with a one- or two-page memo summarizing its contents.[22] The new research report has become such a staple of Washington lobbying that some lobbyists feel awkward and disadvantaged without one. In Washington a small industry of consulting firms has emerged to produce sophisticated reports to meet the needs of interest group lobbyists.[23] In an interview done for another research project, an automobile lobbyist was asked if studies commissioned by his trade group lacked credibility because they're underwritten by car manufacturers? He responded, "No doubt—they're very definitely tainted. But we do it because it gives us something to use as a marker and it gives us something to point to."

Once again the behavior of nonprofits at the state and local level diverges sharply from that of Washington lobbies. The use of information by these nonprofits does not follow this model but, rather, data and research are conveyed to government in many ways, and nonprofits do not depend on the "new report." The fundamental reason for this difference is that by and large the federal government does not need the research provided by Washington lobbies. The national government is already information rich.[24] Members of Congress do like to have studies that support their point of view, and if government offices haven't provided one, they are more than happy to use what is available from interest groups. But unless the research is from a respected citizens group, a think tank, or an academic, such reports are likely to be discounted if not downright ignored.[25]

The contrasting manner in which research from nonprofits is transmitted and consumed at the state and local level springs from a rather different incentive system. State and local bureaucracies as well as state legislatures cannot generally be described as information rich. Their information capacities and needs vary widely, and they find great benefit in drawing on the resources of trusted nonprofits. Nonprofits also find a different opportunity structure than that facing Washington lobbyists. They are not fighting just to get a fifteen-minute appointment with a committee staffer. Those nonprofits with a strong information capacity are able to find many ways of matching their resources to government needs.

Government Benefits

A beginning point for analysis of information politics is to examine the benefits to government from its relationship with nonprofits. Bureaucracies at the state and local level find the research and expertise of nonprofits useful, if not absolutely necessary, to supplement their own scarce resources, increase their flexibility, and provide them with necessary technical and political support.

LEAN BUREAUCRACIES. It is easy to think of government as a giant behemoth, so large, powerful, and rich it can easily develop whatever information resources that it needs. Yet each government bureaucracy competes with others for budget resources, and significant budget increases are hard to come by. The staffing of individual offices and bureaus within a state or local bureaucracy can be surprisingly thin, and the pressure to keep the bureaucratic head count down is intense.[26] In an interview, the head of a statewide sheriff's association was asked if he ever got calls from government asking for data. He replied, "Oh yes. They'll want jail populations for example. We run our own computer company, Sheriffs _____. We run it with the _____ sheriffs. [They] own half and we own half. It links the databases of sheriffs. Through this company we know what the population of our jails is. We know what the number of deputies working on patrols is." When the interviewer expressed surprise that the state department of corrections didn't know how many people were in jail, he replied, "No, it doesn't have it. They only have a few people working there and they don't do data things like this."

In a government bureaucracy, pressed on many sides by demands for services or funding, data gathering may seem like an unaffordable luxury. As one respondent from rural Minnesota put it, the bureaucrats he deals with are people with "42 other jobs that they're trying to do." Moreover, research itself can seem like a bottomless pit: there is always more to be done. And isn't research what universities and think tanks do? Consequently, in the internal bureaucratic politics at state and local agencies, research is often a low priority. Without a strong, built-in constituency, researchers who are employed by a bureaucracy may have little leverage in the ongoing bargaining over the allocation of budgetary resources. As a result, typical state and local bureaucracies may have a very limited information-gathering capacity. Nonprofits take advantage of that gap, as do private interest groups. In discussing the utilization and incidence data that he shared with a state agency, the head of a health-related nonprofit noted, "It startles me sometimes that our state agencies don't have these data but we do."

FLEXIBILITY. If flexibility is the goal, nonprofits are the means. Nonprofits allow government agencies to experiment with new ideas, respond to sudden increases in demand for services, and avoid long-term commitments of resources. Since Ronald Reagan became president, it has been exceedingly difficult for legislators championing new services or programs to create additional bureaucracies. Even during the affluent Clinton years, the collective mind-set of those in government was to keep government from expanding and to use privatization, competition, and nonprofit service providers to keep costs down and government small.

The large pool of respected and competent nonprofits gives government enormous flexibility in addressing the ever-changing needs and priorities of any one community. Take, for example, "Community Services," a multi-service center in northern California. Over the years the state of California, the county, and some local governments have given it responsibility for programs such as shelter for the homeless, citizenship education for immigrants, weekend work for juvenile offenders, mentoring for graduates of weekend work, food distribution, services for seniors, energy services such as emergency utility payments and weatherization, and job training for women on welfare. Some of the time Community Services approached government, seeking out grants and new opportunities. At other times said its director, "We're called on to fill special needs. The county will come to us and say, 'We've got this thing, will you do it for us?'"

A variant of this dynamic comes from devolution. As the federal government has moved more programmatic responsibilities to state and local governments and they, in turn, have relied more and more often on nonprofits, the more difficult it is for all levels of government to monitor performance. In studying the implementation of TANF, Thomas Gais and his colleagues write, "Devolution has moved decisionmaking down to states—and many states have moved important policy and management decisions down to counties and even communities—without creating an information infrastructure that allows local administrators, policymakers, and citizens to understand the magnitude and nature of problems confronting families in their areas."[27]

Whether they are expanding programs they have experience with but do not have the capacity to run, initiating new programs in an attempt to try innovative approaches to problems, or generally devolving responsibilities downward, the funding bureaucracies become dependent on the nonprofits for performance data. Frequently, there is neither agency staff to do data collection nor funds for outside evaluations. As a consequence of its philosophy of trying to avoid large bureaucratic commitments to new programs, government places a premium on the expertise on the nonprofits it contracts with. Government grants create the need for accountability, and accountability creates the need for data collection. The more flexible government wants to be, the more it will depend on nonprofits to tell it what is working in the community.

SUPPORT. The instrumental value of the nonprofits' expertise and data is that their research can provide critical support for an agency's endeavors. Although we often think of government as stable to the point of rigidity, the reality is that government agencies—and especially those at the state and local level—live in a world of uncertainty. Economic downturns, always unpredictable, cause budget problems, and individual agencies may be forced to make real cutbacks in staffing and programming. Emergencies or increased demands for services from particular agencies can lead to budget pressures everywhere else. Scholars have long understood that agencies look to their client groups for political support, but our usual conception of this process involved business lobbies and the agencies that regulate them.[28] As we argued earlier, at the community level it is often nonprofits that agencies must look to for outside support. The executive director of the "Housing Coalition," described a number of different ways his organization supported local agencies in his Midwestern state:

> We just finished a project with the _____ mayor for a housing trust fund. It [will have] $15-20 million in it. The mayor asked me to sit on a committee to figure out how to do this. They know we're advocates. The thing is, they want our support. It becomes an endorsement from the advocates. They also know that we've done this elsewhere. How did they do it in _____? We know that because we were there. We also have training funds from HUD so that if there's an application a city needs to write, we can help.

He added that sometimes agencies are "looking for new initiatives or out-of-the-box thinking and they need outside help. The current system is difficult to change. People have stakes in the present system. Outsiders change the equation."

In these two short passages, the executive director mentioned five forms of support that his nonprofit provides to the government agencies and offices it works with. The Housing Coalition offers general political support for political leaders who want to be known for their support for low-income housing; it's a repository of knowledge about existing programs for policymakers interested in developing a proposal; it supplies technical expertise to city agencies writing grants to the federal government; it provides "out-of-the-box" thinking to agencies looking for innovation; and it provides leverage for policymakers who need to overcome the opposition of entrenched forces inside or outside of government. All of these separate, supporting roles, all of this value to government is built on the expertise that the Housing Coalition has developed over the many years it has been working on behalf of the poor.

And Nonprofit Opportunities

Nonprofits are only too aware of all the needs of the agencies and policymakers they deal with. To further their goal of becoming a valued partner, jointly producing public policy, and gaining respect for their capacity so they can win more grants and contracts, nonprofits look strategically for opportunities to provide something of value to those in government. Some of what they offer has already been detailed, but here we rotate the prism slightly and look at this relationship from the perspective of nonprofits.

IDENTIFYING NEEDS. As nonprofits interact with government they cannot help but become aware of the data agencies need but do not have easy access to. It is not rocket science for a nonprofit director to recognize how data they have at their disposal or could acquire from sources they work with, could be packaged for government's use. It is to any interest group's advantage to find a niche for itself and to exploit that niche with whatever resources or tactics it has at its disposal.[29]

When interviewees were asked about information they provided government, they sometimes cited statistics gathered in the course of their work and supplied on an ongoing basis to agencies they work with. Said one executive director, "If they're asking us, they're asking for statistics that we have. How many people [use] child care, how many requests [do] we get?" But it is no accident that those statistics are assembled in an attractive and easily usable format. The child care organization designed its data gathering with government's needs in mind and makes a conscious effort to pull together the numbers quickly so its data are ready long before the government agency's reporting requirements eventually yield the same information. As interest groups often do, it tries to frame the issues in its own terms.[30] A more ambitious effort, requiring a sophisticated research staff, is to create a database and set of social or economic indicators that are of such high quality that they are difficult for government to ignore. At one nonprofit working in social services, the executive director said it devoted substantial resources to establishing a statistical "trend line on health and insurance and on welfare reform." These indicators have gained attention for the organization at the local and state level. These hard data, easily usable by government, and transmitted in a form unencumbered by the editorializing of a report, are the most prized by agencies.

Not all nonprofits can provide raw data directly to an agency, and some use reports to attract attention to their cause. The issuance of a report critical of some policy lapse on the part of government may seem antithetical to the goal of nurturing a partnership. Yet a cooperative stance should be backed up by some capacity to inflict costs when an agency's policies or processes cross the threshold of what is acceptable. One of the shrewdest information strategies we observed was that of a nonprofit attacking a bureaucracy in the hopes of getting the agency a larger budget. An environmental group working in a relatively poor state was frustrated by the governor's resistance to increasing his Department of Agriculture's budget for helping farmers with waste management problems. Using money from various sources, the environmental group produced an ambitious study of waste management by farms in the state. The report generated support in the legislature for funds for the Department of Agriculture so it could expand its work on the issue. "We can be helpful in moving that agenda along by taking a more hard-nosed stance in the legislature than the agency can," said the executive director. The state's Department of Agriculture couldn't ask for a funding increase that the governor had not approved, but there was no such inhibition against the nonprofit.

COORDINATION. Nonprofits are quick to identify coordination problems in government. In a metropolitan region coordination problems exist not only among agencies within a city but among various federal, state, county, regional, and city governments. Sometimes this difficulty involves jurisdictional questions when a problem crosses the authority of different agencies from different layers of government. Recall, for example, the watershed task force discussed in chapter 5. Governments in the six affected counties had not moved effectively on their own because there was a thicket of conflicting agency jurisdictions. By the time the Nature Conservancy got a local nonprofit to take the leadership in convening a joint working group, all the stakeholders were ready to come to the bargaining table.

More often than not, nonprofits are not directly trying to bridge conflict or negotiate an agreement. Frequently, their goal is simply to solve the problem of the left hand of government not knowing what the right hand is doing. In large metropolitan areas in particular, there are a lot of oblivious left hands. The executive director of a nonprofit in a large, midwestern city noted, "We have 57 police departments [and] 31 school districts." His nonprofit is an ongoing source of planning documents and studies provided to local agencies. Government is the primary source of grant money to do the studies, even though the source of much of the data the nonprofit collects is the government itself. "You see, the dots don't connect. We connect the dots," he explained.

ADVOCACY. The ultimate goal of allocating resources for research and data collection is, of course, to influence government. As argued already at length, the most efficient way to do so is through the joint production of public policy. Information is a means to that end. Information is a many-splendored thing, and nonprofits can collect, analyze, package, and disseminate it in endless ways. For one statewide association of nonprofits serving poor senior citizens, it became apparent that the state's Medicaid office could not always model the effects of regulatory changes on nursing homes and other nonprofit vendors. Its research staff built a sophisticated database with the capacity to "plug in different scenarios" for reimbursement rates. As a result said the executive director, the state office now relies "on us for information about how their policies impact our members." He said the organization's database was critical in changing a proposed regulation that resulted in a better reimbursement rate for nonprofits. The draft version of the regulations would have improved the reimbursement rate only for for-profit nursing homes and would have brought down the rate for nonprofits.

Whatever the cooperation by government or interest in the nonprofit's research, the nonprofit must always be prepared to push for attention to its work. As good as this organization's database is, it still had to lobby the Medicaid office to look at its calculations to see how they contrasted with the bureaucracy's projections. Even when a nonprofit is incorporated into the policymaking process, it has to work to get policymakers to recognize the value of its information. Even in the most cooperative of relationships, nonprofits must maintain the capacity to be aggressive. Information can be used as leverage, but only when it is being pushed.

Conclusion

In their classic study of foreign trade politics, Raymond A. Bauer, Ithiel de Sola Pool, and Lewis Anthony Dexter described interest groups in Washington as service bureaus.[31] "Service bureau" suggests responding to requests or anticipating needs.[32] What do you need? How can I help? This model still seems to fit Washington politics very well, and certainly nonprofits at the state and local level provide a service to agency officials and legislators with the data and reports they provide to them. Yet nonprofits entering the policymaking process can aspire to being much more than a service bureau. Indeed, they can hope to be partners in policymaking, helping to design programs and policies rather than just implementing them. And while this is the optimum relationship for an interest group with government, it is not an unrealistic goal for nonprofits at the state and local level. Although they will never be equal partners with government officials, they can be incorporated into the policymaking process, consulted as well as listened to.

The boundaries between government and client groups are much more porous outside of Washington. This not only makes government more accessible to state and local lobbies, it means that they have to devote comparatively fewer resources just to get a hearing. And when government approaches a lobbying organization instead of the other way around, the costs are less expensive still.

Nonprofits wanting this kind of relationship must be prepared to invest some of their scarce resources into building the kind of organization that government agencies find attractive. Effectiveness with government is easy enough to understand. To be sure more money is better than less, but for effectiveness with government. wealth helps only because it facilitates the development of particular organizational capacities. Neither is the size of membership a key to success, which is fortunate because many social service providers do not have real memberships and may have only a limited circle of donors.

Nonprofits greatly enhance their chances of gaining access to government and influencing public policy if they commit to investing resources in developing the organizational capacities important in the political world. First and foremost is to make government relations someone's responsibility. It has to be somebody's job. If it is the responsibility of the executive director, then the board of directors must clearly acknowledge and value the work. If it is someone else's, the executive director and others in the nonprofit must support those efforts and make sure that those individuals are not overwhelmed with other assignments and incapable of spending much time on government relations. This objective may seem overly structured for the typical, modest-sized nonprofit, but when executives or staffers know they are going to be evaluated on a task, they are going to treat it more seriously. The payoff is high: the data show that organizations that put someone in charge are rewarded with a high level of contact with government.

A nonprofit's research or information capacity seems critical in contributing to the organization's relationship with government. In looking at both samples, this variable is the one with the most powerful impact. Research capacity is surely a proxy for the policy expertise possessed by an organization. When we think of expertise, we can think of many reasons why officials in government will find the knowledge embedded within an organization of value to them. Of all the resources that an interest group can offer policymakers, information is the most specialized. It is not a commodity, but, rather, is endlessly varied, highly differentiated in quality, and constantly in demand. As such, it is a way that a nonprofit can distinguish itself from the pack, drawing the attention of the government officials it wants to cultivate. Again, the reward is substantial.

Bureaucracies at the state and local level have many needs that nonprofits can help to fill. The raw data and other information that nonprofits generate not only help bureaucrats make more intelligent decisions about the programs they administer, but that information can have political value as well. Nonprofits offer a voice in support of what those bureaucracies do. This is especially critical in social services, where there may be no private industry to back the agency. Identifying the needs of bureaucracies and the opportunities to aid them is not difficult. Developing the expertise and investing the resources over a long period of time is what's challenging.

CHAPTER SEVEN

The Rules
Are Never
Neutral

As budget woes from the recession and other factors began to worsen at the beginning of the twenty-first century, the solution in state after state was an all-too-familiar one: reduce funding for social services. In Massachusetts, for example, one of the first cuts was to reduce Medicaid rolls by 50,000 people. There was no rationale other than budgetary problems; no one in the state government made a serious claim that the newly disqualified did not merit Medicaid coverage. Yet at the same time the state continued funding for many other programs for union and business interests, some of dubious value.

This is a familiar, even mundane, tale of human services taking the brunt of budget cuts while better-organized constituencies win support for their programs. Political scientists have a simple explanation for this dynamic. Programs for the poor, disabled, sick, jobless, and frail suffer because those people have no money to support interest groups to work on their behalf. And even if they did have some discretionary income, they would not contribute to such interest groups because of the free rider problem: let others pay for the lobby. The disadvantage of the poor in the policymaking process is so enduring, and these underlying reasons so clear, that interest group scholars have long been satisfied with their answer and have moved on to other research problems.

Surprisingly, perhaps, it's the wrong answer.

The Interest Group Universe

The poor and other disadvantaged constituencies certainly do not have the discretionary income to join interest groups. If interest representation in the political system were dependent on voluntary associations, then this part of the conventional political science answer would be correct. The interest group universe is not dominated by voluntary associations though. Much of the representation by interest groups comes instead from institutions and other nonmembership organizations. Corporations, state and local governments, trade associations, some public interest groups, and nonprofits of various sorts do not depend on individuals to provide them with financial support. Indeed, only a minority of active interest groups are voluntary associations.[1] Are there institutions capable of adequately representing those who are politically weak and have no funds to support lobbying? Of course there are: 501c3 nonprofits.

The flip side of this coin is that the free rider problem is not the obstacle either. There is no collective action problem because most 501c3 nonprofits do not rely on dues-paying members or large numbers of donors to support them. They do actively pursue patrons—individuals or institutions who are willing to make large gifts—but this is not uncommon in interest group politics.[2]

Significant representation for the disadvantaged already comes from the nonprofit sector. The 501c3s, their trade associations, and other tax-exempt organizations (chiefly 501c4s) lobby on behalf of the constituencies that would otherwise have no representation.[3] But they lobby with one hand tied behind their back. Tax-exempt nonprofit trade groups cannot hope to provide sufficient representation because their resource base is generally too small. The 501c3s must provide the bulk of the lobbying if the underrepresented are to be adequately represented before legislatures. Collectively, 501c3s have an impressive array of assets. But they are forbidden by law from making campaign contributions, mounting substantial grass-roots campaigns, and lobbying legislators to any substantial degree. Worse still, many nonprofits are socialized by their understanding of the law to believe that they should not be politically active. Other types of organizations with interests before government do not have similar restrictions and, like rational actors, they take advantage of the freedoms they are given under American law to lobby as aggressively as they like for policies that benefit their constituents.

Thus the underlying answer to why the 501c3s' constituencies are at a severe competitive disadvantage in legislative policymaking is that government has decided that nonprofits should be constrained in their lobbying. The prohibitions and limits mentioned are regulations: government rules that influence market behavior. The lobbying rules are never neutral, and the regulations restricting nonprofits ensure their ineffectiveness in the legislative process.

Why Regulation?

There is little question that government needs to closely regulate some of the policy areas that nonprofits work in, such as health care and education. Yet the need for regulating *nonprofits* regardless of the area they work in may seem counterintuitive. What general protections does society need against nonprofits? What, exactly, are the threats that they pose?

There are certainly some issues on which agreement is widespread on the need for government regulation of 501c3s. Foundations must, by law, give away a minimum of 5 percent of their assets each year. A business with no legitimate charitable focus cannot claim eligibility for tax-deductible contributions. Otherwise, they are committing fraud. The reasons for regulating nonprofits in regard to lobbying may not be as obvious. Regulating the political activities of nonprofits springs from the desire to protect a sound and popular policy: promoting private giving to charitable organizations. It is in the nation's interest to have public charities do as much as they can to take care of the dispossessed in society. There is also widespread agreement that the country should support educational and religious organizations. Thus, since the relevant legislation was passed in 1917, there has been little question that tax deductibility for donations to Yale University, the United Way, the American Cancer Society, or other such nonprofits should continue.

Distinguishing charitable institutions and awarding them the right to receive tax-deductible donations means, conversely, identifying organizations that should not receive this coveted designation. Differentiating organizations qualifying for 501c3 status from those that do not is a tricky piece of public policy. The Internal Revenue Service has recognized from the time the tax deduction was first enacted that support for the law could be seriously compromised by granting 501c3 to the wrong kinds of organizations. Imagine the consternation of liberals if the Christian Coalition had applied for and been awarded tax-deductible status.

The focus in this book is on the regulation of lobbying, and little is said about restriction on electoral activity by 501c3s. Regulation in this area is warranted as political parties, interest groups, and candidates will be quick to exploit any loophole they identify or any weaknesses in enforcement of the laws governing nonprofits. Most of the abuses in this area have involved other types of tax-exempt nonprofits and not 501c3s. So-called 527 committees, tax-exempt nonprofits classified as political organizations, emerged as a source of controversy in the late 1990s because they became vehicles for hiding the identity of donors who wanted to support a political cause. A reform bill passed in 2000 ended anonymity for 527 donors. The ink had hardly dried on the new McCain-Feingold campaign finance law, aimed at stopping the flow of soft money to political parties, when tax-exempt organizations emerged to raise soft money for issue ads.[4] It seems evident that if the general prohibition against electoral activity by 501c3s were relaxed, it would have a devastating effect on the legitimacy of tax deductibility for public charities. The IRS must remain vigilant so that permissible election-related activity for 501c3s, such as holding candidate debates, allowing candidates to visit facilities and speak, or writing nonpartisan issue analyses, are not used as veneers for tax-deductible contributions given with the intent to support individual candidates or parties.

Justifiable Subsidy

Unlike the restriction on electoral activity, the regulatory standards for the participation of 501c3s in the legislative process should be reconsidered because they significantly limit representation of the most underrepresented constituencies in the American political system. The greatest obstacle to such change is the opposition from conservatives who see the tax benefits of 501c3 as an advantage for liberal organizations. Since 501c3 is a tax expenditure—we all must pay additional taxes to compensate for the revenue lost by tax-deductible contributions—the provision of the law constitutes a subsidy to nonprofits. Conservative legislators wonder why their constituents should be paying to support organizations they don't like. Part of the motivation behind conservatives' push for greater grant funding for faith-based organizations is surely to balance government's financial support of liberal social service agencies.[5] (Since the faith-based organizations with the most success in gaining government grants are inner city black churches, there is some question about whether conservative churches will actually gain the most from a broadening of grants available to the religious sector.)[6]

Among 501c3 nonprofits there is an overwhelming tilt toward the liberal side of the political spectrum. Nonprofits in health care, social services, education, environment, and the arts tend to prefer what conservatives call "big government" and prefer the spending that conservatives decry. Good government groups also tend to be on the liberal side of the fence. Indeed, the only major sector of the 501c3 world that does not seem to have a decidedly liberal outlook is religion.

Despite the ideological tilt, the 501c3 subsidy is a justifiable one. Government does not follow a principle prohibiting subsidies for interest groups, and it is not unusual for policymakers to find ways of helping groups to participate in the governmental process. There was no intent in the initial law to help liberal organizations—the purpose is to support charities and organizations that perform a public service regardless of ideology. The reality is that people with liberal sentiments are more interested in the kind of work that nonprofits do than are conservatives.[7] These organizations still do the good work that warrants a tax expenditure.

Voice and Democracy

Although the First Amendment explicitly grants Americans the freedom to "petition the government for a redress of grievances," petitioning the government turns out to be a regulated activity. The regulatory framework for interest groups is studded with privileges for different interest group sectors. Restrictions against various activities are common. Over time the accumulation of this assortment of advantages and disadvantages represents not so much a twisted, tilted playing field as a rusty Rube Goldberg contraption.

A common assumption is that a balanced system—a system in which all relevant interests are represented—will produce the best public policy decisions. This idea seems only logical (if impossible to prove empirically). An even more compelling argument for rethinking 501c3 is normative: we'll have a fairer political system if the disadvantaged in society are adequately represented in public policymaking. The United States is a pluralist democracy: the public policymaking process facilitates interest group politics, and lobbies work strenuously to influence government decisions. The basic policymaking system is not going to change, and no sector of society can maximize its influence unless it is heavily involved in interest group politics.

In an ideal pluralist democracy, all relevant interests have a voice in the policymaking process. Robert Dahl, the preeminent pluralist theorist, defines "the 'normal' American political process as one in which there is a high probability that an active and legitimate group in the population can make itself heard effectively at some crucial stage in the process of decision."[8] Thus Dahl is not defining a pluralist system as one in which interest group sectors have equal influence. Having a voice means simply that preferences can be effectively articulated and that policymakers hear that voice. The second condition should be easily met as a consequence of the first. Legislators spend their day listening to the voices of interests, and they are usually eager to hear what constituents have to tell them. So the underlying problem is amplifying the voice, not improving legislators' hearing.

It is nonprofits' duty to do the amplifying. It is no other interest group sector's responsibility. It is not the job of corporations or labor unions. Professional associations must represent their professionals. It would be nice if liberal citizen groups provided some of this voice, but donors who have willingly contributed to environmental groups have not found the same urgency to support lobbies for the homeless.[9] In short, the only way that the voice of the disadvantaged in American society will be raised is if nonprofits do it.

Why is it assumed that these constituencies need more representation than they are currently getting? Indeed, the revolution in welfare produced a wide variety of programs for providing social services to the needy. The United States is not a heartless mean-spirited culture, impervious to the suffering of the indigent and the sick. The welfare state is extensive and consumes a good deal of the budget at the federal and state levels. Moreover, policymakers are not like billiard balls on a table, standing stationary until struck by the cue ball. They do not have to be told by interest groups what to do, and clearly there are many legislators who would keep pushing for policies to benefit these constituencies even if they never heard from nonprofits working on their behalf.

Without reviewing all the evidence presented in the previous chapters and in other relevant works on interest groups, let one central point provide the answer as to why a pluralist democracy requires more representation— more voice—by nonprofits: 501c3s lobby less (at the legislative level) than other interest group sectors. No other interest group sector faces the restrictions that public charities do, and all other sectors have substantial representation of lobbying organizations before Congress and the state legislatures. In a democracy, it is only natural that organizations will lobby legislators to further their self-interest. James Madison told us long ago that the causes of "faction" are "sown in the nature of man," and that in a free society government should not restrain factions but instead let them all compete against one another.[10] Madison's argument in the *Federalist* is our constitutional guide to interest groups, and its underlying principles should apply to nonprofits just as they do to all other interest group sectors.[11]

Fundamental Differences

The behavior of nonprofits toward administrators and legislators is so strikingly different that some may wonder if something more than regulation is at work. Maybe nonprofits prefer administrative lobbying because it's easier, more cost effective, or more important to the maintenance of the orga-nization. These are all plausible explanations, but the data in table 5-2 suggest that regulation is central. Recall that the data show that conven-tional nonprofits lobby legislators at a considerably lower frequency than they lobby administrators. Yet the H electors lobby legislators at the same level of frequency that they lobby administrators. Logically, these differences between the two samples should not be evident if 501c3s simply preferred administrative lobbying.

The survey is unable, however, to answer another important question about the lobbying behavior of 501c3s: if nonprofits are making their voices heard at the administrative level, does it really make that much difference that they do not do as much advocacy work before legislatures? Adminis-trators communicate with their legislative overseers and surely transmit the views of client groups in such discussions. Moreover, legislators are hardly isolated or unaware of the problems facing nonprofits. Do legislators really need to be told by lobbyists for community health centers that they should spend more on community health?

Administrative lobbying is not enough; it is not an adequate substitute for the amount of lobbying that is stifled by government regulation of non-profits. There are fundamental differences in advocacy at these two different venues:

LEGISLATURES SET PRIORITIES. Although agency administrators make many important decisions, one thing they do not do is set the broad spend-ing and programmatic priorities of the federal and state governments. Interest groups of all types go to Congress or their state legislature and argue for more spending for the programs they support. The process is a lit-tle more complicated than the stereotype of the squeaky wheel getting the grease, but not being engaged is a severe liability.[12] Nonprofits are already at a disadvantage with legislatures because they can't make campaign con-tributions. And any disadvantage is significant in an arena where the stakes are so high and the competition so abundant. In some years a budget is close to a zero-sum game and not to press the urgency of one's cause is to make it easier for legislators to accede to other pressing demands.

Another key difference is that most lobbying of agencies by nonprofits takes place at the local level. Some takes place at the state level. In com-parison very little of the lobbying by 501c3s takes place at the federal level. To get the message across, this distribution is far from ideal. For example, many low-income housing nonprofits have developed a close working rela-tionship with their local housing bureaucracy. As a partnership develops with that bureau, influence will be extended as local officials come to understand problems from the viewpoint of the nonprofits and the nonprofits' clients. But none of that directly influences Congress's funding levels for housing programs.

EDUCATING LEGISLATORS. By shying away from legislative lobbying, nonprofits lose an opportunity to educate legislators and their staffers. By law—by section 501c3—nonprofits can do all the educating of legislators that they want. The nonprofits that do lobby often defend such endeavors as educational in nature and thus not subject to the substantial limitation. The difference between educating and lobbying is, of course, an artifact of law; they are conceptually difficult to distinguish because to try to educate policymakers about a problem is to try to influence them. But when nonprofits do not understand what the law says, and they are wary of what they do and how it might be interpreted as lobbying, they pull back much farther than necessary.

To take just one simple example, if a nonprofit shies away from the legislative process and makes little effort to influence local state legislators or representatives in Congress, it may not ever ask those individuals to come by the facility to meet the staff, give a talk, or have their picture taken at some contrived ceremony. What is lost? It's not so much the opportunity to lobby for more money or try to sway an upcoming vote—the traditional conception of legislative lobbying. That kind of aggressive lobbying would not usually be done at such occasions even if the nonprofit were oriented toward legislative advocacy. Rather, what is lost is the chance to broaden legislators' understanding of the programs they fund, the impact of the policies they have set, and, most important, the problems that need addressing.

Educating legislators extends beyond conveying information and enhancing awareness. Part of what interest groups do is to try to make legislators accept their definition of the problem at hand.[13] If a legislator views social services from the viewpoint of budget problems, that is not advantageous to service providers. If they see the problem as one of waiting lists for frail elderly, or disease contagion, or unvaccinated children, or deinstitutionalized mental patients, or of other such vivid reminders of what budget dollars go for, that is much better for the nonprofits.

MOBILIZING CONSTITUENTS. One type of lobbying that the IRS regards as falling within 501c3s' limitations is grass-roots advocacy. Conventional nonprofits occasionally engage in such efforts, though they encourage members to write or call legislators at less than half the frequency rate of the H electors. This may seem to be an appropriate tactic for nonprofits with middle-class constituents, such as environmental or good government groups. In contrast clients of human service providers may not seem to be the ideal candidates for political mobilization. Yet to need services is not necessarily to be incapacitated, and being poor does not mean one is apathetic.

Although mobilization of clients over regulatory issues is certainly possible, explaining administrative rulemaking and assigning appropriate responsibility is generally more complicated than analogous legislative campaigns. Agencies are not impervious to public opinion, but lobbies usually target grassroots advocacy toward legislators or chief executives. Even when an agency is legally responsible for a decision, the underlying force on the issue may be the legislative committee overseeing that agency. By limiting grassroots advocacy because of concerns over 501c3, nonprofits not only lose an opportunity to increase their influence but they also lose the chance to educate their constituents about how government works and enhance those individuals' civic engagement and sense of efficacy.[14]

Whose Fault?

Unfortunately, clear thinking about advocacy is compromised by gross ignorance of what section 501c3 actually says. If one believes that lobbying is generally forbidden by tax law and the consequence of being caught is the loss of tax deductibility, it makes perfect sense to exclude advocacy as one of the missions of the organization. As table 7-1 demonstrates all too well, the level of misinformation about 501c3 is startlingly high. (As chapter 3 notes, especially in table 3-1, on many of the provisions of the law listed in the quiz respondents did not do much better than they would have by flipping a coin before checking off their yes or no answers.)

Given the ignorance about 501c3, the obvious question to ask is who is to blame. There is no shortage of candidates. It may be willful ignorance by nonprofit leaders—they may not understand the law because they cannot be bothered to learn about it. Perhaps nonprofit leaders are badly advised. Since 501c3 is tax law, accountants and lawyers are frequently called on to give advice on what is allowable. There should be no assumption that these professionals offer accurate interpretations of 501c3, especially if they do not specialize in nonprofit law or nonprofit accounting. Finally, and most obviously, there's the Internal Revenue Service. Does it do what it can to communicate clear standards and regulations?

Table 7-1. *Nonprofits and the Effect of Consultation on Their Expertise*

Can your organization	Correct answer	Percent correct, all respondents	Percent difference in correct response between respondents who consulted various sources and all respondents			
			Consulted lawyers	Consulted accountants	Consulted nonprofits	Did not consult anyone
Support or oppose federal legislation under current IRS regulations	Yes	54	+11	+9	+16	-6
Take a policy position without reference to a specific bill under current regulations	Yes	61	+13	+12	+22	-8
Support or oppose federal regulations	Yes	62	+12	+9	+20	-9
Lobby if part of your budget comes from federal funds	Yes	32	+6	0	+12	-1
Talk to elected public officials about public policy matters	Yes	80	+8	+4	+16	-5
Sponsor a forum or candidate debate	Yes	45	+10	+4	+13	-9
Percent of sample indicating that they consulted someone in this category	...	...	36	17	26	27

Q.9. Does your organization consult experts about the legality of any efforts you make to influence government? Check all that apply.

Note: "All respondents" refers to the sample of "conventional nonprofits"—those 501c3s that do not take the H election and do not list any lobbying expenditures on their tax form 990s. Respondents could check more than one category (for example, they could indicate that they consulted someone in this category). The n for each crosstabulation generally ranges from 460 to 475.

Our survey asked respondents if they consulted "experts about the legality of any efforts you make to influence government?" Of those who responded, 36 percent said they consulted a lawyer; 17 percent said they consulted an accountant, and 26 percent said they consulted experts at other nonprofits. (Respondents could check more than one box in case they consulted different types of experts.) Table 7-1 crosstabulates the survey's quiz about section 501c3 with this question about consultation. There were six statements that a significant percentage of respondents answered incorrectly, and they are listed along with the correct true/false answer in the two columns on the left.[15] The numbers in the four columns on the right are the differences between the percentage of those who consulted the various experts giving the correct answer and the percentage of all respondents giving the correct answer.

For example, those who consulted a lawyer scored 11 percentage points higher than all respondents in correctly answering the question on whether it is permissible to "support or oppose federal legislation under current IRS regulations." Those respondents who had consulted someone at another nonprofit do better than those who sought advice from lawyers or accountants, but all three sources of advice were associated with higher scores. What isn't clear from these data is whether the advice given by people at other nonprofits is more accurate than that given by lawyers and accountants, or that their advice is more trusted. Those who didn't consult anyone scored lower than all respondents on all questions and thus receive negative percentage scores in the column on the far right.

Explanations of why accountants and lawyers may not do as well as nonprofit leaders emerged from the interviews and focus groups. Nonprofits may draw on the services of these professionals because of their expertise on any number of problems. They may later be consulted more broadly, including questions about 501c3. Or the lawyer or accountant may be tied to the organization through a connection or through a member of the board. Lawyers and accountants for small nonprofits may even be members of the board and volunteer their time. Or they may be hired because they are inexpensive or work in the same neighborhood. For lawyers and accountants who occasionally advise nonprofits, there is little incentive to seriously study the case law on section 501c3. If they are rarely asked about it, they will build up little expertise. This is a real problem because a cursory reading of the law can lead one to be overly cautious in advising nonprofits about political involvement. The end result is bad advice and misinformed executive directors, like the head of a good government group who told us that its lawyer said, "Above and beyond anything else, you can't lobby government." That's not even close to a correct interpretation of the law.

The Internal Revenue Service is a major cause of the ignorance over 501c3 because it resolutely refuses to define what "substantial" lobbying is. There is so much ambiguity about what that word means, it cannot help but leave nonprofit executives puzzled when they begin to learn about the law that governs public charities. An underlying problem is that the office handling tax-exempt organizations has long been an IRS backwater. The IRS in general is chronically underfunded as it lacks a supportive constituency, and members of Congress have demonstrated little interest in giving it the technological capability and personnel resources that it needs. Within its internal organization and priorities, nonprofits rank relatively low. The Tax-Exempt Division is, again, the office that took fourteen years to write the regulations to implement the H election. It makes no significant effort at all to publicize the H election, and it makes no effort to help nonprofits understand why other nonprofits have been reprimanded for violating the lobbying prohibitions in 501c3. In an interview for this book, an IRS official firmly restated the organization's position, "Officially we don't care whether a charity takes the election or not."[16]

If the IRS deserves blame for the ignorance of nonprofit leaders about 501c3, it is also true that too many of those executives are willing accomplices. When we showed the results of the survey's 501c3 quiz to a long-time academic observer of nonprofits, he responded angrily saying "that [information] should be part of Nonprofit Management 101. If leaders don't get these [answers] right, they shouldn't get the job." This may be a bit harsh. Like any leaders, the executives of nonprofits have an enormous range of responsibilities, and many come into their jobs with little or no experience in advocacy. There is a lot to learn in managing a nonprofit, and it comes as no surprise that 501c3 will be easily misunderstood by those who make only a minimal effort to learn its content. Adding to the confusion is that some states have their own set of lobbying regulations, thus adding to the homework of learning the relevant law.

The failure to master the content of 501c3 is compounded by the reality of audits by the IRS and retribution by agencies upset with grantees. Chapter 4 notes that 18 percent of those interviewed indicated that they had a problem with the IRS or a state agency linked to their political activity. Since politically active nonprofits were deliberately oversampled in the interviews, the true percentage in the entire population of 501c3s is not known.

But this figure still says something very important: being threatened by the government because of political activity happens often enough to send a message to the nonprofit community at large. Nonprofits do get punished, and a very small number even lose their tax deductibility. In essence, a little knowledge about what happens to nonprofits that violate the law is a disincentive to lobby. And if you don't lobby, you don't need to spend time trying to understand the subtleties of the complex set of rules that govern the political activity of public charities.

Nonprofit, Heal Thyself

The impact of government regulation on the representation of disadvantaged constituencies is clear. But if the law is a problem, how should it be changed? With any reform of 501c3, care must be taken not to do anything to weaken the integrity of the tax deduction for charitable contributions. The solution, therefore, is not to change the basic law but to fully implement one of its provisions: the H election. Extending the H election to the broader universe of 501c3s does not extend tax deductibility to any new class of organizations, does not broaden the definition of lobbying, and does not grant any new privileges or rights to nonprofits. The H election is part of 501c3—an alternative way for nonprofits to determine if their lobbying falls within the limits of the law.

Currently, if an application for 501c3 status is approved by the Internal Revenue Service, that organization is bound by the substantial standard unless it takes action to select the H option. It is not informed by the IRS that it has a choice between the two standards. Thus a new 501c3 must learn on its own that it has an alternative, determine that it is to its advantage, fill out the form, and send it to Washington.[17] With a bit of perseverance form 5768 can be found on the Internal Revenue Service's website.[18] It is so short that it can be filled out in less than a minute or two. As has been emphasized throughout, relatively few nonprofits know about the H election, and the proportion of nonprofits taking the election remains tiny more than a decade after the law was implemented.[19]

Making the H election the default would in one Washington lawyer's words, "put charities on clearer legal ground." He added, the H election should be "an opt out rather than an opt in." In this way 501c3s would have to file a form to elect the substantial standard. If the H election were the default, only a small percentage of nonprofits would instead choose the substantial option. A handful of extremely large nonprofits might avoid

Table 7-2. *The H Election Lobbying Limits*

Annual budget	Total direct lobbying expenditures ceiling	Total grass-roots lobbying expenditures ceiling
Up to $500,000	20% of the budget up to $100,000	One-quarter of the total direct lobbying expenditures ceiling
$500,000 to $1 million	$100,000 + 15% of excess over $500,000	$25,000 + 3.75% of excess over $500,000
$1 million to $1.5 million	$175,000 + 10% of excess over $1 million	$43,750 + 2.5% of excess over $1 million
$1.5 million to $17 million	$225,000 + 5% of excess over $1.5 million	$56,250 + 1.25% of excess over $1.5 million
More than $17 million	$1 million	$250,000

Source: Adapted from "How to Estimate Whether Your Organization Might Be Close to the Maximum It May Spend on Lobbying under the 1976 Lobby Law," Washington, Charity Lobbying in the Public Interest, n. d.

Note: For purposes of making these calculations, an H elector's annual budget is computed by subtracting costs for investment management, unrelated businesses, and certain fund-raising expenses.

the H election because of the ceiling on lobbying expenditures. The sliding scale under the H election limits the largest organizations—those with an annual budget of more than $17 million—to spending $1 million on lobbying and an additional $250,000 in grass-roots expenditures.[20] In a given year no more than a handful of 501c3s spend more than this amount.

A virtue of making the H election spending limits the default is that the change would act as a socializing agent to teach nonprofit leaders about the law on lobbying. The lawyers, accountants, and other nonprofit leaders that advise nonprofits would likely give organizational leaders a handout similar to table 7-2, which shows the five levels of revenue on the sliding scale along with the amounts that can be spent at each rung. They would also likely learn the more precise definitions of lobbying provided under the H election. What constitutes lobbying for purposes of accounting is quite narrow, and it would be helpful if nonprofits learned some of the basics of the IRS's expensing rules.

How might this change be made? Conceivably, the IRS could do what it has never done and define what "substantial" means, offering the ceilings in the H election as quantitative indicators of the thresholds that divide substantial from insubstantial. The grounds for this change can be expressed simply. There are now two administrative standards to address the same issue of lobbying by 501c3s. Logically, the standards should not represent different intent. Unifying the standards makes sense because nonprofits are confused about the ambiguity in the default definition. Moreover, the 1976 amendment has clearly failed because despite the problem of an ambiguously worded standard, relatively few 501c3s take the election.

The legal argument against a regulatory change instituted by the IRS is straightforward. When Congress took up the issue in 1976, it had the opportunity to replace the substantial standard with something else. It decided not to, selecting instead an alternative accounting mechanism for those 501c3s concerned with the imprecision of the default standard. Which side would prevail in court is interesting speculation but just that since the IRS's Tax-Exempt Division is not about to redefine the substantial standard by adopting the H ceilings.[21] It knows it would be attacked by conservatives in Congress, and sensible as this revision may be, political realities and the office's excessive caution mean no such administrative change is in the offing.

A second way of achieving this change is for Congress to do the job. This is not a complicated change—literally only a few words in a tax bill would be necessary. Yet interviews with nonprofit mavens in Washington reveal reluctance to go ahead with any such effort to convince Congress that a change in the default standard is necessary. As one lawyer pointed out, even though this change "seems logical," nonprofit leaders "would have to be careful not to do something that draws out the Istooks of the world or creates opportunities for mischief by tax writing committees." By the same reasoning another nonprofit advocate in Washington concluded, "We want to stay the course." And a third said simply, it's "not doable." All these strategists recognize that to get a bill through that made the H election the "opt out," would require a deal that gave conservatives some significant concessions. For example, some conservatives in Congress want legislation making it easier for churches to become involved in political activities, including endorsing candidates and spending money on their behalf. Under the proposed legislation, the churches could do this without losing their tax-deductible status as long as the spending did not constitute the bulk of the congregation's budget.[22]

A less problematic reform is for the Internal Revenue Service to eliminate the default and force applicants or those just awarded 501c3 status to make a choice. A form with a brief explanation of both options could be included in the 501c3 paperwork, and the executive director would be forced to make a decision. One shortcoming with this option is that brand new nonprofits tend to be tiny, operating with minimal accounting and legal assistance. Executives would have to make this decision when they have not begun to focus on the advocacy that they may want to do later. A great benefit, however, is that the number of H electors would grow, and the lawyers and accountants who advise nonprofits would be forced to learn more about the H election. The word would spread, and the option would certainly become more popular than it is today. Unfortunately, the Tax-Exempt Division of the IRS shows no inclination to make such a move.

Nonprofits' Work

Neither the executive nor legislative branch of government is likely to make these reforms, so any substantive change will have to come from the nonprofits. Nonprofit leadership organizations that lobby on behalf of nonprofits or conduct training for nonprofits, should do what they can to educate other 501c3s about the H election. This is a considerable challenge given the number of nonprofits in this country. It is also a challenge because there are so many other issues facing nonprofits that the typical executive director surely has other priorities.

Even though it is an uphill climb, pushing the H election is an important project for nonprofit leadership groups. There has never been any broadscale effort to educate nonprofits about the H option for 501c3s, so pessimism about its likelihood of success is surely premature. The findings of table 7-1 offer a starting point in strategy. Despite recommendations that are often made in the nonprofit community for better training of lawyers and accountants about 501c3, our data indicate that such efforts should be directed instead at nonprofits that play a leadership role in their states or communities. It is also hard to isolate the lawyers and accountants who must be educated. They are diverse, tend to work outside of the nonprofits, and are hard to reach in an efficient manner. A particularly promising strategy is to focus on trade associations whose membership is made up of public charities. If they can convince their members to convert to the H election, they can enhance their own advocacy by being better able to mobilize their constituent organizations to lobby in tandem with them. Such collaborative lobbying is one of the key strengths of business lobbying.

Inertia will work against change, and raising money to fund a campaign to educate trade associations and nonprofit leadership organizations about the H election will not be easy. At the same time the H alternative itself costs nothing, so nonprofit leaders learning about the H election do not need to find new resources before change can take place.

Two other solutions may seem obvious. One is to encourage those 501c3s that want to become more politically active but are afraid of the IRS to form an affiliated 501c4. The 501c3 can continue to attract tax-deductible donations while all the lobbying can be carried out by the 501c4. This is not uncommon, and some 501c3s have found this arrangement a satisfactory route to getting around the substantial standard. This approach, however, is not without problems. It requires a separate set of books, careful accounting to ensure that there is no commingling of funds, an additional annual outside audit, and a separate board of directors. The additional costs constitute a tax on such combinations—a tax on nonprofit lobbying. Despite the legality of these combinations, there is also an element of deviousness to them. Interviewees who led such two-headed nonprofits were frank to acknowledge that their only purpose was to foil the IRS and dodge the law. Why should nonprofits have to utilize an accounting scheme to exercise what is ostensibly a constitutional right? As noted earlier, despite the huge upsurge in the numbers of 501c3s in recent years, there has been no increase in the numbers of 501c4s (figure 1-3). Clearly the fact that 501c4s cannot offer tax deductibility is a serious constraint on the growth of such organizations.

Finally, an alternative to fighting the inertia working against the H election is to better educate nonelectors about 501c3 and what it allows under the substantial limitation. When executives make a guess as to how much they can lobby, they usually guess on the low side. The strategy is to confront this ignorance head on. The reality is, if nonprofits correctly understood what the law said, they could do significant lobbying. Eliminating risks means keeping careful records and taking care not to provoke an agency or adversaries who might try to initiate an investigation by the IRS.

The best that can be said for a strategy aimed at improving nonelectors' understanding of 501c3 is that it is better than nothing. No amount of training can undo the inherent problem of a standard that the Internal Revenue Service refuses to define. This law has been confusing since it was first adopted, and it is no less confusing today. Trying to broaden the number of nonprofits that elect the H option, even though it will difficult, should be the preferred strategy. Electing the H option will make nonprofits feel freer to lobby, and this result cannot help but enhance the representation of the chronically underrepresented.

Mission

During the interviews and the conduct of focus groups, we met nonprofit leaders who said that advocacy was not part of their mission. These leaders—leaders of nonprofits that clearly had interests before government—

indicated that they were dedicated to serving their clients, and lobbying fell outside of that commitment. The implication was that adding advocacy to what they were doing was to take away from their underlying purpose.

The reality of running a nonprofit is to recognize that it cannot do everything it needs to. Indeed, the first lecture in Nonprofit Management 101 might be about setting hard priorities: decide what is really important and what the organization can realistically hope to accomplish.[23] To say advocacy is not your organization's mission is not to say that politics is irrelevant or that the nonprofit sector is incapable of influencing government. Rather, it reflects a belief that the nonprofit's central mission is what is truly important and that work, not government relations, is its raison d'être.

Administering a nonprofit is difficult, and the demands on leaders are extensive. From the perspective of executive directors, budgets are always too tight, salaries too low, demands too high, and the future too uncertain. Executive directors often feel like they are in a struggle just to stay afloat. Boards of directors may be a source of pressure on executive directors to stay away from political activity too. Whether it be a concern about 501c3, worry that the organization is being stretched too thin, or believing that lobbying will not yield much, board members may send a clear message that they don't see advocacy as one of the organization's essential tasks. Nonprofit leaders may also feel that neither they nor other staff members have the skills to be effective in the political process. For all these reasons and others, some executive directors may reach the conclusion that despite their organization's substantive interest in some government policy or appropriation, advocacy is not one of their missions.

It is hard not to have sympathy for this view. But as reasonable and as understandable as this position is, nonprofit leaders who believe that advocacy before government is not one of their missions should think long and hard about this question: *if it's not your mission, whose mission is it?*

And Capacity

Beyond the nonprofits that reject advocacy as a mission are many more that believe advocacy is one of their jobs but sharply limit it because they lack the funds necessary to make advocacy a significant part of their work. This is no easy problem to solve; there is no formula to determine how much advocacy is the right amount for different kinds of nonprofits. Nevertheless, the reality of tight resources should not become an excuse for inaction. All nonprofits feel constrained by their finances. All have pressing needs for the programs they administer and the fixed costs they must pay every month.

For most nonprofits, developing their orientation toward advocacy is an incremental process. As the organization grows, or grants and contracts with government become more important, or proposed program cuts at the state level galvanize nonprofits in the sector, a more concentrated focus on government relations may emerge. Although it is not possible to prescribe how government relations should be handled at each stage of a nonprofit's development, a few general guidelines might be useful.

Nonprofits should acknowledge what effective government relations requires and make it someone's job. As already discussed, nonprofits that put someone in charge of government relations were much more likely to have government approach the organization. It was one of the strongest variables in predicting a nonprofit's success in advocacy. Before this step can take place, the executive director or the board of directors has to validate government relations as instrumental to the organization's mission. Part of this process is recognizing that government relations includes legislative lobbying. Pretending that lobbying is "education" or that there's a difference between "advocacy" and "lobbying" is counterproductive because that perpetuates ignorance of 501c3.

Nonprofits must focus on building relationships. To be successful over the long term, the organization has to get beyond seeing lobbying as something it does when there's an emergency or a grave threat. It is an everyday job, and the foundation of that task is to build trust and respect with legislators and administrators. Working relationships with agencies may develop naturally out of grant and contract work, but nonprofits can be aggressive in finding reasons to interact with administrators besides the discussions about projects being done under an agency's aegis. No one nonprofit is going to move the entire state legislature, but each nonprofit can become a good friend of its state representative, state senator, U.S. representative, and maybe even one or both of the U.S. senators. Legislators want the respect of the nonprofit's director, board, and employees, as well as their votes. Relationships take time, but the payoff is high.

Organizations need to develop an information capacity. Local agencies are small, and many are highly dependent on nonprofits for information. State agencies can be surprisingly lean. Few public charities have the resources to develop an independent research office, but nonprofits can be strategic in thinking about how to package data that flow to them from the programs they administer. Having an agency utilize an organization's data base is the optimum position for an interest group.

Even as overloaded, underfunded, and understaffed as nonprofits may be, lobbying can be done without compromising critical programs. Meeting with administrators, legislators, and staffers periodically, bringing them by the facility, sending them information, cooperating with the trade association when asked, and prompting board members to contact policymakers, costs relatively little. Such activities do require time but not so much that they would degrade the nonprofit's performance in other areas.

Conclusion

The ultimate impact of expanded nonprofit lobbying from an increase in H elections or redefining 501c3s' default lobbying standard is certainly unclear. If the law were different, there surely would be more lobbying of state legislatures by nonprofits when budgets for the programs they depend on are being cut. But would it make a difference in any legislature's decisionmaking? There is reason to be cautious in assuming that advocacy will change legislative outcomes. To begin with, there is far more to policymaking than lobbying. And an altered 501c3 will not generate more dollars for budget writers in the legislature to allocate. So in the end, maybe nothing different would happen when the budget is tight and a legislature feels it must cut Medicaid or other social programs. However, generations of political scientists have attested to the importance of lobbying in influencing public policy outcomes. As chapter 5 mentions, nonprofits that lobby often find that they have no direct interest group opponents. In the case of Medicaid appropriations, no lobbies are going to try to convince the state legislature that cutting Medicaid rolls is a good thing.

Since our concern is with a fair process and equal treatment of the lobbying laws for the disadvantaged, we need not speculate further about outcomes. If nonprofits were free to lobby aggressively but a state legislature still makes a decision to cut social service programs, so be it. Those decisions should be the outcome of an impartial democratic process, not of a perverse and misguided regulatory standard that limits nonprofits to insubstantial lobbying.

What is safe to assume is if there is widespread adoption of the H election or a comparable redefinition of the substantial standard, the socialization process for nonprofit employees and leaders will be fundamentally altered. Take, for example, *Speak Up*, a recently published pamphlet for use in training nonprofits in advocacy. It makes a convincing case for the importance of advocacy but is also blunt in warning readers that their organization needs to be "clean" in case it is audited by agencies it might offend with such efforts. The publication also quotes the director of a food bank about the dilemma she faces: "You have to ask is it worth it to open your mouth and take the risk that the funding will be taken away and these families will be out in the street?"[24] Nonprofit trainers must be candid in outlining the risks of advocacy, and thus such stark warnings are not inappropriate. As is also common, the publication mentions the H option only in passing and makes no strong recommendation for its adoption.

Growing use of the H election or a revised default standard would mean that relevant educational material and training need not send such a mixed message. The emphasis should be on the means to represent constituents, not on the violation of the rules or the threat of government retribution. Any such change in 501c3 or use of the H election will not directly lessen the chances of retribution by administrative agencies and the ever-present concern that contracts or grants may not be renewed. Yet strengthening the position of nonprofits in the legislative process can only help to strengthen them at the administrative level too. Enhancing the advocacy capacity of 501c3s and the development of stronger relationships with legislators will raise the stature and prowess of the nonprofits in general. For the administrative process, however, the central strategy for nonprofits remains the same: to nurture partnerships.

An increase in H elections or a change in the default definition will keep nonprofits from self-induced ineffectiveness in the legislative process. When nonprofit leaders understand that they can do more, that it is permissible for them to lobby aggressively, the United States will have a much less biased interest group system.

Section 501c3 of the tax code is a poorly conceived regulatory standard that discriminates against the most disadvantaged in our society. It reduces the representation in the policymaking process of the frail elderly, unemployed, mentally ill, the disabled, and many other politically dispossessed constituencies. The law socializes too many nonprofit leaders into believing that advocacy should not be a significant mission of their organization. The limit on lobbying in section 501c3 is not just bad public policy. It's unjust.

Survey and Interview Methods

W e chose to minimize discussion of methods in the text and concentrate instead on communicating our results. We apologize to readers who would have preferred more discussion of the data gathering at the appropriate points in the body of the work.

Conducting mail surveys of nonprofits is no easy task, and we hope that others in the field might profit from our experience. Specialists working on nonprofits or interest groups may want to consult a separate monograph, *Surveying Nonprofits: A Methods Handbook*, written by Jeffrey M. Berry, David F. Arons, Gary D. Bass, Matthew F. Carter, and Kent E. Portney.[1] It is a step-by-step guide to conducting a random sample survey of 990 filers, and it uses this study as an illustration of how to design and carry out such a research enterprise.

The central design feature of the survey was stratifying the public charities into four separate samples. At the outset it was decided that a separate survey of H electors should be conducted so that cohort could serve as a comparison group to the "conventional nonprofits" (nonelectors listing no lobbying expenses on their 990). The only reason for a public charity to take the H election is to escape the confines of the "substantial" limitation on lobbying. There is no other rationale for becoming an H elector; it provides no other benefits. Since H electors self-select, a sample of such nonprofits offers a relatively clear contrast to conventional 501c3s bound by the substantial standard. In previous studies some researchers have used the lobbying expenditures listed on tax form 990 as an indication of a non-profit's predisposition toward lobbying. Although conventional nonprofits have every reason *not* to be candid about any amount they list for lobbying on their 990, it is reasonable to hypothesize that the tiny percentage of public charities that do list lobbying expenditures might exhibit different behavior and a more sophisticated understanding of the law. Consequently, we added this dimension to the sampling framework and moved from two samples to four.

The four samples and their percentage in the population of all public charities filing a tax return are as follows: non-H-electing 501c3s with no listed lobbying expenditures on their 990 (97.1 percent of all public charities); non-H-electing 501c3s with lobbying expenditures (0.5 percent); H-electing 501c3s with no listed lobbying expenditures (2.0 percent); and H-electing 501c3s listing lobbying expenditures (0.4 percent). Owing to the size of these three small cohorts, it was necessary to survey them separately as relatively few nonprofits in these categories would appear in any reasonably sized random sample of the universe of all 501c3s. The sample size of the four cohorts was set to produce a plus/minus 3 percent level of precision with a 95 percent confidence interval.

The organizations surveyed were selected from the 220,622 public charities that filed a tax return with the Internal Revenue Service in 1998. The Urban Institute let us select variables from tax form 990 for inclusion in the data set and then its staff prepared electronic records of each 501c3 tax return with the requested information. The individual nonprofits to be surveyed were then drawn randomly by computer for each of the four samples.

Preliminary analysis of the results of the four survey samples indicated that all three of the small pools of 501c3s were largely similar to one another in their political behavior. As a group the three cohorts were also clearly different from the behavior of the conventional nonprofits. Since the primary purpose of the research was to explore the behavior of conventional nonprofits and to determine if section 501c3 had an impact on their ability and willingness to represent their clients and members before legislatures, the data analysis in the text does not focus on the differences among all four samples. Had that been done, the statistical presentation would have been much more complicated and less reader friendly. Since the three small samples were not dramatically different from one another, choosing only one to serve as a comparison was not a problematic decision. Given our interest in the H election as an alternative to the default substantial standard, those two samples best served our interests. In comparing the two H cohorts, the cohort listing lobbying expenditures would appear to be a more convincing case of self-selection based on the desire to lobby legislatures. Given that their intent appears unambiguous, that was the sample chosen. Again, though, the differences between the two H samples were not great, and scholars with limited resources may not want to spend the additional funds or add the additional complexity by splitting an H elector sample on the basis of the 990 expenditure record.

The H electors' self-selection meant that we could not consider this cohort as a control group. Yet the self-selection was not an obstacle to the research since one of our goals was to build a political profile of those public charities wanting to lobby legislatures and having freed themselves of the substantial restriction. With this in mind differences and similarities could be explored. One of the central findings of this study, detailed in chapter 3, is that the H electors in the area of human services—the largest nonprofit sector—did not look appreciably different than the nonelectors except in their willingness and interest in legislative lobbying.

The consequence of choosing this sampling frame meant that a very large number of organizations had to be surveyed to produce a sufficient "n" for statistical analysis of each of four separate cohorts. In the end 2,738 public charities were sent questionnaires. Since a chronic problem with mail surveys of nonprofits is the low percentage of organizations that fill them out, considerable attention and expense went into trying to gain a respectable rate of return. Poor return rates have undermined confidence in the nonprofit surveys conducted by social scientists. The broader problem is not with researching nonprofits but in making *organizations* the unit of analysis. Political surveys of individuals, like those done around election time, are relatively easy to conduct. All that is needed is randomly generated residential phone numbers. There is no need to know the name of the people who are interviewed.

Organizations are difficult because the survey must be directed at the person most appropriate for filling it out. Presuming the questionnaire gets to the appropriate person's desk, there is the even larger problem of getting that person to fill it out and mail it back. That is no easy task, and these two related problems are the source of low return rates. The person signing a 990 before it is sent on to the IRS can be any officer in the 501c3, and sometimes this person is the comptroller, hardly an appropriate respondent for a survey on the organization's involvement in the public policy process. The 990 requires a listing of the major officers along with trustees, but this information was not in our electronic data file. The earliest a researcher can acquire such a data file is two years after the tax filing date. (It takes time for the IRS to turn the data over to GuideStar; it then takes time for the Urban Institute to receive those data and prepare them for distribution to scholars who approach it.) Because of this substantial time lapse not only may some of the officers listed leave the organization, but its address can change as well. Furthermore, some organizations in the data file will have ceased operations in the interval between the 990 filing and the time researchers launch their survey.

Since the 990s do not include a phone number, just acquiring a number to call to confirm the address and acquire the name of the executive director, was a major undertaking given the combined size of the four samples. Tufts University undergraduates working for the project spent months working with Internet search engines, web-based phone directories, and making phone calls to do what they could to acquire this information. This process was so laborious, time consuming, and expensive, that in the end only 39 percent of the surveys were addressed to a specific person. The rest were addressed to the "executive director."

The process used for the multiple mailings of the questionnaire followed the sequence recommended in Don Dillman's excellent text, *Mail and Internet Surveys.*[2] The initial mailing was followed up a week later with a reminder postcard. Approximately four weeks after the first mailing those who had yet to respond were sent a second copy of the questionnaire. Four weeks after that, those who still had not responded received a third copy of the questionnaire, sent by certified mail to attract attention and make the recalcitrant executive directors feel guilty for not yet filling it out. By itself this was all logistically complex, but since the study used an experimental design question with three alternatives (question 5), every mailing had three different subsamples for each of the four stratified samples. For all intents and purposes this meant that twelve different surveys had to be administered over a period of two months. In addition, a replacement sample was run for bad addresses (surveys returned to us unopened by the post office). Bad addresses were approximately 5 percent of the organizations originally surveyed, and a replacement sample followed the same time line for mailings once it was initiated.

In the end the return rate was 64 percent, exceptionally high for a survey of nonprofits. Each of the many steps taken to enhance the return rate involved various trade-offs and in the more detailed *Surveying Nonprofits* that we have prepared, each of these costs is spelled out.[3] The generosity of the foundations that supported this project allowed us to take the necessary measures to enhance the return rate and thus the reliability of the survey.

One of the trade-offs affecting the return rate is whether a survey asks respondents to only check boxes and circle numbers, or whether it asks them to write out answers. Requiring respondents to write out answers means that the survey will be perceived as taking a lot of time to answer, and this will have a negative effect on the return rate. Since interviews were always part of the research design for this study it was relatively easy to forgo questions that required written answers. If a substantial number of interviews are not coupled with a survey, this could become a much more problematic decision since not all information that the researcher may need can be easily reduced to checked boxes and circled numbers. There were, in fact, a handful of questions in our survey that asked respondents to write in their own number rather than choosing an alternative from a scale. These questions on staffing levels and revenue sources appear to have been easy to answer as there was no significant fall-off in the response rate from the questions with boxes or a scale.

A more difficult question was how to ask about "lobbying." Since a significant percentage of nonprofits like to pretend that their legislative advocacy isn't "lobbying" and isn't "political," the question wording in this area was particularly challenging. The general strategy was to use multiple, overlapping questions to reduce the chances that the findings would be compromised by validity concerns. One approach (Q.6) was to ask about a series of tactics, one of which included the term "lobbying." The other forms of advocacy listed would, implicitly, seem to constitute something other than lobbying, and respondents uncomfortable with that term because of 501c3 would presumably be more comfortable acknowledging utilization of these additional tactics. Another method was to ask about how often government approached the nonprofit (Q.4), thereby removing the onus of responsibility for this interaction from the shoulders of the nonprofits. The experimental design question (Q.5) rotated the terms "lobby," "advocate," and "educate" in an otherwise similarly worded statement. By cross-checking responses from these and other questions, we were confident that our generalized findings were not an artifact of question wording. To further minimize chances that question wording might be misunderstood, an informal advisory board of experts and activists in the nonprofit field was asked to comment on multiple drafts of the questionnaire.

A unique feature of the research design was the integration of each organization's 990 tax return with its survey responses. Although it turned out to be quite difficult to meld the two data sets, for certain kinds of research on nonprofits the effort is well worthwhile. Each 990 contains a huge array of financial data about the organization. For those studying advocacy, however, the value is modest since because of 501c3 the very limited information on lobbying on a 990 is not even close to being an accurate representation of what those organizations do in the political process. What is useful is the NTEE coding, and scholars utilizing the entire universe of returns filed for a given tax year can use a more highly specified level of coding than we were able to.[4] Whatever the imperfections of the NTEE system, designing something better is difficult to do. We tried and were never satisfied that we had come up with something more effective or reliable, especially in light of the space that would have been required on the questionnaire to allow respondents a full array of choices.

Unfortunately, making broad use of the data encompassed in the 990s requires some sophistication in accounting and some knowledge about how the IRS defines certain variables. In the end we relied on the data from the survey and took very little from the tax returns. Scholars focusing on such topics as finance or fund-raising rather than advocacy will surely find the 990s to be of more value.

Two types of interviews were conducted for this study. The first set of approximately forty interviews was intended to complement the survey. At the most basic methodological level, multiple indicators enhance confidence in the validity of findings when the data point in the same direction. Yet the interviews were always seen as much more than a means of confirming or qualifying the findings of the survey. They were a way of learning more about subjects we knowingly left off the survey and subjects we had not thought about. The basic strategy in the interviewing was to ask a limited number of open-ended questions and allow the respondent to answer at length. The interviewers used unscripted probes to ask interviewees to elaborate when questions did not elicit as complete an answer as we would have liked. Even more valuable were the follow-ups when respondents took us down a road we hadn't anticipated but found intriguing.[5] Every effort was made to try to keep the tone conversational rather than make the session feel like questions and answers; the dynamic sought was for the executive director to take on the role of the teacher.

And teach they did. The executive directors we talked to were a goldmine of information. Their lengthy descriptions of their relationships with government were rich in detail and often demonstrated sophistication and insight. Their descriptions of problems they had had with the IRS and state agencies not only confirmed the most important finding of the survey, but also enabled us to understand the depth of the chilling effect of 501c3 in a way we could not have possibly understood from the survey printouts or from the literature on nonprofits in the political process.

These subjects were drawn from those executive directors who sent back their survey and who answered affirmatively to the question or the last page asking if they would be willing to be interviewed. That required them to give us their name and phone number. Each responding organization was then scored on a scale of political advocacy and divided into three categories of high, medium, and low activity. (The scale went across many of the survey questions and was not limited to legislative lobbying.) Samples of each were drawn randomly from the three cohorts. In retrospect we set the bar a little too low for the lowest level of political activity. Interviewing executive directors of nonprofits that had virtually no political activity was much less valuable than talking to the respondents in the other two categories. We were not naïve enough to think that the directors of the low-activity nonprofits would have a lot to say about an activity they didn't engage in, but as the interviews progressed we recognized that we were spending too much time talking with these directors about subjects that were not going to receive much attention in our book. More time was subsequently devoted to interviewing subjects from the other two cohorts. Since there was never any intention to quantify the results of the interviews this was not seen as a problem. Yet the unexpected and striking finding about the frequency of problems that nonprofits involved in public policy matters have with the IRS and state agencies led to a summary calculation that we cite in the text. The appropriate qualifications are included at those points because of the selection bias and sampling issues.

Approximately twenty-five interviews were also conducted with specialists in the field of nonprofits or with current or former government officials. These interviews are hard to categorize in any general way since they had many different purposes. Some were conducted with people who were involved in the policymaking for the H election or currently work for the IRS. Others were done with local government officials to discuss the administration of citizen participation requirements. A handful of these interviews were conducted in person in Washington, D.C., while the rest were done by telephone. All the interviews with the executive directors were done over the phone. Both sets of interviews were conducted on a not-for-attribution basis so that respondents could feel more comfortable talking about sensitive subjects.

The third part of this study's data gathering was a set of seventeen focus groups, held with panels of executive directors or board members. The individual members of each focus group were recruited with the help of a local nonprofit association in that community. Some of these sessions were conducted with panels of individuals who worked in the same policy area. Others were with people affiliated with nonprofits working on behalf of a particular minority group. The focus groups were conducted after the survey and the interviews with executive directors had been completed. This allowed us to ask respondents to react to some of our earliest impressions of the data. The particular value of focus groups is that participants spark one another, and the interaction among them is much different than the interaction between interviewer and interviewee.

The focus groups were videotaped, but because of the expense, not all were transcribed into written text. Participants were required to sign a waiver allowing them to be identified since segments of the videotapes were to be made available for training purposes. How this may have compromised the candor of recipients cannot be determined. The detail that emerged from these sessions enriched the study, but since the focus groups were sequenced last in field research, they were less revealing than the other two sources of data.

Figure A-1.

Facing the Next Century
Strengthening America's Nonprofits.

Thank you for taking the time to help us learn more about the nonprofit world. As noted in our cover letter, your answers will be held in the strictest confidence.

Part I

We start by asking for some basic background on your organization.

1. In what year was the organization founded? _____

2. Is the current executive director or board chair the founder or one of the founders of this organization?
   Executive Director ☐ Yes   Board Chair ☐ Yes
                     ☐ No   ☐ No

3. If your organization has a membership, is that membership comprised of any of the following? (Check all that apply.)
   ☐ Individuals   *Estimate number of individual members_____*
   ☐ Other nonprofits   *Estimate number of all organizations that are members_____*
   ☐ Government agencies
   ☐ Corporations or business trade associations
   ☐ No membership

Part II

We'd like to learn a little about any interaction your organization has with government. By "government" we mean officials at any level (local, state, federal) who work at any government institution (legislative, executive, administrative agency, boards and commissions, judicial, etc.)

4. In some cases contact with those in government comes about at the initiative of the policymakers themselves. How often on average would you say that people in government approach the executive director, staff, or members of the board to discuss matters of mutual interest?

     ☐ Never   ☐ Two, three times a month
     ☐ Once a month or less   ☐ Four or more times a month

5. For some nonprofits, there is a need to advocate new policies before those in government so that policymakers will have a better understanding of the problems facing the community. How often does your organization undertake an effort to advocate with government officials at any level?

     ☐ Never   ☐ Two, three times a month
     ☐ Once a month or less   ☐ Four or more times a month

Figure A-1. (continued)

6. A variety of means of communicating and interacting with those in government are listed below. Please use the scale on the right to indicate how frequently, if at all, your organization engages in these activities. (By "your organization" we mean the executive director, other staff, volunteers, or members of the board.) In this scale, "0" means never, "1" is relatively infrequent interaction, and "4" is ongoing interaction.

	Frequency				
	Never	*Low*			*High*
Testifying at legislative or administrative hearings	0	1	2	3	4
Lobbying on behalf of or against a proposed bill or other policy pronouncement	0	1	2	3	4
Responding to requests for information from those in government	0	1	2	3	4
Working in a planning or advisory group that includes government officials	0	1	2	3	4
Meeting with government officials about the work we are doing	0	1	2	3	4
Encouraging members to write, call, fax or email policymakers	0	1	2	3	4
Releasing research reports to the media, public or policymakers	0	1	2	3	4
Discussing obtaining grants or contracts with government officials	0	1	2	3	4
Interacting socially with government officials	0	1	2	3	4

7. Thinking generally about those in government that your organization deals with, please select the description below that typically describes those officials' attitudes.

   ❑ Not really interested in hearing our views
   ❑ Sometimes interested in what we have to say
   ❑ Usually interested in what we have to say
   ❑ Interested in what we have to say and interested in actively working with us to achieve a common goal

8. There is a good deal of confusion about whether various activities by nonprofits relating to the policymaking process are permissible. Based on your understanding, can your organization:

Support or oppose federal legislation under current IRS regulations	❑Yes ❑ No
Take a policy position without reference to a specific bill under current regulations	❑Yes ❑ No
Support or oppose federal regulations	❑Yes ❑ No
Lobby if part of your budget comes from federal funds	❑Yes ❑ No
Use government funds to lobby Congress	❑Yes ❑ No
Endorse a candidate for elected office	❑Yes ❑ No
Talk to elected public officials about public policy matters	❑Yes ❑ No
Sponsor a forum or candidate debate for elected office	❑Yes ❑ No

9. Does your organization consult experts about the legality of any efforts you make to influence government? Check all that apply.

❑ Attorney	❑ Accountant
❑ Experts at other nonprofits	❑ Never make any effort to influence government
❑ None	❑ Other_____

Part III

These questions are about your organization's capacity.

10. How many full-time equivalent staff members does your organization employ?
___ Professionals   ___ Clerical/support staff   ___ Volunteers   ___Other

11. Does your organization have one or more persons who have responsibility for government relations or public policy?   *If "yes" please check all that apply.*
   ❑ No   ❑ Yes➔   ❑ Executive Director
                           ❑ Staff Member
                           ❑ Volunteer
                           ❑ Board Member
                           ❑ Board Committee
                           ❑ Lobbyist or other outside professional on retainer

12. What are the sources of your organization's annual income? *Rough estimates are perfectly fine—you don't need to consult your organization's records for a precise answer.*
   Percent
   ___% Individual donors or membership dues
   ___% Government (any level)
   ___% Foundations
   ___% Corporate Contributions
   ___% Income from services provided to clients or others
   ___% Fundraising Events
   ___% Other _____
   100% Total

13. Is your organization a dues-paying member of one or more associations that represent you before government?
   ❑ Yes   ❑No   ❑ Don't Know
   If yes (check all that apply): ❑ Local Associations   ❑ State   ❑ National

14. (If you answered "no" to the previous question, skip to #15). How often do these associations contact you and urge you to contact policymakers about pending matters of importance? And how often do you respond to these requests?

We're contacted by Associations:	*We act upon these requests:*
❑ Never	❑ Never
❑ Once a month or less	❑ Once a month or less
❑ Two or three times a month	❑ Two or three times a month
❑ Four times a month or more	❑ Four times a month or more

Figure A-1. (continued)

15. In the previous section we asked you about your direct involvement in the public policymaking process. Now we would like to know about factors that you feel are barriers to your organization's involvement in the policymaking process and how significant those barriers are. In the scale below, 0 represents no barrier, 1 a low barrier, and 4 represents a major barrier.

	Size of Barrier				
	No Barrier	Low			Major
Tax law or IRS regulations	0	1	2	3	4
Organization receives government funds	0	1	2	3	4
Organization receives foundation funds	0	1	2	3	4
Staff (or volunteer) skills	0	1	2	3	4
Organization's limited financial resources	0	1	2	3	4
Advice from attorneys or accountants	0	1	2	3	4
Your board or staff's attitude toward involvement in the policymaking process	0	1	2	3	4
The public's attitude toward involvement in the policymaking process	0	1	2	3	4
Other_____	0	1	2	3	4

16. Turning from barriers to inducements, what factors motivate your organization to become involved in the public policymaking process?

	Significance of Motivating Factors				
	No Influence	Low			High
Opportunities to obtain government funding	0	1	2	3	4
Protecting government programs that serve our clients, constituents or community	0	1	2	3	4
Promoting government policies that support our mission	0	1	2	3	4
Raising public awareness of important issues	0	1	2	3	4
Defending nonprofits' advocacy rights	0	1	2	3	4
Other_____	0	1	2	3	4

17. How would you describe the capacity of your organization to conduct and disseminate research?

	Capacity				
	None	Low			High
Conduct issue research	0	1	2	3	4
Disseminate research	0	1	2	3	4

18. Do you use any of these communications tools? Do you use them in your involvement in the public policymaking process?

	Use?	Used in policymaking process?
Email	❑ Yes ❑ No	❑ Yes ❑ No
World Wide Web	❑ Yes ❑ No	❑ Yes ❑ No
Fax	❑ Yes ❑ No	❑ Yes ❑ No
Video conferencing	❑ Yes ❑ No	❑ Yes ❑ No
Telephone conferencing	❑ Yes ❑ No	❑ Yes ❑ No
Internet video phone	❑ Yes ❑ No	❑ Yes ❑ No

19. In thinking about the major decisions your organization makes *concerning government relations,* how would you estimate the relative influence of the following participants?

	Influence	None	Low			High
Executive Director		0	1	2	3	4
Chair of the Board of Directors		0	1	2	3	4
Board of Directors or Board Committee		0	1	2	3	4
Professional staff		0	1	2	3	4
Important donors and funders		0	1	2	3	4
Other_____		0	1	2	3	4

20. In thinking about the major decisions your organization makes *concerning program strategy or implementation,* how would you estimate the relative influence of the following participants?

	Influence	None	Low			High
Executive Director		0	1	2	3	4
Chair of the Board of Directors		0	1	2	3	4
Board of Directors or Board Committee		0	1	2	3	4
Professional staff		0	1	2	3	4
Important donors and funders		0	1	2	3	4
Other_____		0	1	2	3	4

21. What is your title?

❑ Executive Director/President   ❑ Staff (specify position)_____
❑ Board Member   ❑ Other_____
❑ Volunteer (other than Board)

Thank you for taking the time to help us. To further our understanding of nonprofits we will be interviewing some of the people who filled out this questionnaire. If you would be willing to be interviewed, please give us the following information:

*Name of person filling out the questionnaire*_____

*Organization*_____

*Phone Number*_____

**Please mail back the completed survey in the supplied Business Reply Envelope or mail to:
Professor Jeffrey Berry, Department of Political Science, Tufts University, 175 Packard Ave, Medford, MA 02155**

Notes

Chapter 1

1. Murray S. Weitzman, Nadine T. Jalandoni, Linda M. Lampkin, and Thomas H. Pollak, *The New Nonprofit Almanac and Desk Reference* (Jossey-Bass, 2002), p. 69.

2. Stephanie Strom, "Charitable Contributions in 2001 Reached $212 Billion," *New York Times*, June 21, 2002, p. A19.

3. Weitzman and others, *The New Nonprofit Almanac and Desk Reference*, pp. 52–89.

4. Robert D. Putnam, *Bowling Alone* (Simon and Schuster, 2000); Theda Skocpol and Morris P. Fiorina, eds., *Civic Engagement in American Democracy* (Brookings, 1999); Bob Edwards, Michael W. Foley, and Mario Diani, eds., *Beyond Tocqueville* (Tufts/University Press of New England, 2001); and Theda Skocpol, *Diminished Democracy* (University of Oklahoma Press, 2003).

5. Lester M. Salamon, *Partners in Public Service* (Johns Hopkins University Press, 1995); and Steven Rathgeb Smith and Michael Lipsky, *Nonprofits for Hire* (Harvard University Press, 1993).

6. See www.youthranch.org.

7. The 501c3 nonprofits are also restricted from engaging in partisan political activity. As argued in chapter 7, such restrictions are justifiable. Public charities can engage in nonpartisan electoral activities such as voter registration and sponsoring candidate debates. It is the lobbying restrictions that are problematic, and thus attention here is focused only on these limitations.

8. To be more specific, they are half of all tax-deductible nonprofits large enough to file a tax return. The universe of tax-filing nonprofits is discussed more fully in the appendix.

9. See Peter Frumkin, *On Being Nonprofit: A Conceptual and Policy Primer* (Harvard University Press, 2002).

10. In addition, the nonprofit can not be a sham: a for-profit company hiding behind an ostensible public-spirited organization.

11. An excellent, nontechnical introduction to nonprofits and the sometimes bewildering nomenclature used to classify these organizations is Lester M. Salamon, *America's Nonprofit Sector: A Primer*, 2d ed. (New York: Foundation Center, 1999). For a broader and more thorough overview of the field, see Lester M. Salamon, ed., *The State of Nonprofit America* (Brookings, 2002).

12. There are another ten types of organizations that are tax exempt under other sections of the IRS code. A complete listing can be found at http://www.irs.gov/tax-stats/article/0,,id=97186,00.html.

13. Since we sometimes refer to those nonprofits that qualify as public charities as "501c3s," for consistency's sake we will also use the more informal notation of 501c3 rather than 501(c)(3) when referring to the tax code.

14. See generally, Burton Weisbrod, "Toward a Theory of the Voluntary Non-Profit Sector in a Three-Sector Economy," in Edmund S. Phelps, ed., *Altruism, Morality, and Economic Theory* (Russell Sage, 1974), pp. 171–95; Avner Ben-Ner, "Nonprofit Organizations: Why Do They Exist in Market Economies?" in Susan Rose-Ackerman, ed., *The Economics of Nonprofit Institutions* (Oxford University Press, 1986), pp. 94–113; and Henry Hansmann, "Economic Theories of Nonprofit Organization," in Walter W. Powell, ed., *The Nonprofit Sector* (Yale University Press, 1987), pp. 27–42.

15. Ryan White, an Indiana teenager, died of AIDS in 1990 contracted from blood transfusions. As an early victim of the disease, he was initially treated with hatred and discrimination in his hometown.

16. Frank R. Baumgartner and Bryan D. Jones, *Agendas and Instability in American Politics* (University of Chicago Press, 1993); Jeffrey M. Berry, *The New Liberalism* (Brookings, 1999); and Frank R. Baumgartner and Beth L. Leech, "Issue Niches and Policy Bandwagons: Patterns of Interest Group Involvement in National Politics," *Journal of Politics*, vol. 63 (November 2001), pp. 1191–213.

17. Weitzman and others, *The New Nonprofit Almanac and Desk Reference*, pp. 8,12.

18. Ibid., p. 91.

19. Joel L. Fleishman, "Public Trust in Not-for-Profit Organizations and the Need for Regulatory Reform," in Charles T. Clotfelter and Thomas Ehrlich, eds., *Philanthropy and the Nonprofit Sector in a Changing America* (Indiana University Press, 1999), p. 174.

20. Again health care nonprofits are excluded. Weitzman and others, *The New Nonprofit Almanac and Desk Reference*, p. 94.

21. Salamon, *America's Nonprofit Sector*, p. 69.

22. Lester M. Salamon, "The Resilient Sector: The State of Nonprofit America," in Salamon, *The State of Nonprofit America*, p. 30.

23. Charles Gilbert, "Policy-Making in Public Welfare: The 1962 Amendments," *Political Science Quarterly*, vol. 81 (June 1966), pp. 196–224.

24. *Public Welfare Amendments of 1962*, hearings before the Committee on Ways and Means, House of Representatives, 87 Cong. 2 sess. (1962), p. 165.

25. Ibid., p. 166.

26. Kirsten A. Grønbjerg and Steven Rathgeb Smith, "Nonprofit Organizations and Public Policies in the Delivery of Human Services," in Clotfelter and Ehrlich, eds., *Philanthropy and the Nonprofit Sector in a Changing America*, p. 146.

27. Martha Derthick, *Uncontrollable Spending for Social Service Grants* (Brookings, 1975), p. 9.

28. Gilbert Y. Steiner, *The State of Welfare* (Brookings, 1971), p. 37.

29. See Daniel Patrick Moynihan, *The Politics of a Guaranteed Income* (Vintage, 1973).

30. See Anne Schneider and Helen Ingram, "Social Construction of Target Populations," *American Political Science Review,* vol. 87 (June 1993), pp. 334–47.

31. Nicholas Lemann, "The Unfinished War," part 2, *Atlantic Monthly,* January 1989, p. 58.

32. Steiner, *The State of Welfare,* p. 32.

33. Derthick, *Uncontrollable Spending for Social Service Grants,* p. 8.

34. Ibid., pp. 7–14, 72.

35. Steiner, *The State of Welfare,* pp. 36–40.

36. Derthick, *Uncontrollable Spending for Social Service Grants,* pp. 17–19.

37. Smith and Lipsky, *Nonprofits for Hire,* p. 55.

38. Ibid., pp. 55–56.

39. Lisbeth B. Schorr, with Daniel Schorr, *Within Our Reach* (Anchor, 1988), p. 256 (emphasis in the original).

40. The definitive work is R. Kent Weaver, *Ending Welfare as We Know It* (Brookings, 2000).

41. Grønbjerg and Smith, "Nonprofit Organizations and Public Policies in the Delivery of Human Services," pp. 142–43.

42. Steven Rathgeb Smith, "The New Politics of Contracting: Citizenship and the Nonprofit Role," in Helen Ingram and Steven Rathgeb Smith, eds., *Public Policy for Democracy* (Brookings, 1993), pp. 198–221.

43. Pressure has grown on nonprofits, too, to become more businesslike. See Paul C. Light, *Pathways to Nonprofit Excellence* (Brookings, 2002).

44. Philip K. Howard, *The Death of Common Sense* (Warner Books, 1994), p. 172.

45. Michael J. Rich, *Federal Policymaking and the Poor* (Princeton University Press, 1993), p. 29.

46. Richard P. Nathan, Allen D. Manvel, Susannah Calkins, and associates, *Monitoring Revenue Sharing* (Brookings, 1975), pp. 14–18.

47. Rich, *Federal Policymaking and the Poor,* pp. 29–34. There was some preliminary movement toward block grants in the Johnson administration as well. See Richard P. Nathan with the assistance of Elizabeth I. Davis, Mark J. McGrath, and William C. O'Heaney, "The 'Nonprofitization Movement' as a Form of Devolution," in Dwight F. Burlingame, William A. Diaz, Warren F. Ilchman, and associates, *Capacity for Change? The Nonprofit World in the Age of Devolution* (Indiana University Center on Philanthropy, 1996), p. 31.

48. Nathan and others, "The 'Nonprofitization Movement' as a Form of Devolution," p. 34.

49. Harrison Donnelly, "Reagan Changes Focus with Federalism Plan," *Congressional Quarterly Weekly Report*, January 30, 1982, p. 148.

50. Ross Evans, "State, Local Officials Assess Void Left by Budget Cuts; Ask Program Swap, Tax Turnback," *Congressional Quarterly Weekly Report*, October 24, 1981, p. 2047.

51. David R. Beam, "New Federalism, Old Realities: The Reagan Administration and Intergovernmental Reform," in Lester M. Salamon and Michael S. Lund, eds., *The Reagan Presidency and the Governing of America* (Washington, D.C.: Urban Institute, 1984), p. 424.

52. Lester M. Salamon, "The Nonprofit Sector and the Evolution of the American Welfare State," in Robert D. Herman, ed., *The Jossey-Bass Handbook of Nonprofit Leadership and Management* (Jossey-Bass, 1994), p. 87; and Beam, "New Federalism, Old Realities," pp. 422–27.

53. Nathan and others, "The 'Nonprofitization Movement' as a Form of Devolution," p. 34.

54. Much to the consternation of those in the nonprofit community, Reagan's tax cuts reduced the tax incentive for charitable gifts for itemizers because his plan lowered the marginal income tax rates. See Burton Weisbrod, *The Nonprofit Economy* (Harvard University Press, 1988), p. 88.

55. See Donald F. Kettl, *Sharing Power* (Brookings, 1993).

56. Paul C. Light, *The True Size of Government* (Brookings, 1999), p. 1.

57. Ibid., pp. 177–78, 198–99.

58. See E. S. Savas, *Privatization and Public-Private Partnerships* (Chatham House, 2000).

59 See Edward Skloot, "Privatization, Competition and the Future of Human Services," www.surdna.org/speeches/private.html.

60. Lester M. Salamon and Alan J. Abramson, *The Federal Budget and the Nonprofit Sector* (Washington, D.C.: Urban Institute, 1982), pp. 1–2.

61. David Osborne and Ted Gaebler, *Reinventing Government* (New York: Plume Books, 1993), p. 109.

62. Margaret Gibelman and Harold W. Demone Jr., "The Evolving Contract State," in Harold W. Demone Jr., and Margaret Gibelman, eds., *Services for Sale* (Rutgers University Press, 1989), pp. 17–57.

63. As noted earlier, all interviews were done on a not-for-attribution basis, and interviewees are usually identified as a "health care executive," "housing leader," or by some similarly general label. When we use extended examples that draw on our sources, such as with the "Front Street Health Center," a pseudonym has been used for the organization. The quotation marks will always make this evident.

64. See Martha Derthick and Paul J. Quirk, *The Politics of Deregulation* (Brookings, 1985).

65. Nonprofit leaders (as well as academics) have been more searching in their questions about the capacity of nonprofits. See, for example, Brian O'Connell, "A Major Transfer of Government Responsibility to Voluntary Organizations? Proceed with Caution," *Public Administration Review*, vol. 56 (May–June 1996), pp. 222–25.

66. Smith and Lipsky, *Nonprofits for Hire*.

Chapter 2

1. Paul C. Light, *Making Nonprofits Work* (Aspen Institute and Brookings, 2000), pp. 6-43.

2. Among the important works that have been done on the involvement of nonprofits in public policymaking are Elizabeth T. Boris and Eugene Steuerle, eds., *Nonprofits and Government* (Washington, D.C.: Urban Institute, 1999); Elizabeth J. Reid and Maria D. Montilla, eds., *Exploring Organizations and Advocacy* (Washington, D.C.: Urban Institute, 2001); Deborah C. Minkoff, "Organizational Barriers to Advocacy," paper presented to the Nonprofit Sector Strategy Group, Aspen Institute, Wye River, Maryland, November 1998; Carol J. De Vita and Rachel Mosher-Williams, eds., *Who Speaks for America's Children?* (Washington, D.C.: Urban Institute, 2001); Susan Rees, *Effective Nonprofit Advocacy* (Washington, D.C.: Aspen Institute, 1998); and Elizabeth T. Boris and Jeff Krehely, "Civic Participation and Advocacy," in Lester M. Salamon, ed., *The State of Nonprofit America* (Brookings, 2002), pp. 299-330.

3. Lester M. Salamon, *Partners in Public Service: Government-Nonprofit Relations in the Modern Welfare State* (Johns Hopkins University Press, 1995); Steven Rathgeb Smith and Michael Lipsky, *Nonprofits for Hire* (Harvard University Press, 1993); Lester M. Salamon and Alan J. Abramson, *The Federal Budget and the Nonprofit Sector* (Washington, D.C.: Urban Institute, 1982); Carol J. De Vita, "Nonprofits and Devolution: What Do We Know?" in Boris and Steuerle, *Nonprofits and Government*, pp. 213-35; and Steven Rathgeb Smith, "Social Services," in Salamon, *The State of Nonprofit America*, pp. 149-86.

4. Robert D. Putnam, *Bowling Alone* (Simon and Schuster, 2000); Gerald Gamm and Robert D. Putnam, "The Growth of Voluntary Associations in America, 1840-1940," *Journal of Interdisciplinary History* 29 (Spring 1999), pp. 511-57; Bob Edwards, Michael W. Foley, and Mario Diani, eds., *Beyond Tocqueville: Civil Society and the Social Capital Debate in Comparative Perspective* (Tufts/University Press of New England, 2001); Theda Skocpol and Morris P. Fiorina, eds., *Civic Engagement in American Democracy* (Brookings, 1999); Theda Skocpol, Marshall Ganz, and Ziad Munson, "A Nation of Organizers: The Institutional Origins of Civic Voluntarism in the United States," *American Political Science Review*, vol. 94 (September 2000), pp. 527-46; and Theda Skocpol, *Diminished Democracy* (University of Oklahoma Press, 2003).

5. As explained at the end of this chapter, the survey excludes those nonprofits too small to file a tax return so this figure may not be generalized to all 501c3s. Thirteen percent of the sample have other nonprofits as members.

6. Putnam, *Bowling Alone*, pp. 18-24.

7. See, for example, Jack L. Walker Jr., *Mobilizing Interest Groups in America* (University of Michigan Press, 1991).

8. On institutions as lobbies, see Robert H. Salisbury, "Interest Representation: The Dominance of Institutions," *American Political Science Review*, vol. 78 (March 1984), pp. 64-76.

9. Jeffrey M. Berry, *Lobbying for the People* (Princeton University Press, 1977); Robert Holbert, *Tax Law and Political Access* (Sage, 1975); and Beth L. Leech,

"Federal Funding and Interest Group Lobbying Behavior," paper delivered at the annual meeting of the American Political Science Association, September 1998.

10. See Debra C. Minkoff, "The Emergence of Hybrid Organizational Forms," *Nonprofit and Voluntary Sector Quarterly*, vol. 31 (September 2002), pp. 377–401.

11. Jeffrey M. Berry, *The New Liberalism* (Brookings, 1999); David Vogel, *Trading Up* (Harvard University Press, 1995); Andrew McFarland, *Common Cause* (Chatham House, 1984); Walker, *Mobilizing Interest Groups in America*; Lawrence S. Rothenberg, *Linking Citizens to Government* (Cambridge University Press, 1992); and Ronald G. Shaiko, *Voices and Echoes for the Environment* (Columbia University Press, 1999).

12. Murray S. Weitzman, Nadine T. Jalandoni, Linda M. Lampkin, and Thomas H. Pollak, *The New Nonprofit Almanac and Desk Reference* (Jossey-Bass, 2002), pp. 4–5.

13. The state of the subfield is critically evaluated by Frank R. Baumgartner and Beth L. Leech, *Basic Interests* (Princeton University Press, 1998).

14. Kay Lehman Schlozman and John T. Tierney, *Organized Interests and American Democracy* (Harper and Row, 1986), p. 77.

15. Berry, *The New Liberalism*, p. 20.

16. Hanna Fenichel Pitkin, *The Concept of Representation* (University of California Press, 1972), p. 116.

17. Robert A. Dahl, *Who Governs?* (Yale University Press, 1961), p. 311.

18. Peter Bachrach and Morton S. Baratz, "Two Faces of Power," *American Political Science Review*, vol. 56 (December 1962), pp. 947–52.

19. "Federalist #10," *The Federalist Papers* (New York: New American Library, 1961), pp. 77–84; Alexis de Tocqueville, *Democracy in America*, ed. J. P. Mayer, trans. George Lawrence (Doubleday, 1969).

20. See, for example, C. Wright Mills, *The Power Elite* (Oxford University Press, 1956); G. William Domhoff, *The Powers That Be* (Vintage, 1979); and Michael Useem, *The Inner Circle* (Oxford University Press, 1984).

21. Mancur Olson Jr., *The Logic of Collective Action* (Schocken, 1968).

22. Ibid., pp. 165–66.

23. Sidney Tarrow, *Power in Movement*, 2d ed. (Cambridge University Press, 1998).

24. Doug McAdam, *Political Process and the Development of Black Insurgency, 1930-1970* (University of Chicago Press, 1982).

25. See, for example, Virginia Gray and David Lowery, *The Population Ecology of Interest Representation* (University of Michigan Press, 1996). They link the population size of any interest group sector to the amount of available resources.

26. The registration requirements for nonprofits lobbying Congress are spelled out in Bob Smucker, *The Nonprofit Lobbying Guide*, 2d ed. (Washington: Independent Sector, 1999).

27. Andrew C. Revkin, "Law Revises Standards for Scientific Study," *New York Times*, March 21, 2002, p. A24.

28. Richard B. Freeman and James L. Medoff, *What Do Unions Do?* (Basic Books, 1984), pp. 221–45.

29. See Ian Brodie, *Friends of the Court* (State University of New York Press, 2002).

30. *Association of Data Processing Service Organizations v. Camp*, 397 U.S. 150 (1970).

31. Steven J. Balla and John R. Wright, "Interest Groups, Advisory Committees, and Congressional Control of the Bureaucracy," *American Journal of Political Science*, vol. 45 (October 2001), p. 802.

32. Ibid.

33. Jeffrey M. Berry, "Citizen Groups and the Changing Nature of Interest Group Politics," *Annals of the American Academy of Political and Social Science* 528 (July 1993), pp. 38–39.

34. David B. Truman, *The Governmental Process* (Knopf, 1971), pp. 90–91.

35. Federal Trade Commission, "Rulemaking under the Magnuson-Moss Warranty-Federal Trade Commission Improvement Act," Washington, 1979.

36. James T. Bennett and Thomas DiLorenzo, *Destroying Democracy* (Washington: Cato Institute, 1985), pp. 407, 448, 453.

37. Derek Willis, "Critics Say Political Groups Formed to Evade New Fundraising Rules," *CQ Weekly*, November 30, 2002, pp. 3112–13.

38. As chapter 5 discusses, there are some states that regulate nonprofits' lobbying of administrative agencies as well.

39. More extensive discussion of methods can be found in the appendix. Specialists in the field are encouraged to consult *Surveying Nonprofits*, written by the authors and others associated with this project. The book uses this survey as an example, offering readers a detailed step-by-step set of instructions for conducting a mail survey of nonprofits. See Jeffrey M. Berry, David F. Arons, Gary D. Bass, Matthew F. Carter, and Kent E. Portney, *Surveying Nonprofits: A Methods Handbook* (Washington, D.C.: Aspen Institute, 2003).

40. Some registered nonprofits whose income falls below $25,000 choose to file tax returns. They are just a tiny proportion of 990 filers, and there are very few in the sample.

41. A statewide census of all nonprofits, registered and not, is described in Kirsten A. Grønbjerg and Laurie Paarlberg, "Extent and Nature of Overlap between Listings of IRS Tax-Exempt Registration and Nonprofit Incorporation: The Case of Indiana," *Nonprofit and Voluntary Sector Quarterly*, vol. 31 (December 2002), pp. 565–94.

42. Putnam, *Bowling Alone*.

43. For background on the utility of the 990 to researchers, see Elizabeth Boris and Rachel Mosher-Williams, "Nonprofit Advocacy Organizations: Assessing the Definitions, Classifications, and Data," *Nonprofit and Voluntary Sector Quarterly*, vol. 27 (December 1998), pp. 488–506; Karen A. Froelich and Terry W. Knoepfle, "Internal Revenue Service 990 Data: Fact or Fiction?" *Nonprofit and Voluntary Sector Quarterly*, vol. 25 (March 1996), pp. 40–52; Karen A. Froelich, "The 990 Return: Beyond the Internal Revenue Service," *Nonprofit Management and Leadership*, vol. 8 (Winter 1997), pp. 141–155; and Jeff Krehely, "Assessing the Current Data on 501(c)(3) Advocacy: What IRS Form 990

Can Tell Us," in Reid and Montilla, *Exploring Organizations and Advocacy*, pp. 37–50.

44. The public may view the 990 of specific nonprofits they are interested in at www.guidestar.org or www.nccs.urban.org/990/.

45. Another question (#5) used an experimental design and one-third of those surveyed received a questionnaire that used the term. The other versions substituted "educate" and "advocate."

Chapter 3

1. William P. Browne, *Groups, Interests, and U.S. Public Policy* (Georgetown University Press, 1998), p. 81.

2. Anthony J. Nownes, *Pressure and Power* (Houghton Mifflin, 2001), p. 8.

3. Jeffrey M. Berry, *The Interest Group Society*, 3d ed. (Longman, 1997), p. 6.

4. Kay Lehman Schlozman and John T. Tierney, *Organized Interests and American Democracy* (Harper and Row, 1986), pp. 150–51.

5. John R. Hibbing and Elizabeth Theiss-Morse, *Congress as Public Enemy* (Cambridge University Press, 1995), p. 63.

6. Alan Rosenthal, *The Third House* (Washington, D.C.: CQ Press, 1993), p. 7.

7. U.S. Code, Title 26, sec. 501.

8. See Henry Hansmann, "Economic Theories of Nonprofit Organization," in Walter W. Powell, ed., *The Nonprofit Sector* (Yale University Press, 1987), pp. 28–29; and Evelyn Brody, "Charities in Tax Reform: Threats to Subsidies Overt and Covert," *Tennessee Law Review*, vol. 66 (Spring 1999), pp. 687–763.

9. Evelyn Brody and Joseph J. Cordes, "Tax Treatment of Nonprofit Organizations: A Two-Edged Sword?" in Elizabeth T. Boris and C. Eugene Steuerle, eds., *Nonprofits and Government: Collaboration and Conflict* (Washington, D.C.: Urban Institute, 1999), p. 141.

10. *Bob Jones University* v. *United States*, 461 U.S. 574 (1983).

11. John G. Simon, "The Tax Treatment of Nonprofit Organizations: A Review of Federal and State Policies," in Powell, *The Nonprofit Sector*, p. 79.

12. *Regan* v. *Taxation with Representation of Washington*, 461 U.S. 540 (1983). Further support for this position came in *Rust* v. *Sullivan*, 500 U.S. 173 (1991). See also Miriam Galston, "Lobbying and the Public Interest: Rethinking the Internal Revenue Code's Treatment of Legislative Activities," *Texas Law Review*, vol. 71, no. 6 (1993), pp. 1269–354.

13. For the IRS view of this history, see Judith E. Kindell and John Francis Reilly, "Lobbying Issues" (www.irs.gov/pub/irs-tege/topic-p.pdf).

14. Janne G. Gallagher, "Charities, Lobbying, and Political Activity," background paper prepared for the Nonprofit Sector Strategy Group, Aspen Institute, October 19, 1998, p. 1.

15. *Slee* v. *Commissioner*, 42 F.2d 184 (2d Cir. 1930).

16. Ibid.

17. *Revenue Act of 1934*, sec. 517, 48 Stat. 760; and Kindell and Reilly, "Lobbying Issues," pp. 264–67.

18. On an accompanying revocation of tax-exempt status, see James J. Fishman and Steven Schwarz, *Nonprofit Organizations: Cases and Materials* (Westbury, Conn.: Foundation Press, 1995), p. 515.

19. *Christian Echoes National Ministry, Inc.* v. *United States*, 470 F. 2d 849 (10th cir. 1972).

20. Jeanne Cummings and Jacob M. Schlesinger, "Christian Coalition's Robertson Vows to Press Forward despite IRS Setback," *Wall Street Journal*, June 11, 1999, p. A20.

21. For a thorough, legally precise explanation of all the exemptions to 501c3, see Bruce R. Hopkins, *Charity, Advocacy, and the Law* (John Wiley, 1992). For an excellent short, nontechnical primer on what is allowed under the law, see Bob Smucker, *The Nonprofit Lobbying Guide*, 2d ed. (Washington: Independent Sector, 1999), pp. 51–77.

22. As chapter 5 discusses, some states define advocacy on rulemaking as lobbying. This is not a prohibition, just guidelines for purposes of determining who must register under state law.

23. Frederick Andrews, "Tax Reform Act to Make Dec. 31 Landmark Date," *New York Times*, December 29, 1976, p. 1.

24. "House Unit Votes Bill on Lobbying Outlays by Charitable Groups," *Wall Street Journal*, May 27, 1976, p. 5.

25. P.L. 94-455, sec. 4911.

26. Smucker, *The Nonprofit Lobbying Guide*, p. 55.

27. Some of the exceptions were already allowed in practice under 501c3, but additional confusion arises as to how all the 501h exceptions apply to 501c3s. See Thomas Raffa, "Advocacy and Lobbying without Fear: What Is Allowed within a 501(c)(3) Charitable Organization," *Nonprofit Quarterly*, vol. 7 (December 2000), p. 46. Eight exclusions as to what constitutes lobbying under the H election are spelled out in Smucker, *The Nonprofit Lobbying Guide*, pp. 53–54.

28. *New IRS Rules: The End of Nonprofit Advocacy* (Washington: OMB Watch, 1987).

29. William Montague, "IRS's New Proposed Regulations on Lobbying Show Improvement, Charity Officials Say," *Chronicle of Philanthropy*, January 10, 1989, p. 1.

30. Raffa, "Advocacy and Lobbying without Fear," pp. 44–47.

31. Smucker, *The Nonprofit Lobbying Guide*, p. 64.

32. For an alternative approach see *Advocacy & Lobbying by NYS Nonprofits: An Investigation of the Need for Education and Reform*, report submitted to the Nonprofit Sector Research Fund, Aspen Institute, January 15, 1998.

33. Another half percent are nonelecting 501c3s listing lobbying expenditures on their 990 and the remaining 2 percent are H electors listing no lobbying expenditures on their 990. For shorthand purposes, when the text refers to H electors, it is referring only to our sample of H electors that list lobbying expenditures. See the appendix for additional discussion of the four survey samples.

34. The question asked for the aggregate support from all levels of government.

35. A related question, whether increasing levels of government funding are neg-

atively correlated with advocacy because of concerns about political retribution, is taken up in chapter 4.

36. The analysis here utilizes the NTEE's Major Categories (level three). Using an NTEE level with anything more discrete or expansive is difficult to do with our sample size. See "Guide to the NTEE Classification System: The National Taxonomy of Exempt Entities," National Center for Charitable Statistics, Urban Institute, n.d. See also Virginia Ann Hodgkinson and others, *Nonprofit Almanac* (Jossey-Bass, 1996), pp. 271–309.

37. The NTEE category includes a broad range of other kinds of health organizations, such as mental health centers, community health centers, and senior medical facilities.

38. The aggregate figures for those from conventional nonprofits who said they advocated/lobbied/educated "two, three times a month" or "four or more times a month" were 19.5 percent, 9.8 percent, and 24.3 percent; significant at .000.

39. For an analysis of the impact of 501c3 on the lobbying of nonprofits in comparison to business groups and other private sector lobbies, see Beth L. Leech, "Federal Funding and Interest Group Lobbying Behavior," paper delivered at the annual meeting of the American Political Science Association, 1998.

40. Chapter 5 offers additional evidence refuting the idea that the conventional nonprofits lobby less because they have less need to.

Chapter 4

1. The average is for five items: "Responding to requests," "Working in a planning group," "Meeting with government officials," "Discussing grants," and "Interacting socially." See table 5-2 in chapter 5 and the accompanying text for further discussion of more aggressive and less aggressive tactics. See, as well, *Advocacy & Lobbying by NYS Nonprofits: An Investigation of the Need for Education and Reform*, report submitted to the Nonprofit Sector Research Fund, Aspen Institute, January 15, 1998.

2. Years ago some accountants told their nonprofit clients that 5 percent was acceptable to the IRS because a 1955 court decision indicated that 5 percent didn't violate the substantial rule. Court decisions in the early 1970s ruled that a percentage test was an unacceptable way for determining compliance with the substantial restriction. See Bob Smucker, *The Nonprofit Lobbying Guide*, 2d ed. (Washington, D.C.: Independent Sector, 1999), p. 63.

3. Technically, it is not a percentage of the entire budget but of "exempt purposes expenditures." This base figure is the entire budget minus investment management expenses for consultants who spend a majority of their time fund-raising, unrelated business income, and expenses related to making capital improvements to raise the value of property. See David Arons, "Lobbying, Advocacy and Nonprofit Management," in Victor Futter, ed., *Nonprofit Governance and Management* (Chicago: American Bar Association and the American Society of Corporate Secretaries, 2002), p. 375.

4. Under the substantial test the rules are generally vague as to what lobby preparatory activities are considered "lobbying" under the law.

5. "Choosing Accounting Software," *Nonprofit Quarterly*, vol. 8 (April 2001), pp. 34–41.

6. As a matter of clarity, the interviewee's use of the terms "hard" and "soft" money was not an allusion to campaign finance but to nondeductible and deductible contributions by individuals.

7. *Regan v. Taxation with Representation of Washington*, 461 U.S. 540 (1983).

8. Evelyn Brody and Joseph J. Cordes, "Tax Treatment of Nonprofit Organizations: A Two-Edged Sword?" in Elizabeth T. Boris and C. Eugene Steuerle, eds., *Nonprofits and Government: Collaboration and Conflict* (Washington, D.C.: Urban Institute, 1999), p. 146.

9. There was no specific questioning about audits, though we did ask respondents how 501c3 affected their organization. Although this question and follow-ups may have been a cue, this information about audits was essentially volunteered, and conceivably the figure could be higher. The small number of interviews (around forty) is also a caution against any reliance on the 18 percent figure. Pinning down the exact number is less important than substantiating that it happens with some frequency, thus sending out periodic reminders to the broader nonprofit community about the teeth of the government.

10. This includes charity regulators in state attorney generals' offices. They also have the power to audit and conduct investigations.

11. Bauer, Pool, and Dexter capture this period well. In their monumental study of foreign trade legislation, they found an active citizen group, the League of Women Voters, but then document how the group was ignored by policymakers and other interest groups. Raymond A. Bauer, Ithiel de Sola Pool, and Lewis Anthony Dexter, *American Business and Public Policy* (Atherton, 1963), pp. 388–95.

12. John McPhee, *Encounters with the Archdruid* (Farrar, Straus, and Giroux, 1971).

13. Jeffrey M. Berry, *Lobbying for the People* (Princeton University Press, 1977), p. 49.

14. "I.R.S. Threatens the Sierra Club," *New York Times*, June 12, 1966, p. 50.

15. See Ronald G. Shaiko, *Voices and Echoes for the Environment* (Columbia University Press, 1999). The membership and budget data come from *The Encyclopedia of Associations, Part I*, 37th ed. (Farmington Hills, Mich.: Gale Group, 2001), p. 466.

16. This passage is drawn from Berry, *Lobbying for the People*, pp. 51–55.

17. Richard Corrigan, "Public Interest Law Firms Win Battle with IRS over Exemptions, Deductions," *National Journal*, November 21, 1970, pp. 2541–49; and Richard N. Goldsmith, "The IRS Man Cometh: Public Interest Law Firms Meet the Tax Collector," *Arizona Law Review*, vol. 13 (1971), pp. 857–85.

18. Eileen Shanahan, "Tax Ruling Scores White House Role," *New York Times*, December 12, 1973, p. 1.

19. James T. Bennett and Thomas DiLorenzo, *Destroying Democracy* (Washington, D.C.: Cato Institute, 1985), pp. 407, 448, 453. Labor unions are not 501c3 nonprofits, but they can support other organizations that are.

20. Marshall Wittman and Charles P. Griffin, *Restoring Integrity to Government: Ending Taxpayer-Subsidized Lobbying Activities* (Washington, D.C.: Heritage Foundation, July 1995), p. 1.

21. Jeff Shear, "The Ax Files," *National Journal*, April 15, 1995, p. 925.

22. Michael S. Greve and James Keller, *Funding the Left: The Sources of Financial Support for "Public Interest" Law Firms* (Washington, D.C.: Washington Legal Foundation, 1987).

23. Michael S. Greve, "Why 'Defunding the Left' Failed," *Public Interest,* vol. 89 (Fall 1987), p. 91.

24. See Bennett and DiLorenzo, *Destroying Democracy*; and Wittman and Griffin, *Restoring Integrity to Government.*

25. Jeffrey M. Berry, *The New Liberalism: The Rising Power of Citizen Groups* (Brookings, 1999).

26. *Federal Register*, July 8, 1980, pp. 46022–034.

27. *Federal Register,* November 3, 1983, pp. 50860–874.

28. Shear, "The Ax Files," p. 927.

29. Gary D. Bass, Shannon Ferguson, and David Plocher, *Living with A-122* (Washington, D.C.: OMB Watch, 1984).

30. Shear, "The Ax Files," p. 927.

31. Jeffrey M. Berry, "Maximum Feasible Dismantlement," *Citizen Participation,* vol. 3 (November–December 1981), pp. 3–5.

32. Walter A. Rosenbaum, "Public Involvement as Reform and Ritual: The Development of Federal Participation Programs," in Stuart Langton, ed., *Citizen Participation in America* (D.C. Heath, 1978), pp. 81–96.

33. Greve, "Why 'Defunding the Left' Failed," p. 93.

34. Shear, "The Ax Files," p. 925.

35. See Elizabeth J. Reid, "Nonprofit Advocacy and Political Participation," in Boris and Steuerle, *Nonprofits and Government*, pp. 316–18.

36. See, for example, David E. Williams and Elizabeth L. Wright, *Phony Philanthropy* (Washington, D.C.: Citizens Against Government Waste, 1998).

37. "The Istook/McIntosh/Ehrlich Federal Grant Reform Amendment: Righting a Wrong," fact sheet, House Republican Conference, July 25, 1995 (provided by Congressman Istook's office to the authors).

38. William Tucker, "Sweet Charity," *The American Spectator*, February 1995, pp. 39–40.

39. "The Istook-McIntosh-Ehrlich 'Grants Reform' Amendment Provisions by Version," fact sheet provided by Congressman Istook's office to the authors.

40. Many of the most visible national environmental groups are actually c4s or c4-c3 combinations. Table 4-2 also shows that environmental groups have a stronger tendency to make use of the H election, presumably to allow them to lobby more freely. Environment/animals constitute 19 percent of the H electors but only 4 percent of the conventional nonprofits.

41. "Guide to the NTEE Classification System: The National Taxonomy of Exempt Entities," Washington, D.C., Urban Institute, National Center for Charitable Statistics, n.d.

42. The variables used for these correlations are Q.12 (the respondent's estimate of the percentage of their annual budget derived from government) and Q.6b (the frequency on a five-point scale of "lobbying on behalf of or against a proposed bill or other policy pronouncement").

43. Although some of the inducements listed in Q.16 may appear to overlap, tests for multicollinearity all proved negative.

44. For a look at the Istook claims from the perspective of welfare spending, see Robert C. Lowry, "Was Istook Right? Analyzing the Simultaneous Evolution of Public Welfare Spending and Private Human Services Organizations in American States," paper delivered at the annual meeting of the Association for Public Policy Analysis and Management, 2001.

45. Paul C. Light, *Making Nonprofits Work* (Washington, D.C.: Aspen Institute and Brookings, 2000), p. 17.

46. Karen M. Paget, "The Big Chill," *American Prospect* (May-June 1999), pp. 26–33. In our focus groups we heard complaints from participants about such foundation restrictions. Unfortunately, we were unable to include much of anything on foundations in the survey and are not in a position to offer any significant empirical analysis of their impact on lobbying. Question 12 on sources of income included foundations and the simplest of tests suggests that there may be something to the foundations chill nonprofit lobbying thesis. However, further research with a fuller statistical specification is necessary to confirm the view we heard in our focus groups.

Chapter 5

1. Paul E. Peterson, *City Limits* (University of Chicago Press, 1981), p. 116.

2. Mancur Olson Jr., *The Logic of Collective Action* (Schocken, 1968).

3. In some contexts small size can be an advantage. See Olson, *The Logic of Collective Action*, pp. 53–65.

4. Jeffrey M. Berry, *The Interest Group Society*, 3d ed. (Longman, 1997), pp. 17–43; Robert H. Salisbury, "The Paradox of Interest Groups in Washington—More Groups, Less Clout," in Anthony King, ed., *The New American Political System*, 2d ed. (Washington, D.C.: AEI Press, 1990), pp. 203–29; and John P. Heinz, Edward O. Laumann, Robert L. Nelson, and Robert H. Salisbury, *The Hollow Core* (Harvard University Press, 1993).

5. On lobbying in state politics, see Alan Rosenthal, *The Third House*, 2d ed. (Washington, D.C.: CQ Press, 2001); and Anthony J. Nownes and Patricia Freeman, "Interest Group Activity in the States," *Journal of Politics*, vol. 60 (February 1998), pp. 86–112.

6. Robert H. Salisbury, "Interest Representation: The Dominance of Institutions," *American Political Science Review*, vol. 78 (March 1984), pp. 64–76.

7. Kirsten Grønbjerg and Laurie Paarlberg, "Community Variations in the Size and Scope of the Nonprofit Sector: Theory and Preliminary Findings," *Nonprofit and Voluntary Sector Quarterly*, vol. 30 (December 2001), pp. 684–706.

8. John P. Kretzmann, John L. McKnight, and Nicol Turner, *Voluntary Associa-*

tions in Low-Income Neighborhoods: An Unexplored Community Resource (Evanston, Ill.: Institute for Policy Research, Northwestern University, n.d.).

9. Grønbjerg and Paarlberg, "Community Variations in the Size and Scope of the Nonprofit Sector," p. 699.

10. Kay Lehman Schlozman and John T. Tierney, *Organized Interests and American Democracy* (Harper and Row, 1986), p. 350.

11. See *Michigan Public Policy Handbook* (East Lansing: Michigan Nonprofit Association and Michigan Public Policy Initiative, 2000); and *Advocacy & Lobbying by NYS Nonprofits: An Investigation of the Need for Education and Reform*, report submitted to the Nonprofit Sector Research Fund, Aspen Institute, January 15, 1998.

12. See Zoltan L. Hajnal and T. N. Clark, "Interest Group Politics: Who Governs and Why?" *Social Science Quarterly*, vol. 79 (March 1998), pp. 227–41.

13. Schlozman and Tierney, *Organized Interests and American Democracy*; and Berry, *The Interest Group Society*.

14. There are numerous surveys of interest groups that included a battery of questions about the utilization or efficacy of various tactics. There is little commonality in the questions as each survey has used the author's own list of tactics. Even crude comparisons to this sample of 501c3 nonprofits are difficult because few other surveys isolate 501c3s in a distinct grouping in the statistical analysis. We are guilty, too, of not matching our list of tactics to previous studies. Our feeling was that valid comparisons would still be problematic, and our priority was keeping our survey short—most lists of tactics are much longer than ours—and wording the items in a way that communicated what we were asking about in terms that would be unambiguous to those who work for 501c3s. See, for example, Richard Hoefer, "Human Services Interest Groups in Four States: Lessons for Effective Advocacy," *Journal of Community Practice*, vol. 7 (September 2000), pp. 77–94; *Advocacy and Lobbying*; Jack L. Walker Jr., *Mobilizing Interest Groups in America* (University of Michigan Press, 1991); Schlozman and Tierney, *Organized Interests and American Democracy*; Nownes and Freeman, "Interest Group Activity in the States"; and Jeffrey M. Berry, *Lobbying for the People* (Princeton University Press, 1977).

15. Elizabeth Drew, "Charlie," *New Yorker*, January 9, 1978, pp. 32–58.

16. See Rosenthal, *The Third House*.

17. Melissa Middleton, "Nonprofit Boards of Directors: Beyond the Governance Function," in Walter W. Powell, ed., *The Nonprofit Sector* (Yale University Press, 1987), p. 146.

18. Sharon L. Harlan and Judith R. Saidel, "Board Members' Influence on the Government-Nonprofit Relationship," *Nonprofit Management and Leadership*, vol. 5 (Winter 1994), pp. 173–96.

19. Judith R. Saidel, "Advocacy, Interdependence, and Public Policy," paper delivered at the annual meeting of the Association for Research on Nonprofit Organizations and Voluntary Action," 2000, p. 4; and Judith R. Saidel, "Expanding the Governance Construct: Functions and Contributions of Nonprofit Advisory Groups," *Nonprofit and Voluntary Sector Quarterly*, vol. 27 (December 1998), pp. 421–36.

20. See Jennifer M. Brinkerhoff, "Government-Nonprofit Partnership: A Defining Framework," *Public Administration and Development,* vol. 22 (February 2002), pp. 19–30.

21. This literature is voluminous, and no effort will be made to list the important works in the field. Two excellent books that provide a broad overview and sharp analysis are Lester M. Salamon, *Partners in Public Service* (Johns Hopkins University Press, 1995); and Steven Rathgeb Smith and Michael Lipsky, *Nonprofits for Hire* (Harvard University Press, 1993).

22. Jennifer Alexander, Renee Nank, and Camilla Strivers, "Implications of Welfare Reform," in J. Steven Ott, ed., *Understanding Nonprofit Organizations* (Westview, 2001), p. 279.

23. Salamon, *Partners in Public Service,* p. 144.

24. See Smith and Lipsky, *Nonprofits for Hire*; Steven Rathgeb Smith and Deborah A. Stone, "The Unexpected Consequences of Privatization," in Michael K. Brown, ed., *Remaking the Welfare State* (Temple University Press, 1988); and Walter W. Powell and Rebecca Friedkin, "Organizational Change in Nonprofit Organizations," in Powell, *The Nonprofit Sector,* pp. 180–92.

25. Francis X. Clines, "Safety Net Helps Make Leaving the Welfare Rolls Permanent," *New York Times,* March 19, 2001, p. A10.

26. Ibid.

27. E. S. Savas, *Privatization and Public-Private Partnerships* (Chatham House, 2000), pp. 63–107; and Margaret Gibelman and Harold W. Demone Jr., "The Evolving Contract State," in Harold W. Demone Jr., and Margaret Gibelman, eds., *Services for Sale* (Rutgers University Press, 1989), pp. 17–57.

28. See, generally, Pauline Vaillancourt Rosenau, "The Strengths and Weaknesses of Public-Private Policy Partnerships," in Pauline Vaillancourt Rosenau, ed., *Public-Private Policy Partnerships* (MIT Press, 2000), pp. 217–41.

29. Francis E. Rourke, *Bureaucracy, Politics, and Public Policy,* 3d ed. (Little, Brown, 1984), pp. 48–90.

30. On the adaptation of interest groups to government, see Virginia Gray and David Lowery, *The Population Ecology of Interest Representation* (University of Michigan Press, 1999).

31. See Alice O'Connor, *Poverty Knowledge* (Princeton University Press, 2001), pp. 124–36; Daniel P. Moynihan, *Maximum Feasible Misunderstanding* (Free Press, 1969); and Walter A. Rosenbaum, "Public Involvement as Reform and Ritual: The Development of Federal Participation Programs," in Stuart Langton, ed., *Citizen Participation in America* (Lexington Books, 1978), pp. 81–96.

32. 104 CMR 26.00.

33. Health Centers Consolidation Act, P. L. 107-186.

34. Richard C. Hula and Cynthia Jackson-Elmoore, "Governing Nonprofits and Local Political Processes," *Urban Affairs Review,* vol. 36 (January 2001), pp. 324–58.

35. Peterson, *City Limits*; and Stephen L. Elkin, *City and Regime in the American Republic* (University of Chicago Press, 1987).

36. Clarence N. Stone, *Regime Politics* (University Press of Kansas, 1989).

37. See Clarence N. Stone, "Urban Regimes and the Capacity to Govern," *Journal of Urban Affairs*, vol. 15, no. 1 (1993), pp. 1–28.

38. Rufus P. Browning, Dale Rogers Marshall, and David H. Tabb, *Protest Is Not Enough* (University of California Press, 1984).

39. Jeffrey M. Berry, Kent E. Portney, and Ken Thomson, *The Rebirth of Urban Democracy* (Brookings, 1993).

40. Barbara Ferman, *Challenging the Growth Machine* (University of Kansas Press, 1996).

41. Ferman, *Challenging the Growth Machine*.

42. Sara E. Stoutland, "Community Development Corporations: Mission, Strategy, and Accomplishments," in Ronald F. Ferguson and William T. Dickens, eds., *Urban Problems and Community Development* (Brookings, 1999), p. 200.

43. See Richard C. Hula and Cynthia Jackson-Elmoore, "Nonprofit Organizations, Minority Political Incorporation, and Local Governance," in Richard C. Hula and Cynthia Jackson-Elmoore, eds., *Nonprofits in Urban America* (Quorum Books, 2000), pp. 121–50.

44. See Steven Rathgeb Smith, "The New Politics of Contracting: Citizenship and the Nonprofit Role," in Helen Ingram and Steven Rathgeb Smith, eds., *Public Policy for Democracy* (Brookings, 1993), pp. 198–221.

45. On collaboration by nonprofits as an indicator of effectiveness, see Paul C. Light, *Pathways to Nonprofit Excellence* (Brookings, 2002), pp. 46, 173.

Chapter 6

1. The official, if less memorable, name of the welfare reform law is the Personal Responsibility and Work Opportunity Reconciliation Act of 1996.

2. V. O. Key Jr., *Public Opinion and American Democracy* (Knopf, 1961), p. 503.

3. See John R. Wright, "PACs, Contributions, and Roll Calls: An Organizational Perspective," *American Political Science Review*, vol. 79 (June 1985), p. 401.

4. Richard L. Hall, "Buying Time: Moneyed Interests and Mobilization of Bias in Congressional Committees," *American Political Science Review*, vol. 84 (September 1990), pp. 797–820; and John R. Wright, "Contributions, Lobbying, and Committee Voting in the U.S. House of Representatives," *American Political Science Review*, vol. 84 (June 1990), pp. 417–38.

5. Elisabeth S. Clemens, *The People's Lobby* (University of Chicago Press, 1997), p. 11.

6. See James Q. Wilson, "Democracy and the Corporation," in Robert Hessen, ed., *Does Big Business Rule America?* (Washington, D.C.: Ethics and Public Policy Center, 1981), pp. 35–39.

7. See, generally, Melissa M. Stone, Barbara Bigelow, and William Crittenden, "Research on Strategic Management in Nonprofit Organizations," *Administration & Society*, vol. 31 (July 1999), pp. 378–423.

8. John Simons and John Harwood, "For the Tech Industry, Market in Washington Is Toughest to Crack," *Wall Street Journal*, March 5, 1998, p. A1.

9. Ken Kollman, *Outside Lobbying* (Princeton University Press, 1998); and Kenneth M. Goldstein, *Interest Groups, Lobbying, and Participation in America* (Cambridge University Press, 1999).

10. In his study of twenty-six nonprofits, Paul Light found that information resources were highly "uneven" among the organizations. "Some of the Surviving Innovation organizations had state-of-the-art computers, whereas others were still using notepads and adding machines." *Sustaining Innovation* (Jossey-Bass, 1998), p. 195.

11. Jeffrey M. Berry, *The New Liberalism* (Brookings, 1999).

12. See Jeffrey H. Birnbaum, "The Power 25: The Influence Merchants," *Fortune*, December 7, 1998, p. 134.

13. On the difficulty of measuring power, see Peter Bachrach and Morton S. Baratz, "Two Faces of Power," *American Political Science Review*, vol. 56 (December 1962), pp. 947–52; and John Gaventa, *Power and Powerlessness* (University of Illinois Press, 1980).

14. Stephen Engelberg, "Business Leaves the Lobby and Sits at Congress's Table," *New York Times*, March 31, 1995, p. A1.

15. John P. Heinz, Edward O. Laumann, Robert L. Nelson, and Robert H. Salisbury, *The Hollow Core* (Harvard University Press, 1993).

16. As chapter 2 notes, "membership" is a slippery concept since it covers a range of possible meanings. Often, "members" have no role in the governance of the organizations and would be more accurately described as donors. The survey instrument makes no such distinction, but respondents could indicate that their organization had no individual members. Cases in which there was no membership were not included in these regression equations.

17. The supposition that the two samples themselves are significantly different in respect to the frequency of government-initiated contact is validated by pooling the H electors and the conventional nonprofits and using a dichotomous variable for organizational type in an otherwise similar regression equation. Organizational type is highly significant (.003), indicating a substantial difference.

18. See Zoltan L. Hajnal and T. N. Clark, "Interest Group Politics: Who Governs and Why?" *Social Science Quarterly*, vol. 79 (March 1998), pp. 227–41.

19. Lester W. Milbrath, *The Washington Lobbyists* (Rand-McNally, 1963).

20. See, for example, Scott Ainsworth, "Regulating Lobbyists and Interest Group Influence," *Journal of Politics*, vol. 55 (February 1993), pp. 41–56; David Austen-Smith, "Information and Influence," *American Journal of Political Science*, vol. 37 (August 1993), pp. 799–833; John E. Chubb, *Interest Groups and the Bureaucracy* (Stanford University Press, 1983); and John Mark Hansen, *Gaining Access* (University of Chicago Press, 1991).

21. Hansen, *Gaining Access*, pp. 13–17.

22. See William P. Browne, *Private Interests, Public Policy, and American Agriculture* (University Press of Kansas, 1988), p. 54.

23. Hilary Stout, "One Company's Data Fuel Diverse Views in Health Care Debate," *Wall Street Journal*, June 28, 1994, p. A1.

24. The argument here is restricted to information relating to public policy. Interest groups can also provide information in the form of political intelligence. We don't

explore that because nonprofits at the state and local level seem to place little emphasis on gathering and distributing political intelligence to legislators or administrators.
In Washington, however, there appears to be value to interest groups who develop
this information capacity. See Raymond A. Bauer, Ithiel de Sola Pool, and Lewis
Anthony Dexter, *American Business and Public Policy* (Atherton, 1968), pp.
350–57; and Hansen, *Gaining Access*.

25. Berry, *The New Liberalism*, pp. 119–52.

26. Paul C. Light, *The True Size of Government* (Brookings, 1999).

27. Thomas L. Gais, Richard P. Nathan, Irene Lurie, and Thomas Kaplan,
"Implementation of the Personal Responsibility Act of 1996," in Rebecca Blank and
Ron Haskins, eds., *The New World of Welfare* (Brookings, 2001), p. 64.

28. See Francis E. Rourke, *Bureaucracy, Politics, and Public Policy*, 3d ed. (Little, Brown, 1984).

29. See Virginia Gray and David Lowery, *The Population Ecology of Interest
Representation* (University of Michigan Press, 1999); and William P. Browne,
"Organized Interests and Their Issue Niches," *Journal of Politics*, vol. 52 (May
1990), pp. 477–509.

30. Gary J. McKissick, "Interests, Issues, and Emphases: Lobbying Congress
and the Strategic Manipulation of Issue Dimensions," paper delivered at the annual
meeting of the Midwest Political Science Association, 1995.

31. Bauer, Pool, and Dexter, *American Business and Public Policy*, pp. 350–57.

32. Matthew N. Beckmann and Richard L. Hall, "Lobbying for Protectionist
Trade Policy," paper delivered at the annual meeting of the Midwest Political Science Association, 2001.

Chapter 7

1. Robert H. Salisbury, "Interest Representation: The Dominance of Institutions," *American Political Science Review*, vol. 78 (March 1984), pp. 64–76; and
Frank R. Baumgartner and Beth L. Leech, "Interest Niches and Policy Bandwagons:
Patterns of Interest Group Involvement in National Politics," *Journal of Politics*, vol.
63 (November 2001), pp. 1191–213.

2. Jack L. Walker Jr., *Mobilizing Interest Groups in America* (University of
Michigan Press, 1991).

3. Trade associations composed of 501c3s could be a either 501c3 or 501c4.

4. Thomas B. Edsall, "New Ways to Harness Soft Money in Works," *Washington Post*, August 25, 2002, p. A1.

5. See *Unlevel Playing Field: Barriers to Participation by Faith-Based and Community Organizations in Federal Social Service Programs* (Washington, D.C.: White
House Office of Faith-Based and Community Initiatives, 2001).

6. Mark Chaves, "Religious Congregations and Welfare Reform: Who Will Take
Advantage of 'Charitable Choice'?" *American Sociological Review*, vol. 64 (December 1999), pp. 836–46; and Arthur E. Farnsley II, "Can Faith-Based Organizations
Compete?" *Nonprofit and Voluntary Sector Quarterly*, vol. 30 (March 2001), pp.
99–111.

7. See Peter Frumkin, *On Being Nonprofit: A Conceptual and Policy Primer* (Harvard University Press, 2002), pp. 16–19.

8. Robert A. Dahl, *A Preface to Democratic Theory* (University of Chicago Press, 1956), p. 145.

9. The citizen lobbies active on the national level have demonstrated little interest in the programs administered by health and human service providers. They are, of course, nonprofits too (c3s and c4s) even though they are not the organizations that come to mind when we speak of nonprofits. Jeffrey M. Berry, *The New Liberalism* (Brookings, 1999).

10. From *Federalist*, No. 10, *The Federalist Papers* (Mentor, 1961), pp. 78–79.

11. See Burt Neuborne, "Madison's Nightmare: The Tax-Driven Exclusion of Disinterested Voices from the Legislative Process," available at www.law.nyu.edu/ncpl/libframe.html; and Miriam Galston, "Lobbying and the Public Interest: Rethinking the Internal Revenue Code's Treatment of Legislative Activities," *Texas Law Review*, vol. 71, no. 6 (1993), pp. 1269–354.

12. John P. Heinz, Edward O. Laumann, Robert L. Nelson, and Robert H. Salisbury, *The Hollow Core* (Harvard University Press, 1993).

13. Gary J. McKissick, "Interests, Issues, and Emphases: Lobbying Congress and the Strategic Manipulation of Issue Dimensions," paper delivered at the annual meeting of the Midwest Political Science Association, 1995; and Beth L. Leech, Frank R. Baumgartner, Jeffrey M. Berry, Marie Hojnacki, and David C. Kimball, "Organized Interests and Issue Definition in Policy Debates," in Allan J. Cigler and Burdett A. Loomis, eds., *Interest Group Politics*, 6th ed. (Washington, D.C.: CQ Press, 2002), pp. 275–92.

14. Sidney Verba, Kay Lehman Schlozman, and Henry E. Brady, *Voice and Equality* (Harvard University Press, 1995); and Joe Soss, "Lessons of Welfare: Policy Design, Political Learning, and Political Action," *American Political Science Review*, vol. 93 (June 1999), pp. 363–80.

15. The two statements that almost all respondents gave the correct answer to were whether it was legal to use government funds to lobby (93 percent correct) and whether it is legal to endorse candidates for public office (84 percent correct). Both are impermissible. Since there were too few incorrect responses to these statements to analyze, they were left out of the table.

16. Detailed IRS documents offering historical background and explaining what is allowable under 501c3 are Judith E. Kindell and John Francis Reilly, *Lobbying Issues* (www.irs.gov/pub/irs-tege/topic-p.pdf; and Judith E. Kindell and John Francis Reilly, *Election Year Issues* (www.irs.gov/pub/irs-tege/topici02.pdf.).

17. The IRS does send all new public charities a publication that, in small print on page 43 of this dense, highly technical document, informs readers that the H election can be substituted for the substantial test. Without some background on this matter, someone reading this section would have trouble understanding what the H election is. This document also offers various definitions and expenditure ceilings for H electors. See Publication 557, *Tax-Exempt Status for Your Organization*, rev. (Washington, D.C.: Internal Revenue Service, July 2001), pp. 43–44.

18. www.irs.gov/pub/irs-pdf/f5768.pdf.

19. For technical reasons time series data on the number of electors is difficult to obtain. The Urban Institute is able to provide time series data on the number of electors that report lobbying expenditures on their 990s, but electors that don't report such expenses are far more numerous. The increase in electors with lobbying expenditures seems to parallel the growth in 501c3s overall. The Urban Institute figures fix the number of H electors reporting lobbying expenses at 1,694 for 1999. Interpolating from our sampling frame means that there were fewer than 7,000 electors among 990 filers that year. Memorandum from the Urban Institute: "Lobbying Expenses Reported on Form 990's Schedule A," June 18, 2001.

20. The spending limits under the H election are not indexed and have never been raised since the law was first implemented. Although the effective decline in the value of the money at the spending limits due to inflation is only a problem for a small number of electors, the ceilings at each interval should be raised in line with increases in the cost of living.

21. The case law offers differing views of what criteria might better define the current substantial standard. Two federal cases argued for a percentage test to be used in determining whether activities are substantial, *Seasongood v. Commissioner,* 227 F.2d 907 (6th Cir. 1955), and *Haswell v. United States,* 500 F.2d 1133 (Ct. Cl. 1974). A third case, *Christian Echoes National Ministry, Inc. v. United States,* 470 F.2d. 849 (10th Cir. 1972), cert. denied, 414 U.S. 864 (1974), rejected the use of a percentage test and called for a facts and circumstances analysis of whether substantial lobbying occurred. The lack of agreement by the courts clearly makes it more difficult for the IRS to reconceptualize the substantial standard. The case law does not, however, forbid it from defining the standard more clearly. For more information about these cases see the Kindell and Reilly, *Lobbying Issues.*

22. Juliet Eilperin, "GOP Seeks to Ease Curbs on Churches in Politics," *Washington Post,* June 3, 2002, p. A4.

23. See Paul C. Light, *Pathways to Nonprofit Excellence* (Brookings, 2002), p. 61.

24. *Speak Up* (New York: Center for an Urban Future, 2002), p. 10.

Appendix

1. Jeffrey M. Berry, David F. Arons, Gary D. Bass, Matthew F. Carter, and Kent E. Portney, *Surveying Nonprofits: A Methods Handbook* (Washington, D.C.: Aspen Institute, 2003).

2. Don A. Dillman, *Mail and Internet Surveys: The Tailored Design Method* (Wiley-Interscience, 2000).

3. Berry, Arons, Bass, Carter, and Portney, *Surveying Nonprofits.*

4. Instead of using the level 3 coding with broad categories like "human services," researchers can separate out more discrete categories like "family services and adolescent parents" (P45), "family counseling" (P46), and "single-parent agencies and services" (P42). Even a large survey is not large enough to take advantage of such discrete categories, and the database of all filers would probably be required. These examples are NTEE core codes. See Murray S. Weitzman, Nadine T. Jalan-

doni, Linda M. Lampkin, and Thomas H. Pollak, *The New Nonprofit Almanac and Desk Reference* (Jossey-Bass, 2002), pp. 201–13.

5. See Jeffrey M. Berry, "Validity and Reliability Issues in Elite Interviewing," *PS* vol. 35 (December 2002), pp. 679–82.

Index

ACTION-Housing. *See* Allegheny Council for the Improvement of Our Neighborhoods
ADC. *See* Aid to Dependent Children
AFDC. *See* Aid to Families with Dependent Children
Agricultural issues, 38–39
Aid to Dependent Children (ADC), 10
Aid to Families with Dependent Children (AFDC), 10, 12–13, 14, 17–18, 22. *See also* Temporary Assistance for Needy Families; Welfare
Alexander, Jennifer, 105
Allegheny Council for the Improvement of Our Neighborhoods (ACTION-Housing), 116
American Birth Control League, 51, 52, 75
American Farm Bureau Federation, 39
American Political Science Review, 33
Americans for Tax Reform, 83
Armey, Dick, 83
Arons, David F., 167
Arts and culture organizations, 87, 100
Aspinall, Wayne, 76, 77
Association for Retarded Citizens, 84
Atlanta, 115

Baker, James, 83
Bass, Gary, 82, 167
Bauer, Raymond A., 143
Berry, Jeffrey, 29–30, 167
Bob Jones University, 50
Boston, 119, 120. *See also* Massachusetts
Bowling Alone (Putnam), 26
Brody, Evelyn, 50
Brower, David, 75
Bush, George H. W., 10
Bush, George W., 40, 80

Campaigns and campaign finance, 36–37, 40, 48–49, 52, 123. *See also* Section 501c
Carter, Jimmy, 82
Carter, Matthew F., 167
Cato Institute, 81
CDCs. *See* Community Development Corporations
Center for Corporate Responsibility, 78
Centers for Medicare and Medicaid Services (DHHS), 102
Central Valley (Calif.), 118
Charitable giving. *See* Section 501c; Tax issues